WEIRD HIKES

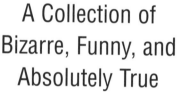

A Collection of
Bizarre, Funny, and
Absolutely True
Hiking Stories

ART BERNSTEIN

FALCON®

GUILFORD, CONNECTICUT
HELENA, MONTANA

AN IMPRINT OF THE GLOBE PEQUOT

A FALCON GUIDE®

All interior photos by the author

Text design by M. A. Dubé

Library of Congress Cataloging-in-Publication Data is available.

ISBN 0–7627–2586–9

Manufactured in the United States of America
First Edition/First Printing

CONTENTS

ACKNOWLEDGMENTS

DO I HAVE ANY ACKNOWLEDGMENTS? ANYBODY I'M DYING TO THANK? I like what Maureen Stapleton said when she accepted the Oscar for Best Supporting Actress several years ago:

"I thank everyone I've ever met."

I'll go Maureen one or two better. I thank everyone I've ever met and then some. I thank everyone who's ever shown me kindness or encouraged me. Or who has enjoyed my writing.

And I thank my lucky stars.

INTRODUCTION

THE LOVELY KATRINA, MY GOOD FRIEND, WAS KIND ENOUGH TO READ THE manuscript for this book before it was published. Her response was, and I quote:

"Yeah, and?"

Katrina is a very special person. Katrina sees auras. And she sees the spirits of dead people. She sees all sorts of things like that. I do not see auras or the spirits of dead people. I have no special psychic talent or unique insights into any other world or alternative universe.

Weird things do not happen to me.

Except on hikes.

The weird thing about weird things is that most of the time, it doesn't occur to you that something weird happened until long after the event, when you get home and think it over.

Even then, weird things don't happen to me very often. As a professional writer of guidebooks to hiking trails, I've been on probably five hundred hikes in thirty years. And on those five hundred hikes, I've had fourteen weird experiences, and two of the weird experiences happened on the same hike. So, actually, it was only thirteen hikes, and thirteen hikes out of five hundred is 2.6 percent.

The fourteen stories that follow are absolutely true. Every one of them. Of course as a writer, I needed to include certain story elements, such as motivating the main character (which can get tricky because I'm the main character in every story) and giving the story a "point." If you don't include story elements, even the most bizarre experience doesn't make very good reading. But aside from that, the stories are absolutely true. And the story elements are mostly true.

Reading back over my manuscript, the only thing I can see that needs clarifying is that I seem to talk about glaciers a lot. When you hike in the western United States, the subject does indeed come up frequently. So rather than explain glacial geology in each story, I'll do it here:

If it snows more than it melts every year for many years in a row, a glacier—a moving sheet of ice—will begin to form. You can always tell where there used to be a glacier in a high-mountain region (there were many more of them ten thousand years ago than there are now) because they leave a distinctive, amphitheater-shaped basin, with a cliff on one end and usually a small lake at the bottom. Such formations are called "cirques." I love cirques.

If the glacier got a little too big for its britches and spilled out of the cirque and down into the adjacent valley, which it scoured out and widened, then you have a glacial valley. The rock and dirt displaced by the glacier's carving action collects into gravel mounds called "moraines."

And that's all you need to know about glaciers.

HIKE ONE
THE FIRST HIKE

PART 1

THE FIRST PERSON IN THE ENTIRE UNIVERSE THAT I TOLD ABOUT THAT awful party when I was seventeen, and about the Lady in the Woods, was my daughter Sara. The party took place in October 1960, during my second weekend in college. I told Sara in summer of 2000. That's how embarrassed I was about it.

Sara tried to be reassuring. She insisted that my shenanigans fell more or less within the limits of normal freshman experimentation. College freshmen, after all, have been known to pull some pretty goofy and self-destructive stunts. All in all, Sara noted, my self-destructive options were severely limited compared to her freshman college year in 1992. My freshman year, in 1960, was well before the advent of crack cocaine or Ecstasy. Even marijuana was little used and pretty much taboo among college students, who are notorious for being willing to try just about anything.

In my mind, however, that long-ago party represented my first, and possibly worst, episode of overtly alcoholic behavior. The first of many. The first of thousands.

I still have never mentioned to Sara about my second act of overtly alcoholic behavior, which occurred at a dorm party precisely two weeks later. It was even more humiliating than the first party. If it hadn't been for the Lady in the Woods, I might have killed myself; that's how depressed I was after the second party.

Thank goodness for the Lady in the Woods.

The weekend of the first party, a mixer thrown by the sophomore class for incoming freshmen, started out positively enough. I don't know how I pulled it off but I actually landed a date. A really nice date. A sweet, kind, and gentle date. A surprisingly pretty date. I was not used to such good fortune. I was not used to landing dates.

1

The biggest mystery, to me, was how I ended up at a place like Antioch College at all. The tiny southern Ohio liberal arts college had a national reputation for extremely high academic standards and innovative educational programs. Most of the students came from large eastern cities and were highly motivated leadership types with stratospheric grade-point averages, clearly defined interests if not passions, and SAT scores in the upper seven hundreds..

My SATs were in the low six hundreds, my high school grade-point average was a gentleman's 3.00, and my primary objective in life, in the fall of 1960, was to get laid for the first time. Beyond that, I hadn't thought much about what did and did not interest me. If anybody asked, I told them I either wanted to go into engineering or social work, mostly because my father was an engineer and my mother was a social worker. That sounded a little more acceptable than saying I wanted to get laid. Especially to my father and mother.

The truth was that I'd rather have downed a Drano cocktail than follow in the footsteps of my parents. Hell, I didn't even want to go to Antioch. It was my mother's idea. Everything in my life up to then had been my mother's idea. I had been my mother's idea.

"It's a wonderful school," she informed me.

"Okay," I said.

"Very highly rated."

"I said okay. Now leave me alone."

"You'll love it. I promise."

"If you say so."

I did not love it and I did not hate it. Like a lot of things back then, it just was.

If you're wondering how I managed to get into such a prestigious school, I've long puzzled over that. Maybe it was because I was a pretty good student at an exceptionally good high school in Detroit, Michigan. Maybe it was because my mother wrote an outstanding application essay for me. Maybe it was because I told them I was interested in engineering and social work.

In any event, had I not made a complete jackass of myself, my date with Lisa Daugherty for the Freshman-Sophomore Mixer would have been the highlight of my year. Whether I got laid or not.

I might even have ended up with a girlfriend, heaven forbid.

Even my roommate was impressed.

"Nice going, Good Time," he said.

My roommate, Jon Rubinstein from Scarsdale, New York, was blessed with a charm and charisma with the opposite sex that I lacked and envied. Jon called me "Good Time" because I happened to have the same last name as a character in a Damon Runyon story he once read. The character was named Good Time Charlie Bernstein. Jon thought that fit me well.

At the time, it did.

Surprisingly, Jon turned out to be a sensitive and reliable friend when my life rapidly went to hell. Almost as sensitive and reliable as the Lady in the Woods. His approval of Lisa was very important to me.

I met Lisa Daugherty in the college cafeteria. I actually met her roommate, Anna Maria Botticelli, first. Anna Maria introduced me to Lisa a few days later. Anna Maria was lots of fun, an outgoing, chubby, boisterous type. But after one minute with Lisa, I was smitten from the fuzz of my crew cut to the bottoms of my canvas-top sneakers.

Lisa had every attribute of good looks and personality that my seventeen-year-old hormones found irresistible. She was diminutive, blond, and pretty in a wholesome sort of way, with penetrating blue eyes that knew instantly if something was bothering me or if I was not being 100 percent honest with her or with myself. She was also self-effacing and shy, which mystified me, because girls as pretty as Lisa were usually pretty stuck up.

Too stuck up to go out with me.

But most of all, Lisa was kind. Not to mention caring, and generous. She did not have it in her to be anything but kind, caring, and generous.

To my astonishment, Lisa didn't just mumble, "Sure why not?" when I asked her out over lunch in the cafeteria, after Anna Maria had left for class. She said, "I'd be delighted to be your date." And she seemed genuinely pleased. She always seemed genuinely pleased.

Lisa, a freshman like myself, had a part-time job at the college library. She got off at nine o'clock on Saturday nights, so we agreed that I would pick her up at nine-thirty. The party started at eight and would probably go until midnight or later.

By eight-fifteen on the night in question, I was neatly attired in my best narrow tie and corduroy sport jacket and was pacing back and forth in my tiny dorm room, driving Jon crazy. Jon was also headed for the party. Every freshman and sophomore on campus was headed for the party. There just wasn't that much else to do on a Saturday night in Yellow Springs, Ohio. They could have thrown a frog dissecting demonstration and half the campus would have been there.

"Why don't you come with me, Good Time?" said Jon. "It'll keep you occupied."

"But my date isn't until nine-thirty."

"So you'll go to the party, stay for an hour, then pick up Lisa and come back."

I'd never thought of that. Jon Rubinstein was not first in his class at Scarsdale High School for nothing.

PART 2

THE ANNUAL FRESHMAN—SOPHOMORE MIXER WAS HELD IN ONE OF THE NEW dormitories, where sophomores, juniors, and seniors lived. Freshmen lived in the old clapboard dormitories. Since the college's oldest building was constructed in the 1850s, I'm not kidding when I say the dormitories were old. The new dormitories, made of brick and stylishly modern, were much, much nicer than the old ones.

With Antioch's unique nationwide work-study program, and a fairly high dropout rate, nearly the entire campus, that fall quarter, consisted of freshmen and sophomores. There would be many more upper-class people on campus in winter and spring quarters.

Jon and I arrived to find the dormitory commons room bustling with neatly dressed students. There were crepe paper streamers on the walls and ceiling, an overflowing snack table, and loud music from, not surprisingly, the 1950s. The Supremes were popular. And Ray Charles. And the Frankies: Avalon, Valli, and Sinatra.

The room reeked of cigarettes. But I didn't notice because I happened to be a prime contributor to the stench. For the record, I quit smoking in 1967.

As was usually the case at parties, I immediately plopped down on a couch and waited for somebody besides Jon to talk to me. The truth was that the concept of a "mixer," to me, was ludicrous. I could no more mix at a party than mice could mix with coyotes. If anybody wanted to talk to me, they had to make the first move because I was too shy to make the first move myself. Way too shy.

The truth was, I hated parties. I hoped that things would not be so bad later on when Lisa was with me. I didn't plan to stay very long, either now or later on with Lisa. Except that there was nowhere else to go in Yellow Springs.

Jon made an effort to sit with me for a few minutes. But Jon was a gregarious mixer type and pretty soon I was alone and uncomfortable, inhaling one cigarette after another to hide my discomfort, just as I always did at parties.

And then I saw it.

It was large and red and shining. It beckoned to me like an overly made-up prostitute in San Francisco's North Beach. It was the answer to all my problems. How could I resist? I stood up, walked over to the punch bowl, and filled one of the little waxed-paper cups with the sweet red nectar. Then I took a small, tentative sip.

The mixture, as nearly as I could determine, consisted of cherry Kool-Aid, 7Up, and vodka. It was the vodka that interested me most, although I liked cherry Kool-Aid and 7Up well enough. Who doesn't?

That tentative sip was not the first time I'd consumed alcohol, but it was the first time I'd had vodka. Of course, it depends on what you mean by *consumed*. If you don't count Passover wine, it may well have been my first alcoholic drink. My parents didn't drink at all, except for Passover wine and a glass of beer on rare social occasions, perhaps three or four times a year. None of my friends in high school drank. At least not that I knew of. They were pretty dorky, by and large.

That big, beautiful, seductive red punch bowl was the first time I'd ever had a large quantity of alcohol placed directly in front of me, to have my way with as I pleased.

Drink casually in hand, I sidled back to my spot on the couch, sat down, and took another sip. Then I took another sip. Then, when I thought nobody was looking, I downed the rest of the drink in one gulp.

Then I did something that, to this day, I cannot explain. I walked back to the punch bowl and drank nine more glasses of punch, one after the other. Maybe it was because I was very tense and hoped the drinks would settle me down. Maybe it was because I was a latent alcoholic and that first swallow triggered something in my body chemistry. I'll never know.

According to my daughter Sara, college freshman have been known to do that sort of thing. And they pretty much never have a logical explanation.

All I knew, at the time, was that when I finished the ten drinks, I was as sober as a Latin School headmaster. But I also knew, with absolute certainty, that within a few minutes I'd be slobbering drunk or possibly dead. I'd never been falling-down drunk before and I did not look forward to it. Especially since I had to meet Lisa in less than half an hour.

Poor, sweet, kind, beautiful Lisa.

I decided, while still reasonably sober, that it was probably best to leave the party before I made a fool of myself, if I hadn't already made a fool of myself. I entertained a faint hope that I might be able to sober up before my nine-thirty date. A very, very faint hope.

Without saying good-bye to Jon, or to anybody else, I wandered outside, into the warm Ohio night, intending to walk around for a few minutes, or maybe try to score a cup of coffee somewhere, then head over to Lisa's dorm.

PART 3

I REMEMBER ONLY FRAGMENTS OF THE NEXT HOUR. I THINK I SPENT MOST OF IT IN an alcoholic blackout, although at the time I'd never heard of such a thing. I recall walking across the main lawn of the campus, past Antioch Hall. Or "stately old Antioch Hall," as the brochures described it. Then I remember finding myself in what looked like a woods. I had no idea how I got there but I was running along a trail in the dark, panting, gasping, and terrified. I kept tripping and falling. I was dizzy and my legs didn't seem to want to cooperate, but I'd scramble to my feet and start running again.

The only woods I knew of near the campus was Glen Helen, the thousand-acre nature preserve owned by the college. I couldn't imagine how I'd ended up in the Glen while walking across campus from one dormitory to another. The entrance to the Glen was a block out of my way.

Now, you have to understand that I was not a nature person in those days. The Glen Helen Ecological Preserve, shining jewel of the Antioch campus, left me totally cold. I'd never been there before and I regarded it as a place for sissies and ethereal types. I was not a person who communed with nature. I was a big-city kid from the teeming streets of Detroit. Art Bernstein in the woods was like Art Bernstein on the moon. Or Art Bernstein with a beautiful female.

I did not spend much time pondering my situation, however, because the one thing I knew for certain was that somebody or something was chasing me. Or at least I believed that somebody or something was chasing me. Why else would I be running? Since I couldn't recall who or what was chasing me, I just kept going. The main thing I remember is falling down a lot. In fact, I fell down every few steps, which made my flight pretty ineffectual. I wasn't a very good runner even when sober.

It occurred to me afterward that whoever or whatever was or was not chasing me had to have been pretty slow not to catch me.

I did have the presence of mind to realize that the trail was heading downhill, which meant I was going into the Glen, not out. Once I reached the bottom, a maze of pathways would supposedly lead to the park's interior. The only way back to campus, as far as I knew, was to backtrack on the route I was on—the very same trail on which somebody or something was chasing me into the dark, into the unknown, into the woods, with all its ghost trees, shadows, and unfamiliar terrain.

After a while the path came to the bottom of the hill, leveled off, and began following a little creek. I couldn't actually see it but I knew that a creek ran along the bottom of the tree-covered gorge into which the trail led. I'd seen the creek from the deck in front of the nature center, at the trailhead. I'd been on the deck exactly once, during a guided tour of campus my first day, with my parents.

In addition to a terror of getting beaten up, mauled, killed, and/or eaten by my pursuer, I was panicked that if I continued too much farther, I'd never find my way out. At least not in the dark. Among other things, that would mean standing up poor Lisa.

That was when I bumped into somebody. At first I thought it was a tree. Then I concluded that the jig was up and my pursuer had caught me. Except whoever or whatever I'd bumped into was in front of me, not behind me. The impact was pretty violent, knocking the wind out of me and sending me sprawling into the dirt for the hundredth time. I did catch a brief glimpse of the person I'd bumped into. It was a tall, dark-haired, pleasant-looking woman in jeans and a flannel shirt.

I didn't know it then, but I later found out that she was the Lady in the Woods.

Then my alcoholic blackout kicked in again. When I next returned to consciousness, I was back on the main lawn of the campus, walking past Antioch Hall on my way to Lisa's dorm. I didn't feel nearly as woozy as I had in the woods, but I had a horrible headache, I was out of breath, and my gait was still pretty unsteady.

In the light on the front porch of Lisa's dorm, I checked my watch. It was nine-fifty. I could see by the same light that I was covered with dust and dripping with perspiration, there was a hole in the knee of my pants, and my shirt was untucked. I tried to straighten myself up, tuck in my shirt, and dust myself off. When I touched the top of my head, my hand came back with blood on it. I debated going home, calling Lisa and telling her I had suddenly taken ill. That not only would have been the absolute truth, but it would have been the intelligent thing, the compassionate thing, to do. Except I still wasn't thinking very clearly.

Instead I took a deep breath and knocked on the door.

"My goodness," said Lisa, looking horrified. "What happened?"

"Sorry I'm late," I said, trying to smile and act casually. "I went to the mixer a little early with my roommate and had a couple of drinks. It was a silly thing to do and I apologize for being late. I was trying to walk it off before I got here. I tripped on the way."

"Well, come on in," said Lisa, with a sigh. "I'll see what I can do to help."

That was when I noticed Lisa's party dress. It was green and beautiful, a one-piece mini skirt. She'd obviously gone to great lengths to look her best for me, just as I had for her. I wanted to cry.

Lisa's dorm radiated warmth and comfort. It was an older dorm, similar to mine, but it somehow felt nicer. Women's dorms do that. Lisa sat me down at a table in the little community kitchen. She deftly made up a pot of coffee.

My dorm did not have a community kitchen.

"Don't worry about it," she kept telling me. "We don't have to go to the party. Everything will be fine. I'm not mad."

I'd have bought Lisa's reassurances, except for something she said as I was beginning to sober up, along about my fourth cup of coffee. I hinted that perhaps we might consider trying a second date if I swore on a stack of Bibles that I wouldn't show up intoxicated. It seemed like an easy enough promise. And a reasonable suggestion. At that moment, I fully intended never to ingest alcohol again as long as I lived.

"You're very nice, Art. Really. But my father was an alcoholic and I promised my mother I would never date an alcoholic. I just hope you're eventually able to face whatever it is you're running from."

I wanted to reassure Lisa that I was not and never would be an alcoholic. That she was making way too much of this. That it was a fluke, a chance aberration. But deep down there was no denying that the evidence, from her point of view, spoke for itself, no matter how much I believed she was misinterpreting my behavior. So I kept my mouth shut and nodded in sad agreement.

As it turned out, I kept my mouth shut for forty years.

PART 4

THE NOTORIOUS MIXER INCIDENT MY SECOND WEEK OF COLLEGE, AS DEVASTATING as it was at the time, would not have been nearly so embarrassing had I not done exactly the same thing two weeks later. I spent much of the two weeks trying for the life of me to remember how I'd ended up in Glen Helen and what had been chasing me. But the memory was apparently lost forever in the drunken haze.

I also spent considerable time pondering exactly what Lisa had meant by *facing whatever I was running from*. I was fairly certain it had just been a figure of speech. But part of me kept wondering if she somehow knew about my mysterious pursuer in Glen Helen, just before I visited her in the dorm.

The second explanation was not very likely.

For the dorm party, I had no date. Thankfully. It was not the kind of thing to which you would invite a sweet, innocent female. The guys in my dormitory, including myself, had all chipped in and purchased a keg of beer. The college paid little attention to such things in those days. They sure do now, and rightfully so. Purchasing kegs and getting drunk was what freshmen did, part of the ritual. Our dormitory had a resident adviser, a tall, skinny engineering student named Hal. Rather than being a moderating influence, Hal was the one who went to the party store and purchased the keg. The drinking age in Ohio was eighteen.

I'd never tasted beer before, just like I'd never tasted vodka before.

The dayroom in our dormitory was in the attic, on the third floor. It was a run-down old room filled with frayed, overstuffed couches and chairs that looked as though they'd been there since the building's construction in the 1880s. The room smelled of lumber and soiled carpet.

I drank one glass of beer, my first ever, and remember being very analytical about it.

"Not bad," I commented to Jon. "A little bitter, though."

"Beer is an acquired taste," he reassured me.

I wouldn't admit it, but all in all I preferred the Kool-Aid punch. I wasn't much of a connoisseur in those days. I went for potent first and sweet second. Beyond that, I didn't much care. I was the same way with table wine ten years later. I could talk a decent game about vintages and fancy French labels. But if I wanted to get drunk in a hurry, as I often did, there was no appreciable difference between Chateau Rothschild and Boone's Farm.

During the first two hours of the dorm party, I consumed a grand total of twelve glasses of beer. I recall being extremely pleased with myself, elated even, because unlike two weeks earlier, I'd spread my drinks out. At least I was making progress.

Needless to say, I ended up even drunker than I'd been at the mixer. I didn't have a blackout, but I remember giggling like an idiot, falling down the stairs, and throwing up in the hallway. The only thing any of my dorm mates knew to do with somebody who'd overindulged was throw him in the shower, fully clothed, and let the cold water run on him.

That was precisely where I ended up. I'm told I put up a surprisingly spirited fight. As I recall, I didn't particularly object to being thrown in the shower. I just didn't want to make it easy for them.

A few days later Jon related the story of the great Bernstein shower-throwing incident, from his point of view. My point of view, after I sobered up, was that I'd been acting like an idiot and deserved it. In fact, the cold water actually helped a little. Or at least it calmed me down. I didn't admit it to Jon, but all in all I'd sort of enjoyed the experience.

According to Jon, my dorm mates almost abandoned the idea of throwing me in the shower because they were afraid I'd hurt myself in all the ruckus. Once I was in the shower, Jon explained, I went completely limp and kept flopping out. A couple of people had to stand there with a foot on my rear end, holding me in. Some of them ended up almost as wet as I did.

While I was in the shower, five of the people who'd carried me there availed themselves of the opportunity to relieve themselves into the toilet, which was located immediately next to the shower, as toilets often are.

"While they were all standing there peeing," said Jon, "your arm suddenly flopped out of the shower stall and into their line of fire. The five people ended up urinating on your arm. It was funny as hell."

I did not think it was funny.

The night I got drunk the second time, the night they threw me into the shower, was also the night I discovered that Jon was a pretty decent person, at least for a strikingly good-looking, self-assured, probably spoiled, stuck-up rich kid. He helped me to our room and stayed up with me all night. Every time I moaned, he'd grab me by the hair and swing my head out over the wastebasket, in case I was about to throw up, which I did several times.

Jon confided in me a few days later that I was not the drunkest person at the party that evening. Three other people had also been thrown into the shower.

It was scant solace.

PART 5

IT HAPPENS LIKE THAT SOMETIMES. YOU STAY UP LATE PARTYING LIKE MAD, GET roaring drunk, fall into bed, then wake up bright-eyed and raring to go at some ungodly early hour. It happened to me the morning after I was thrown into the shower at the dorm party.

I woke up at five o'clock, which for me was unheard of. I tried to go back to sleep. I even took some aspirin to assuage my throbbing head. I managed to doze off for another twenty minutes, then woke up for good. The aspirin had softened the headache considerably, but I felt an overwhelming need for fresh air (the dorm reeked of vomit). So at five forty-five, I stepped out into the fresh, sweet-smelling, early-morning, midwestern autumn, a few minutes before sunrise.

"A couple of dews before dawn," as the song from *Guys and Dolls* goes.

I didn't recall ever having gotten up that early before. I was pretty much a night person. My main interests in life, hanging out with friends and trying to meet girls, were predominantly nocturnal activities. Or they were as I practiced them. I'd been up at six-thirty or seven before to go to school, or to the lake with my parents. But five forty-five was ridiculous.

I had no idea where I was going when I stepped out of my dormitory. The cafeteria and library were closed. All the stores and restaurants in town were closed. All my friends were asleep. I didn't want to talk to anybody anyhow. I wanted to run away, to never show my face in public again. I was confused and depressed and convinced that something was terribly wrong with me. No human being could possibly be this screwed up.

And yet some unknown factor in the crisp, early-morning air made me feel good. Made me feel elated. Made me feel more at peace with the world and myself than I'd ever felt before. I'd never realized before that simply getting up early could do that to you.

My oddly inappropriate sense of peace and happiness confused me even more than my drinking and depression.

Then I did the unthinkable. With nothing else to do, I headed for the Glen. I wanted to get away from the campus. And the town. I had to think things through and it seemed important to be by myself. The Glen was as good a place as any for a long walk by myself.

Even though I was not a nature person.

I paused at the deck in front of the nature center and looked down into the little gorge that was Glen Helen. When I say *little* it's from the perspective of forty years later, having been to the Grand Canyon and rafted several great whitewater rivers of the West. To a seventeen-year-old Detroiter who'd never been anywhere, Glen Helen was immense.

Basically, the Glen consisted of a fairly steep hillside covered with hardwood trees. The hillside sloped down to a little willow-lined creek. The elevation drop was maybe 150 feet. At the bottom, trails went off in both directions along the creek and up the other side of the gorge. The gorge's far side was more densely wooded (because it faced north instead of south, I later learned), but it wasn't as steep as the slope adjacent to campus and the nature center. The far side of the Glen, I'd been told, contained a number of side creeks and hidden draws. There was also supposed to be a pretty decent waterfall somewhere, but I never did find it.

On that sunny weekend in mid-October, southern Ohio was approaching the height of its color season. The Glen was stupendous in its mantle of vibrant reds, yellows, and oranges. It also smelled really nice. I quickly discovered that long, deep breaths of morning air, filled with the aromas of autumn, though intoxicating in their own way, can get rid of a hangover faster than any commercial medicine.

What amazed me most that morning was how the Glen seemed to embrace me, to clasp me to its breast and reassure me that despite it all, everything would be okay. And yet, a couple of times while I was walking along, thinking about my stupid behavior, and how lonely I was, and how confusing life could be, I started crying. And strangely, even that felt good. I don't cry very often.

I made it down to the creek easily enough. I felt reasonably energetic but couldn't help worrying a little about the hike back up. I also worried about how long my energy would hold out. To this day I worry about the return trek when I go hiking.

I guess I'm just a worrier. I'm told that obsessive worrying is a symptom of the same disorder that caused me to drink too much.

I hiked in the Glen for about thirty minutes. I made it to the bottom of the hill, walked up the creek a ways, and then turned off on a side trail for a considerable distance. Eventually I turned onto another side trail, then another. I kept changing directions because it always seemed as though the scenery would be just a little prettier on the new trail than the trail I was on.

I was pretty sure I'd be able to find my way back. All I had to do was head downhill and downstream.

Surprisingly, I did not worry about things chasing me. It barely crossed my mind to worry about things chasing me. I figured the pursuing demons of night, from two weeks earlier, were long gone, if they ever really existed. The Glen seemed so peaceful and beautiful and charming, I honestly believed that nothing bad could possibly happen there.

At least I believed that until something started chasing me.

I ended up maybe a mile and a half from campus, although I had no way of telling for sure and no prior experience by which to estimate such things. I found myself in a dense stand of woods beside a little side creek near some tan rock outcrops. Anytime you find woods, creeks, and rock outcrops in Ohio, it is a memorable experience.

I was walking up the trail, just finishing my latest crying jag and feeling very foolish, when something rushed out of the bushes immediately behind me. I jumped two feet off the ground and nearly had a heart attack. Adrenaline instantly inundated my body like the Red Sea flooding the Egyptian army.

The first thing I heard was a rustling in the bushes, then a brief turmoil, then loud barking and snarling. Then whatever it was started nipping at my heels. It sounded like a giant, angry Doberman or German shepherd. I instinctively started running, without looking back. I figured I had no chance of outrunning a large angry dog. But I didn't know what else to do. Except maybe turn around and holler at it to go away.

After less than twenty feet of running I was about to do precisely that (honest), when a woman appeared on the trail in front of me. It was the same woman I'd bumped into during my night run two weeks prior.

It was the Lady in the Woods.

"Now you hush, Precious," she said wagging a finger. "Leave the nice man alone."

I looked behind me and discovered a tiny, nervous, fluffy red Pomeranian dog, jumping up and down and yipping. The animal had an unusually deep voice for a miniature lap dog. Or at least that's what I told myself.

I hoped that the silly little dog was not what I had been running from two weeks earlier. That would have been really embarrassing.

"Hi," I said to the lady. "Nice day."

"It's a beautiful day."

"Do you come here often?" I said, nervously trying to make conversation.

The woman laughed when I said that. It wasn't a belittling laugh, but a gentle, sweet laugh that gave me the opportunity to see her wonderful smile for the first time. She appeared to be in her midthirties. Slender and attractive, she had long, dark, free-flowing curly hair, intense brown eyes, and an unusually soft demeanor. She wore an Antioch College jacket, Levi's, hiking boots, and a knitted hat.

Women did not normally wear hiking boots in 1960 and I remember thinking it was a little strange.

"I live here. My name is Helen Burch. Everyone calls me the Lady in the Woods."

That was the first time I'd ever heard the term, *Lady in the Woods.*

"Why do they call you that?"

"Because I live right here in the Glen."

"Really? I didn't know you could do that."

"I'm sort of the caretaker. I have a cabin not far from here. It was built in 1763. Very historic. Would you like to see it? I'm about to cook breakfast."

"Sure."

In a little hollow not five hundred feet from where Helen's dog had jumped out at me, there was indeed a tiny log cabin beneath some dogwood trees.

At least Helen said they were dogwoods.

Twenty minutes later I was inside the cabin sitting at a large pedestal table, which appeared handmade and very, very old. I was devouring a plate of bacon, scrambled eggs, and toasted homemade bread with jam. That was what you had for breakfast back in the days when nobody knew much about nutrition.

Cholesterol notwithstanding, it was a wonderful meal. The aroma of bacon cooked on a woodstove was glorious. My only regret was that after Helen served the meal, she sat down beside me at the table. I'd been enjoying watching her cook.

"So tell me," I asked, between coffee sips and bites of egg, "how does one go about landing the job of Glen Helen caretaker?"

"I don't know, I just applied for it. It sort of helped that my great-grandfather was the person who gave the property to the college. And that my great-great-great-grandparents built this cabin."

That was when I finally made the connection between the names *Helen Burch*, *Glen Helen*, and *Hugh Taylor Burch*. The latter was a revered Antioch icon who had donated the Glen Helen land to the college in the 1920s. As I understand it, he named the land for his daughter, who was born in the 1890s.

"And what are your duties as caretaker?"

"I walk around, talk to visitors, keep the trails up, and phone in trouble to the nature center or the police. It's pretty easy."

"Nifty. How long have you been doing it?"

"A couple of years. It took me a long time to find myself. My father was an engineer and my mother was a social worker. In college I used to tell everyone I wanted to be an engineer or a social worker. But it was a lie. Finally I decided on a direction for my life that was completely mine and not my parents'. And here I am."

The impact of Helen's statement did not sink in right away. She sounded so matter-of-fact that you'd have thought everyone's parents were social workers and engineers. She was so easy to talk to, it was as though I were having a conversation with myself.

Actually, Helen's engineer father drove a train. My engineer father designed machinery.

"So you ended up devoting your life to communing with nature?" I concluded.

"Something like that."

"I don't know very much about nature. I'm from Detroit."

"And I'm from Cincinnati. But don't worry. You don't have to commune with nature if you don't want to. Personally, I enjoy it."

"I've certainly enjoyed this morning."

"Glad to hear it. Come back and visit anytime. I'm usually around. And the cabin is never locked."

Helen and I talked for nearly two hours. I left feeling much better about things. And no, I had no problem finding my way out of the Glen and back to the campus.

"Guess what?" I said to Jon when I got back the dorm. Jon was still in bed. It was only eight forty-five after all. I was starting to get tired myself by then.

"What is it, Good Time?" Jon mumbled. "What are you so happy about?

"I met the Lady in the Woods."

"Congratulations. Who the hell is the Lady in the Woods?"

"She's a caretaker who lives in the cabin in the Glen. She's very nice. She made me breakfast."

"The Lady in the Woods? Never heard of her. And I never heard about a cabin, either. But I'll take your word for it."

PART 6

I NEVER DID MAKE IT BACK TO HELEN'S CABIN, EVEN THOUGH I INTENDED TO JUST about every weekend. I visited Glen Helen frequently because early mornings, woods, and nature had suddenly taken on much more meaning for me. The Glen became "my place" and I spent many happy hours wandering its trails, and the trails of nearby nature preserves and parks. But Helen's cabin was just a little too far away, and I never quite had the time to go that far.

I left Antioch after a year because my parents couldn't afford it. I have never been back.

My visit with Helen Burch was definitely a turning point. It changed many of my attitudes and inspired my love of nature and the outdoors. Much of the impact was gradual, though.

After my year at Antioch, I obtained a B.A. in anthropology from the University of Michigan, fully intending to become a social worker like my mother. Except she was a good social worker. Also, she liked being a social worker. I worked as a social worker, on and off, for eight years.

Then, following memorable trips out west in 1966 and 1967, I made the decision (in 1968) to enroll at the University of Michigan School of Natural Resources. In 1972 I received the degree of master of science in natural resource management.

While I never again drank twelve beers or ten glasses of vodka punch at one sitting, I wrestled with alcoholism until my third child was born. I officially quit drinking in September 1982, and have not consumed alcohol since.

While researching this story, in 2000, I decided to give the Antioch College Glen Helen Nature Center a call from my home in Oregon and see if I could find out anything more about Helen Burch and the old Burch Cabin.

"The cabin's not there anymore," said a pleasant female voice with a strong New York accent.

"That's too bad." I said, "I understand it was very historic. Built in 1763."

"I know, it was a terrible tragedy when the Burch Cabin burned down in 1948. Helen Burch, the caretaker, who lived there with her little dog, died in the fire. The dog died, too, according to the newspaper report. Where in the world did you hear about that?"

The lady on the phone was full of crap. There was a cabin in Glen Helen in 1960 and there was a wonderful woman named Helen Burch living in it. I can prove it, too: Ghosts from 1948 would not wear hiking boots, Antioch jackets, and Levi's.

Of that I am certain.

THE HIKE: *Glen Helen Ecological Preserve, Antioch College, Yellow Springs, Ohio.*

LENGTH *(one way): 1.5 miles.*

DIRECTIONS: *In Ohio, take I-70 to US 68 South, toward Yellow Springs and Xenia. In Yellow Springs, turn left at the second stoplight, onto East Livermore Avenue. Proceed through the Antioch College campus to the east end, where the Glen Helen Ecological Preserve begins. Park at the nature center and trailhead. Day use only.*

HIKE TWO
THE POWER SOURCE

PART 1

THIS STORY, WHICH ENDS WITH THE POSSIBLE IMPENDING DESTRUCTION of Mount Shasta, California's most impressive summit, began on a warm September evening in 1970, when J. Herbert Gumble answered the door naked. J. Herbert Gumble was my coworker at the Siskiyou County Welfare Department, in Yreka, California, where I'd just been hired after moving out from Michigan. He and his wife, Barbara, had invited my wife, Patricia, and me to dinner.

A major reason for my move to Yreka was that I'd seen Mount Shasta for the first time when passing by in my car a couple of years earlier and had become mesmerized by its siren lure. That happens to a lot of people. Mount Shasta is the solitary, 14,161-foot volcano that stands guard over the California Far North. For those who live in Shasta's shadow, I quickly discovered, the influence of the massive, glacier-covered peak is pervasive. Shasta greets you every morning, puts you to bed at night, and enters your awareness frequently throughout the day. You rarely go more than an hour or two without thinking about the mountain.

I did not yet know, when I went to J. Herbert Gumble's house for dinner, about Mount Shasta as a spiritual "Power Source," although I was aware that the summit held deep spiritual significance for many people. It certainly did for me, except I didn't call it "spirituality" back then because the term made me uncomfortable. I just called it a really pretty mountain that made me feel good when I looked at it.

I also did not yet know, when I went to J. Herbert Gumble's house, about the protectors, the Lemurians, the legendary creatures whose job was to watch over the spiritual Power Source and keep the power flowing. I would learn about them very soon. Lemurians are a favorite subject among Mount Shasta spiritual types.

In addition to being my co-worker, J. Herbert Gumble was a New Age guru and self-anointed priest, although he downplayed that particular sideline around my wife and me because we made it clear that we weren't interested in such things. And they didn't call it "New Age" then. J. Herbert called it "Alternative Spirituality." There were a lot of self-anointed and self-appointed gurus in the Mount Shasta area in those days. There still are, as far as I know.

Whatever J. Herbert Gumble's religion, I did not want any part of it. As much as I admired and enjoyed the mountain, I didn't believe in organized religion. I didn't think I needed religion, and I did not want religion. Not J. Herbert Gumble's religion or anybody else's. That was for other people. Religion made no sense to me. I considered it sucker-bait for the gullible. And I most assuredly did not follow gurus. I still don't.

All that notwithstanding, I liked J. Herbert a lot, aside from his religious practices. Otherwise I would not have accepted the dinner invitation. He was by far the most interesting person at the welfare department, jobs neither of us would hold for very long.

In addition to being a welfare worker and a high priest, J. Herbert Gumble was an exhibitionist. These days they'd call him a "flasher." Having heard that about him, I was not surprised when he answered the door naked. I was not pleased, either. He reputedly showed off his body to anyone who would look, especially young women, whom he frequently (I'd been told) picked up in bars or on the street. The rumor was that J. Herbert cheated on his wife constantly, which I considered odd because she was by far the better looking of the couple. She was also by far the nicer of the two. Not that J. Herbert wasn't nice.

Barbara Gumble, a tall, serious, short-haired brunette, was not an exhibitionist and did not cheat on her husband. Or so I'd been told.

J. Herbert was forty years old in 1970 and had curly blond hair, a lean, well-proportioned body, and a great big, long, hooked nose. As to whether any other part of his anatomy was great big, long, and hooked, I cannot say. Despite his best efforts that day, I didn't look.

I think he was trying to shock us. The fact that my wife was twenty-three, good looking, and very shy was probably all the incentive J. Herbert needed to drop his drawers. My wife did not look, either. At least she claims she didn't.

Barbara and J. Herbert Gumble lived in a tidy little house on the edge of town, with pasture on one side, a stand of piney woods on another, and the newly constructed Interstate 5 passing by. It looked sort of like the house in the Andrew Wyeth painting *Christina's World*, a white clapboard structure rising starkly out of a field. Like the painting, at first glance it radiated great rustic charm. Also as with the painting, when you looked more closely there was something not quite right about it.

The official excuse that J. Herbert offered for being naked was that he was in the middle of ironing his pants.

"Come on in," he said, shaking hands with me and wrapping an unctuous and overly familiar arm around Patricia, whom I knew to be immune to his alleged charms (she told me his physical appearance repulsed her). "I'm ironing my pants."

He was, too. There was an ironing board set up in the living room.

What mostly drew J. Herbert and I together as friends were the problems we'd both been experiencing at work. To be accepted by the general populace in Siskiyou County, California, in 1970, it helped to be a narrow-minded bigot, which we were not, although we were pretty bigoted against narrow-minded bigots. Welfare recipients and hippies were particular targets of community scorn. The town boasted a disproportionate share of welfare recipients and hippies in 1970. Anything bad that happened, from lost kittens to lightning striking a tree, was blamed on welfare recipients and hippies. Signs in the windows of some of the stores and restaurants in town proclaimed WE DO NOT SOLICIT HIPPIE PATRONAGE.

It was a tense situation. I'd seen shop owners, upon observing that a hippie-looking individual was approaching their establishment, drop everything and run and lock the door. Normally I did not patronize stores with a NO HIPPIES sign in the window.

J. Herbert, myself, and our supervisor, a secret cocaine addict named Bob Piggins, were all suspected (correctly) of being hippie sympathizers and were considered just a little too liberal and "big city" for decent folks. J. Herbert and his wife hailed from the bustling and cosmopolitan metropolis of Chico, California. But they had lived in San Francisco. So had Bob Piggins, a Yreka native.

I'd met Patricia in Detroit two years earlier, at a party at a friend's house, not long after returning from a two-month stint in Berkeley in 1967, the famous "Summer of Love." The 1967 trip had been preceded, in 1966, by a six-month sojourn in San Francisco, the year the city's flower-child reputation came into full blossom. I'd been more of an observer of the Summer of Love than a participant. J. Herbert claimed he had been a participant. But J. Herbert claimed a lot of things.

The main thing Patricia and I had in common was a burning desire to move out west. I wanted to move there because the winters were milder and there were infinitely more hiking opportunities than in Michigan.

Patricia wasn't particularly interested in hiking but she was obsessed with Oregon and claimed she used to write reports about it in elementary school. Patricia, a gentle blond with the thickest, most beautiful hair I'd ever seen, and her two-year-old daughter accompanied me when I again left Michigan for San Francisco in May 1970. I was hired at the Siskiyou County Welfare Department two weeks later. Given the narrow-mindedness of the folks in Siskiyou County at the time, I saw no reason to mention that Patricia and I weren't actually husband and wife, as everyone assumed. We were married in June 1971, in the Reno Courthouse by a kindly old gentleman who bore the official title of Commissioner of Civil Marriages. The ceremony was very civil indeed. So was the marriage, for the most part.

Yreka, the Wild West, Gold Rush, logging, and cattle ranching seat of California's northernmost county, wasn't quite Oregon, but we were satisfied. Patricia immediately found work as a legal secretary, and the very first cases she handled had to do with claim jumping on gold mines. Talk about culture shock. We finally moved to the Beaver State from the Golden State in 1972.

The very best thing about Yreka, of course, was that Mount Shasta lay only 30 miles away. There were much closer towns, such as Mount Shasta City, but 30 miles was near enough for the town of five thousand to fall well within the mountain's spell and aura. At 14,161 feet, Shasta was not quite the Golden State's highest summit. But it was easily the most prominent. On exceptionally clear days it could be seen from the top of Mount Diablo, east of Oakland, 300 miles south. When I once flew from San Francisco to Michigan, Shasta came into view immediately upon takeoff and remained in view until after we'd crossed into Utah. When the mountain faded from my field of vision, the plane was 800 miles away from northern California's solitary sentinel.

Mount Shasta was visible out the front door of our little rented house in Yreka. The peak was visible from just about every front door in Yreka. I can attest that there is no better way to start your day than by witnessing a glorious Mount Shasta sunrise. It compensates for a lot of things that may be going wrong in one's life.

Since 1970, I have seen Mount Shasta probably five thousand times. I've seen it in summer, fall, winter, spring, morning, noon, and night. I've hiked trails on every side of the mountain and have watched from the summit, huddling in front of my wind-whipped tent, as the mountain's pointed shadow slowly crept across the much lower mountains to the east.

I have come to two conclusions about Mount Shasta:

1. It never looks the same twice.
2. I've yet to see Mount Shasta without experiencing an overwhelming sense of awe.

Although I tend to be pretty much a cynic, if ever a place radiated a spiritual essence, it is Mount Shasta. I certainly understood how the mountain could inspire spirituality in some people.

The mountain's spiritual aura explained why religious crackpots by the thousands found their way to Yreka, and to Mount Shasta City, during the halcyon hippie days of the early 1970s. A lot of noncrackpot religious types also found their way to the area, but the crackpots far outnumbered the noncrackpots. Oddly enough, J. Herbert Gumble was a noncrackpot. At least as far as religion went. My personal theory was that his "church" was simply another way to meet girls.

After a huge turkey dinner, as Pat and Barb washed dishes, Herb and I (I called him Herb, with the *H* properly silent) sat in the living room sipping Rainier beers. He offered me a marijuana joint but I declined. And yes, we both had pants on by then.

"Damned nice country you got around here," I commented, lazing back on the couch as the aroma of turkey gravy continued to waft in from the kitchen. The only things that prevented me from falling immediately asleep were J. Herbert's presence and an intensifying pressure in my bladder from too much beer.

"I'll say," said J. Herbert, with a knowing grin. J. Herbert was the master of the knowing grin. "You got your Mount Shasta. Everybody knows about Mount Shasta. You got your Marble Mountains. You got your Trinity Alps. You got your Crater Lake and your redwoods. If I were a hiking fanatic, which I'm not, I suspect I could hike a different trail every day of my life, all within a hundred-mile radius of Yreka, and never run out of trails."

"I thought you liked hiking," I said.

"I love hiking. But not every day of my life."

"I know what you mean," I lied. I figured there was nothing to be gained by contradicting him, even though I loved the idea of hiking a different trail every day of my life. "But tell me, what's the prettiest natural place in the area? Not counting Mount Shasta, of course."

"That's easy," said J. Herbert, with a knowing, sleepy grin. "Ney Springs."

"What's so special about Ney Springs?" I said, stifling a yawn.

"That's a long story," said J. Herbert, uncapping another brew. "Aside from being incredibly beautiful, Ney Springs is very special."

"I guess I'll have to check it out. How to I get there?"

"Actually, that's kind of complicated. But as it happens, you're in luck. I'm going there next weekend. Our church is having its monthly Full Moon Festival and Ruckus. You and Pat want to come? It'll be lots of fun."

"I'm not sure," I replied with a suspicious squint. "You're not trying to convert me, are you? As much as I like you, I don't believe in gurus."

"You said you wanted to see Ney Springs," said J. Herbert, pretending to look hurt. "It's very scenic and you just might enjoy yourself. You don't have to participate in the rituals. Lots of people come only to watch."

"I'll think about it."

"I'll pick you and Pat up at six o'clock on the evening of the seventeenth. I hope you don't mind a couple of dozen naked young girls running around in a drunken religious frenzy. Can you handle that?"

On reflection, I decided that I did not mind a couple dozen naked girls running around in a drunken religious frenzy. My only problem was trying to think up an excuse for having Patricia stay home.

PART 2

A FEW DAYS AFTER MY DINNER AT J. HERBERT GUMBLE'S HOUSE, AND BEFORE THE big ceremony at Ney Springs, J. Herbert and I met for lunch at the McDonald's in Mount Shasta City. Between burger bites, if we so chose, we could look out the window at the barren, naked peak, which was waiting anxiously for the season's first snowfall. Herb and I were both in the field that day, visiting clients.

"Ever heard of Lemurians?" J. Herbert inquired through a mouthful of half-chewed Big Mac. Had he asked the question twenty-four hours earlier,

I wouldn't have had the faintest idea what he was talking about. As it was, he created a prime opportunity for me to strut out a bit of newly acquired knowledge.

"I have indeed," I replied, pleased with myself for having passed his little pop quiz. "Some guy in the Buckhorn Tavern was telling me about them last night. As I understand it, Lemurians are the descendants of the escapees from the Lost Continent of Mu and they live underneath Mount Shasta. What I can't figure out is, how can someone live underneath a mountain? You don't believe in Lemurians, do you?"

I would have been very surprised to learn that J. Herbert Gumble believed in Lemurians. J. Herbert Gumble believed in J. Herbert Gumble. Everything else was a scam. I knew that and he knew I knew that.

"Of course I don't," said J. Herbert. "But to fully appreciate Ney Springs, and the spiritual power of Mount Shasta, you have to understand the legends hereabouts. Especially the Lemurian legend. It's very fascinating but it's a rather long story so you'll have to bear with me. I may not be able to finish the story today."

"I'm all ears," I announced.

"First of all," J. Herbert explained, "although everybody around here has heard of Lemurians, not many people know how the legend got started. Or what it means. Even fewer people know about the connection between the Lemurians, the spiritual power of Mount Shasta, and Ney Springs. Have you ever heard of the Continental Drift Theory?"

"Umm—sure," I said, somewhat startled by the sudden non sequitur. "In geology class back at the University of Michigan."

"The Continental Drift Theory was first expounded in the 1860s. Its originator, some German guy whose name I forget, gave the name, Gondwanaland to the giant, protocontinent from which all others are derived."

"I know about Gondwanaland," I said, feeling pleased with myself. "Nobody today believes there was ever such a continent as Gondzwanaland."

"Whether there was really such a place is beside the point. What matters is that part of Gondwanaland, a subplate comprised of present-day East Africa, Madagascar, and part of India, was named 'Lemuria' after an animal called a lemur, which lives in all three places. It's the lowest form of primate."

"Are you serious?" I said, laughing. "I made a joke about lemurs and Lemurians last night. The guy I said it to never heard of lemurs."

"That doesn't surprise me. On a subject that silly, you could drown in the sea of misinformation and ignorance. My source happens to be the California State Library in Sacramento. I went to high school in Sacramento. The St. Jerome Prep School. Awful place. But that's also beside the point."

"So you're originally Catholic?"

"I still am Catholic," said J. Herbert with a wink and a knowing grin, "but don't tell anybody. It would ruin my image. Anyhow, about ten years after the subcontinent of Lemuria was first described, a Russian mystic in New York named Madame Helena Blavatsky published a book in which she described 'Seven Races of Man.' Race Number Two were the Lemurians, an apelike people who laid eggs, were hermaphroditic, stood 15 feet tall, and had eyes in the back of their heads and four arms. We're Race Number Five, in case you're interested."

"And this theory, no doubt, was subsequently borne out in archaeological research, along with Piltdown man, bigfoot, and dragons."

"That's about right. As it happens, Madame Blavatsky's big contribution to the Lemurian legend was to mistakenly move Lemuria from the Indian Ocean to the Pacific."

"Interesting," I said, for want of a better comment.

"It gets much crazier," said J. Herbert. "You're probably wondering about the connection between Lemuria and the Lost Continent of Mu."

"Not exactly. Is there a connection?"

"Most people assume they are one and the same because of the name similarity. But they're not. Not at all. The Ancient Continent of Lemuria and the Lost Continent of Mu are connected only by their identical middle syllable. That and the fact that both were supposed to have been in the Pacific. Except for the one that was in the Indian Ocean."

"The guy in the bar last night told me that Lemurians are from Mu. I guess he was wrong."

"People from Mu are called Muvians and people from Lemuria are called Lemurians. It's very confusing. But then it's all nonsense anyhow. The Mu theory traces to the 1500s when a missionary named Diego de Landa, working in Mexico, published an alleged Mayan alphabet, which he claimed proved that the region's native tribes were descended from the Lost Tribes of

Israel. Since Mayan writing was pictographic and not phonetic, his alphabet was completely bogus."

"It certainly would not have been the first recorded incidence of bad archaeology," I commented. I'd taken a couple of archaeology courses in college.

"Nor the last," said J. Herbert. "Anyhow, in 1864, a French mystic named Brasseur used the de Landa alphabet to translate a Mayan inscription into a story about a 'land called Mu, which sank beneath the Pacific in a great catastrophe.' *Mu* is the middle letter of the Greek alphabet. Brasseur thought the Mayans were escapees from this Lost Continent. Actually, they were clearly related to, if a little more advanced than, the tribes around them."

"How does all this relate to Mount Shasta and Ney Springs?"

"I'm getting to that. In 1894 one Frederick Oliver, under the name Phylos the Tibetan, wrote a book called *A Dweller on Two Planets*, about a traveler who meets a Chinese holy man while climbing on Mount Shasta. The holy man runs a temple dedicated to preserving the ancient writings of Mu. The traveler visits the temple, is introduced to the wisdom of Mu, and, incidentally, psychically visits the planet Venus. It was intended as fiction but many people took it seriously. Some still do. You can purchase the book at most bookstores hereabouts."

"I guess some people will believe just about anything."

"Tell me about it. Would you believe there are still followers of Madame Blavatsky around? Anyhow, the story then jumps to 1924 and a man named Edgar Larkin. Larkin was a small-time entrepreneur who operated a little telescopic observatory for tourists, mainly to augment the income from an adjacent inn he managed for the Southern Pacific Railroad. It was called Mount Lowe and it wasn't far from Mount Wilson, a real observatory near Sacramento. Mount Shasta was a favorite target of telescopic observation."

"And still is, no doubt."

"No doubt. Larkin, probably to attract business, and having read the Oliver book, began spreading stories about seeing Lemurians dancing on Mount Shasta in white robes. He described them as 'taciturn' and said they held secret nightly rituals by the light of green campfires."

"Hey, why not? Another inflated advertising claim. But how did he know they were Lemurians? Or Muvians? Did they have four arms and eyes in the back of their head?"

"Larkin never mentioned anything like that. I guess he just assumed they were Lemurians because they were on Mount Shasta dancing around green campfires. In any case, not long after, a San Francisco journalist named Lanseur created a sensation with a story about how he'd observed Lemurians on Mount Shasta as he rode past in a train. Which is pretty observant considering you'd have to be 150 feet tall to even *start* to be visible on Shasta from a passing train. It was pretty odd that nobody else on the train saw them. He described them in great detail."

"Very interesting," I said, noting that J. Herbert had finished his meal and was gathering his briefcase preparatory to leaving. "You sure know a lot about the Lemurians." I looked at my watch and saw that it was indeed time to go back to work. "But you never got to the connection between Mount Shasta, Lemurians, and Ney Springs."

"I guess that will have to wait," said J. Herbert as he dashed out the door, suddenly looking very businesslike.

I felt as though I'd been in the middle of open-heart surgery and the doctors and nurses had abruptly decided to go skiing for a few days and finish the operation when they got back.

PART 3

J. HERBERT GUMBLE FILLED ME IN ON THE REST OF THE STORY A COUPLE OF DAYS later, on the way to the Full Moon Festival and Ruckus. I expected him to be dressed in some sort of garish ceremonial garb when he picked me up, but his clothes were pretty subdued for 1970: widely flared bell-bottomed jeans and a tie-dyed T-shirt. My own apparel wasn't much different (although a swarm of yellow jackets had taught me a rather "pointed" lesson on a hike several weeks earlier about the inadvisability of wearing bell-bottoms in the woods).

It was late in the day, around seven o'clock, when we left for the festival. Soon after, we were traveling in J. Herbert's car on the interstate between Yreka and Mount Shasta City. Ahead of us, and slightly to the southeast, the sun was setting on Mount Shasta. The mountain glowed red like a sunburned Swede who'd swallowed a Mexican hot pepper.

Ditching Patricia for the evening had proved remarkably easy. She didn't want to go. I pretended to beg and plead but she steadfastly insisted she had more important things to do. Barbara Gumble didn't go, either.

"Have fun, sweetheart," Pat said, giving me a gentle peck on the lips as I walked out the door.

"Have you ever heard Mount Shasta spoken of as spiritual 'Power Source'?" J. Herbert asked as I sat beside him in the front seat of his Volkswagen Beetle, watching the mountain grow redder and redder until I thought it would burst.

"Of course," I said. "Everybody has."

"And do you know what it means?"

"Certainly," I replied. Then I paused. I knew that J. Herbert's next question would be to ask me to explain the meaning, which I suddenly realized I could not do. "What does it mean?" I said.

"A spiritual Power Source is a place where the presence of God can be felt more readily than other places. If you're looking for spiritual highs, it helps to find a Power Source. Mount Shasta is one. So they say. Oak Creek Canyon, near Flagstaff, Arizona, is another. And Taos, New Mexico. And Mount Desert Island in Maine. There are a bunch of them."

"I presume that's why there are so many religious nuts wandering around Yreka and Mount Shasta City. No offense."

"None taken. It's exactly the reason. Except there's one thing the religious nuts, as you so aptly put it, don't know."

"And what might that be?"

"Glad you asked," said J. Herbert, grinning and looking pleased with himself for the tidbit of secret wisdom he was about to impart. "According to a Hoopa Indian shaman I know, a fellow named Augie Atteberry, Mount Shasta is only a secondary Power Source. The mountain draws its power from another, much stronger, primary Power Source. Without the primary Power Source, Shasta would be nothing but a big, pretty volcano, like Mount Lassen or Mount Rainier. Its mystical aura would go out like a snuffed candle."

"And where might this primary Power Source be?" I asked, although I had pretty much guessed the answer.

"The primary Power Source from which Mount Shasta draws its spiritual power," J. Herbert Gumble announced, "is Ney Springs. According to the legend, it is the job of the Lemurians to protect Mount Shasta's power, both on the mountain and at Ney Springs. And it is the job of believers in the legend to protect the Lemurians."

"You show me a Lemurian and I promise to protect him," I joked.

"I just might do that," said J. Herbert with a knowing grin.

At Mount Shasta City, Herb turned off the freeway, then drove up a series of paved side roads that headed away from town. Then he drove up a bunch of gravel roads that headed into the mountains. Then he drove up what seemed like an impossible maze of dirt roads, ending at a nondescript spot by a creek where a dozen or so cars were parked. Then he got out and we started walking up a very steep road that was too badly rutted to drive on very far. The road followed high above the creek, which J. Herbert identified as Ney Creek.

It was just about dark when we started walking. J. Herbert brought a flashlight but we didn't really need it what with the wide road and full moon. From what I could see, this was not the prettiest spot in the Mount Shasta region. It was pretty but not extraordinary.

The most striking thing about the walk to the ceremonial site along Ney Creek was the smell, which grew stronger as we drew closer. It was a distinctly sulphurous smell, like rotten eggs or the boiling mud springs I'd seen and smelled while touring Yellowstone Park with my parents fifteen years earlier.

It smelled like the bowels of hell.

J. Herbert explained that even though Ney Springs and Ney Creek were less than 10 miles from Mount Shasta, the two locations weren't even in the same mountain range. Shasta belonged to the Cascades, a string of young volcanic peaks that stretched from northern California to British Columbia. Ney Springs was situated in a much smaller range called the "Trinity Divide," which was considerably older than the Cascades and made up of a massive chunk of granite known as a "pluton." The presence of a hot spring in the Trinity Divide was probably caused by a hot pocket or finger of molten rock from the Cascades that ran underneath the pluton. In any case, hot springs are most common at the edge of mountain ranges, where the deep underground forces—including magma pockets—that cause the mountains to rise come closest to the surface. Ney Springs was situated at the edge of not one but two mountain ranges.

The ceremonial site was a level wide spot at the end of a closed-off road that branched off the first road we walked up. A large, roaring campfire burned on either end of the level spot. In between, three stone circles had been laid out, marked by river cobbles 6 to 8 inches in diameter. The center circle measured 10 feet across, while the side circles were 6 feet. Outside the circles, dozens of stone cairns, or rock piles, dotted the little flat. They ranged from 1 to 3 feet high. Some looked very precarious, as though the stones had been painstakingly balanced.

Everyone seemed glad to see J. Herbert. Especially the members of his "church," who swarmed around him, besieging him with questions and seeking guidance in what seemed to me like very trivial matters, such as where they should stand or how they should wear their hair. J. Herbert grinned knowingly and patiently as he took charge.

It wasn't difficult to distinguish the members of J. Herbert's church from the onlookers. The church members were 80 percent female and nearly all young and pretty. The few male members weren't bad looking, either. Except for J. Herbert.

"Just hang out and have a good time," J. Herbert instructed as he prepared to leave me to my own devices while he concentrated on more pressing issues. "When we finish the ceremony, I'll take you up to the hot spring and waterfall. That's the part that's the prettiest spot I know of. It's only a few minutes' walk from here."

I positioned myself near one of the fires, which a massive logger type fed frequently from a nearby pile of cordwood and small logs. J. Herbert had identified this individual, and a few others, as "security people." As nearly as I could tell, the job of the security people was to (1) tend the campfires, (2) keep an eye on the half-dozen picnic coolers filled with crushed ice and cans of Rainier beer, from which everyone in attendance, including myself, freely helped themselves, and (3) keep unauthorized and overzealous spectators, again including myself, out of the ritual dance.

According to J. Herbert, another of their tasks was to "watch out for trouble." The thought that there might be trouble made me uneasy. I pictured hordes of townsfolk suddenly descending on us, brandishing clubs, not unlike the scene in the movie *Easy Rider*. I looked around for an escape path, just in case.

The ritual began twenty minutes after our arrival. By then thirty or forty spectators, mostly harmless hippie types, had also arrived. The ceremonial participants, J. Herbert and his church members, numbered around twenty.

The proceedings started with J. Herbert standing alone in the middle of the center circle, with the other participants standing in the side circles. J. Herbert raised his arms to the night heavens and chanted, "Oo ram-na, ram-na, te-osh, te-osh, te-osh, praya makooya lemuriati."

Years later I visited a Christian church where some of the members spoke in tongues. They reminded me of J. Herbert's ritual chanting. Except for the *lemuriati* part at the end.

When the chant was done, a fellow sitting at the edge of the ceremonial flat with a set of bongo drums began playing. His rhythm was soon joined by hand clapping from spectators and participants. The participants, by then, had all downed two or three beers, so their inhibitions were, shall we say, diminished. Not that they had many inhibitions to begin with.

If other inhibition-diminishing drugs besides alcohol were being ingested, I wasn't aware of it, although it wouldn't have surprised me. J. Herbert had been known to drop a little LSD now and then. He had also been known to smoke a little marijuana. And hashish. And occasional opium. He considered cocaine and heroin dangerously addictive, however. I did not use any drugs besides alcohol, but most people I knew in Yreka used alcohol, marijuana, hashish, and LSD.

The dancing began innocently enough. The church members performed a chaotic, free-form fandango that looked pretty much like the Frug from the late 1950s. They danced both inside and outside the circles. Since the dancers paid no attention to the circles, I wondered what the circles were for. I figured I'd find out soon enough.

It wasn't long before J. Herbert, predictably, had dropped his drawers. And his shirt. And his underwear. He did keep his shoes on, though, probably because of all the rocks lying around. Needless to say, the parishioners quickly followed suit. Birthday suit.

The nude dancing and chaotic shouting continued for nearly an hour, amid the happy aroma of the fires, pine trees, and sulphur. The rhythm of the bongos grew gradually faster and the dancing became more and more frenzied, with ever-increasing physical contact between dancers. Some enthusiastic spectators tried to get into the swing of things, too, but anyone attempting to crash into the ritual circles was gently but quickly nudged back by the security people.

I would never have admitted it, least of all to J. Herbert, but I would have loved to join the dance. The dancers looked like they were having a fantastic time. As always, though, I contented myself with standing on the sidelines, ogling the naked girls, and making snide comments to myself about how dumb the ritual was.

Still, I couldn't help but admire the stamina of J. Herbert and his friends. I'd have keeled over in exhaustion after ten minutes. It occurred to me to go look for the hot spring and waterfall, which according to J. Herbert were a few hundred feet up the first road. But I wasn't about to wander off by myself in the dark.

The only person I talked to was a young hippie girl with curly red hair, a wool poncho, and an exceptionally vapid smile.

"Nice ceremony," I said.

"Yeah man," she said. "Cool, huh?"

"Ever been to the hot spring and waterfall?"

"Yeah, man. They're really cool."

"The hot spring is cool?"

"Yeah man. It's really cool."

The conversation ended when the two campfires suddenly went green. I'd never seen a green campfire before. With the change in color, the blazes greatly increased in size and intensity. I had to take several steps back away from them and shield my eyes with my hand. I didn't notice anybody tossing chemicals into the fire but I figured that's what had happened. I wondered if the fires could be seen through a telescope from near Sacramento.

Not a chance.

With a brilliant, eerie green glow illuminating the proceedings, the pace of the dancing, shouting, drumming, and hand clapping intensified even more. Then, after a while, somebody, probably J. Herbert, shouted, "Here they come!"

The dancing abruptly stopped and the celebrants stepped out of the circles. Crowding around, they continued their rhythmic clapping and the bongoist kept bongoing.

"They're coming! Fantastic!" J. Herbert yelled. "Here they are! They're doing it. Yes! Yes! Yes! Wow!"

Then the drumming ceased and everybody began cheering. I tried to get a look at the circles to see what was going on but everyone kept crowding and shoving and I couldn't see very well. I was also a bit tipsy from having downed three or four beers. From what I could make out, the circles were completely empty. I did get a sense of something moving in them, though, just out of my field of vision.

Then the ritual was over. The fires stopped being green and had diminished to barely glowing, definitely red embers. And the darkness of the woods, held precariously in check by the festivities, descended on the flat.

I was confused.

"Are you going to show me the hot spring and waterfall?" I asked J. Herbert as soon as I was able to get his attention.

"Oops. I forgot about that. I didn't expect the ritual to take quite so long. Listen, do you mind if I take a rain check? Besides, those things are better when it's light out. Why don't I give you directions and you can bring Pat out here one day and take a bath in the hot spring?"

"Whatever," I said, a little disappointed as we walked back down the road toward J. Herbert's car. During the drive home to Yreka in the dark, J. Herbert asked me what I thought of the ceremony. "It looked like a lot of work," I replied. "What was going on at the end? I couldn't see very well."

"Did you see the stone cairns come alive, turn into Lemurians, and start to dance inside the stone circles?" J. Herbert inquired.

"No," I said. "Did you?"

"Nope. I don't believe in such nonsense. But at least Mount Shasta's spiritual power is assured for another month. Or so I'm told."

J. Herbert Gumble grinned knowingly.

PART 4

I HAD YET ANOTHER INTERESTING DISCUSSION WITH J. HERBERT GUMBLE IN THE car on the way home from the Full Moon Festival and Ruckus, back in the fall of 1970, this time about the rock cairns that allegedly turned into Lemurians. J. Herbert likened the event to the Emperor's New Clothes. When he'd announced that the rock cairns were moving, he said, half the people present actually saw them move and the other half would never admit that they weren't "spiritually advanced" enough to perceive such a thing. I actually scored points with J. Herbert by not seeing the Lemurians and being willing to admit it.

"So tell me," I said, "are Lemurians taciturn?"

"Not in the least. Most of them boogie like a trumpet player in a New Orleans street parade."

"And are they 9 feet tall?"

"Some are. Most are between 3 and 4 feet tall."

"And do they have four arms and eyes in the back of their head?"

"Yes."

"And are you making all this up?"

"Definitely."

I didn't try to look for Ney Springs again until the following spring. I didn't forget about it, though. Not at all. As I visited more and more of the vast, magnificent wilderness around Yreka, including Caribou Lake at the core of the Trinity Alps and the majestic Sky High Lakes in the heart of the Marble Mountains, I found myself increasingly intrigued by the idea of "the most beautiful place of all." There are few locations on earth more beautiful than Caribou Lake at the core of the Trinity Alps or the majestic Sky High Lakes in the heart of the Marble Mountains.

I'd have gone back to Ney Springs much sooner, but it snowed early and to a low elevation in the winter of 1970-71 and most of the mountain roads quickly became impassable. The first snowfall came in late September. It wasn't just a few flurries, either; it was a major blizzard. Look it up. I remember that particular storm because I rescued some stranded southern Californians in a Volkswagen mini-van with flowers painted all over it, on Etna Summit Road. Since I'd wisely chained up a mile earlier, I pulled them out of a snowbank.

In May 1971 J. Herbert Gumble gave me instructions over the phone on how to find Ney Springs. I didn't anticipate that it would be a very difficult task, and I was especially anxious to see the waterfall. I love waterfalls and always fancied myself a connoisseur and gourmet collector of aqueous plummets. Besides, Ney Creek, and all the roads touching it, were indicated on the local national forest map, although Ney Springs itself was not. Having been to the spot before, I figured I could probably find the place even without J. Herbert's instructions.

Boy, was I wrong. On my way home from a hike off the upper South Fork of the Sacramento River—to Cliff Lake, I believe—I started up the paved road to Castle Lake, as J. Herbert instructed, then turned off on the first gravel road to the left. Then I got totally lost. I could have kicked myself for not paying more attention to J. Herbert's driving the night of the ceremony. On this attempt to locate the site, absolutely nothing looked familiar. It was as though they'd moved the place. Packed it up and stashed it away for safekeeping. Lock, stock, and cairn.

After driving up and down every gravel side road along the 8 miles of Castle Lake Road, which frequently flirted with Ney Creek, without finding a trace of Ney Springs, the ceremonial site, the waterfall, or the sulphur smell, I went home feeling very frustrated.

"I don't know what you did wrong, man," said J. Herbert on the phone afterward. "Sounds like you were on the right track."

That was the second to last time I ever spoke to J. Herbert Gumble. I returned to Michigan to get my master's, then I got a job as a case worker for Children's Services in Grants Pass, Oregon, 80 miles away. J. Herbert visited Patricia and me in Grants Pass once. During the visit, he made amorous passes at Pat, her sister, and her best friend. When I called J. Herbert a low-life womanizer, he accused me of being narrow-minded, judgmental, and inhibited.

"You need to expand your awareness and not be so uptight," he said with a knowing grin.

I agreed with his assessment of my attitude and freely acknowledged that he was absolutely correct. That did not, however, prevent me from booting him out of the house and telling him never to come back.

I think my final words to him were, "Take your knowing grin and shove it."

A year or so later, I heard that J. Herbert and his wife had moved back to Chico. I'd be very surprised if their marriage lasted but you never can tell.

It was twenty-six years before my next attempt at sleuthing out Ney Springs. I'd thought about it a lot during the intervening years but never made it back to Castle Lake Road or the upper Sacramento. Then, in late fall of 1997, our oldest daughter, Jennifer, then twenty-nine, decided to rent some rooms at a charming bed-and-breakfast just outside Mount Shasta City. The place boasted a terrific view of Mount Shasta from the living room, through a large picture window. The living room was full of antiques and had a cozy fire in the fireplace and the world's most talkative parrot. A telescope in the living room was permanently pointed at the mountain. I looked for evidence of Lemurians through the telescope, but there was not a green fire to be seen anywhere.

"Tough luck, buster," said the parrot.

Jennifer and her family lived in the San Francisco area. They had come up for the opening day of ski season and to celebrate Thanksgiving with us. My wife and I, and our youngest daughter, Anna, then fifteen, also stayed at the bed-and-breakfast. Our middle daughter Sara, then twenty-three, was finishing up her B.A. at Portland State University and couldn't make it.

Jennifer is a remarkable young woman. In 1997 she had two children, ages thirteen and three, owned a photography studio in Fremont, California, and was married to a high-level business executive. They're energetic and hardworking people.

Now, it so happens that the B&B was located not far from Castle Lake Road, where the mysterious and elusive turnoff to Ney Springs was also supposedly located. With a couple of hours to kill after breakfast on a cold but sunny Sunday morning, while everyone else was busy gabbing and packing to leave, I decided to go for a ride. And while I was at it, to have another go at locating Ney Springs.

I had nothing better to do.

This time I actually made it to a place that looked very promising. And very pretty. I ended up on a dead-end dirt road on the banks of the Sacramento River, a hundred yards from the mouth of Ney Creek. I enjoyed a beautiful cross-country walk to the creek mouth, through willows, red alders, cottonwoods, and big-leaf maples in fall color. I love the smell of colored leaves in the fall.

The creek mouth was impressive and, in fact, contained a very nice waterfall. But it wasn't the right waterfall and it definitely wasn't the site of the 1970 ceremony. For one thing, the sulphur smell was missing.

On the same excursion I tried another side road. This one dead-ended at Ney Creek, a mile upstream from the mouth. I was certain I'd been there before, with J. Herbert Gumble, and I began getting excited. But again, there were just too many side roads and I didn't have the time or inclination to check them all out. Especially the time. I might have made an attempt had I smelled sulphur. But I did not.

Before returning to Oregon, I did one thing that proved immensely helpful. I stopped by Fifth Season Outfitters, a large and bustling outdoors store in Mount Shasta City. The owner, a blond, Nordic-looking type appropriately named Leif, happened to be a friend of mine because his store had been selling the many hiking guidebooks that I'd written since 1989. Fifth Season carried all my books, and they sold pretty well. Leif was a knowledgeable informant on local hiking opportunities.

"So how do I get to Ney Springs?" I inquired.

"Interesting question," Leif replied, with a knowing grin, as he leaned on the glass counter beside the cash register. The store was crammed to the rafters with noisy skiers bearing credit cards. In summer it's crammed to the rafters with rafters with their sights on the Klamath, McCloud, Scott, and Salmon Rivers. "Where did you hear about Ney Springs? Not many people know about it, and those who do prefer to keep it a secret."

"A fellow told me about it years ago. He said there was a fantastic waterfall there."

"There is indeed. And an old bathhouse, too. At the hot spring. "

"So how do you get there?"

Leif proceeded to describe the exact route I'd just taken, the one where the road dead-ended at Ney Creek, a mile above the mouth. He said there were a bunch of old roads in the vicinity, most of them closed off, but that if I simply walked upstream for a quarter mile, I couldn't miss it.

My next visit to the Mount Shasta area came the following summer, on the Fourth of July 1998. My wife and I had been trying to reach the trailhead to a place called Deadfall Lake, a favorite hike of ours along the Pacific Crest Trail. But despite the magnificent summer weather, we found the road blocked by a 15-foot-deep snowbank 2 miles before the trailhead. So our plans for the day were quickly changed.

Driving back toward Mount Shasta City, we decided to give Ney Springs yet another shot. Following Leif's directions, I parked where the gravel road dead-ended at Ney Creek, a mile upstream from the creek mouth. Then Pat and I started hiking upstream, along the creekbank.

It was fairly rough going for the initial 200 feet or so. The bank was extremely rocky and choked with willow, alder, and sundry other impediments to rapid movement. The creek was fast moving and very pretty. What impelled us to continue, five minutes into the excursion, was the faint smell of sulphur. All we had to do was follow the odor.

Not long after, we came out on a narrow, steep road that had obviously been closed off years earlier. Trees and shrubs slowly encroached at the edges. We continued upstream, following the road for perhaps an eighth of a mile. The road dead-ended at a little shaded flat beside the creek.

On the shaded flat Pat and I encountered three stone circles and hundreds of rock cairns, obviously the site of the 1970 Ruckus. The place looked exactly as it had all those years earlier. It appeared as though the most recent ceremony had been held only a couple of days before.

Most of the hippies and religious mystics from the 1970s were long gone from Mount Shasta City. Either that or they had grown up and blended in with the general populace (where they contributed significantly to the local economy and culture). J. Herbert Gumble hadn't been around in years. Nevertheless, somebody, somewhere, somehow was still watching out for the Lemurians and "protecting Mount Shasta's Power Source."

That pleased me very much.

I had told my wife and kids many times about the ceremony and the vision of the dancing Lemurians. It was a family legend. One of Patricia's great regrets was that she hadn't accompanied me on that balmy night, twenty-eight years earlier.

"Barbara Gumble told me I probably wouldn't enjoy it," she explained.

"Barbara Gumble was wrong," I replied.

Since the closed-off road did not continue upstream, where the hot spring was supposedly located, we explored the flat with the stone circles for a while, then continued our journey along the creekbank. As we progressed, the sulphur smell grew distinctly stronger.

A few hundred feet beyond the ceremony site, I noticed another road, up the hill from where we were walking. It wasn't the same road as the one with the stone circles, but it probably connected to it. I scrambled up the extremely steep slope. Within five minutes Pat and I were walking side by side up the high road, looking for the hot spring. We could tell from the aroma that it was very near.

The high road was extremely rough and rutted but obviously still driven on. I had no idea how it connected with either the ceremonial road or the spot where we'd parked. I intended to find out on the way back.

After five minutes, or twenty-eight years and five minutes, we arrived at Ney Springs, a beautiful little grotto overgrown with horsetails and skunk cabbage, with a little stone wall built into the hillside. A pipe emerged from the wall, and milky, sulphurous-smelling water emerged from the pipe. The water dropped into a little concrete washbasin, which it overflowed. Below the basin, the water collected around the horsetails and skunk cabbage, then ran across the road and down the forested hillside to the creek. I could tell from looking at the water that it was hot because of the steam. But I still felt compelled to feel it. Poking a finger into the washbasin, I had to admit: The water was hot.

Not scalding but hot enough.

It also reeked of sulphur.

The grotto containing the pipe and skunk cabbage lay on the right side of the road. On the road's left side, a steep, 100-foot-long path led sharply

down to the creek. At the bottom of the path, there was more concrete work, which Leif at Fifth Season Outfitters had said was the foundation of an old bathhouse, built in the 1920s. The top of the bathhouse was long gone. In the middle of the concrete foundation was a small cistern, perhaps 4 feet in diameter, with a plywood lid. The cistern was filled with warm water and had two submerged wooden benches inside.

Despite the water's noxious aroma and murky whitish color, it looked very inviting. Where the water overflowed the cistern and ran into the creek, the rocks were stained with a white calcite patina. Immediately downstream, the creek had been dammed into a clear, sapphire-blue, ice-cold pool. The pool had no doubt been built for the benefit of those desiring to shock their system with a sudden leap from the warmth of the cistern. Hot-spring fanatics love to do things like that.

Pat and I didn't partake of the hot-spring bath, but we just had to tell our daughters about it. They liked stuff like that. Especially Anna, then sixteen.

After checking out the hot spring, we hiked back to the road and continued following it uphill, in search of the most elusive and purportedly beautiful prize of all, the legendary Ney Creek waterfall, J. Herbert Gumble's "most scenic place."

Beyond and above the hot spring, the road became much steeper and even more deeply rutted. It was almost a quarter mile from the spring to the spot where the narrow trail to the waterfall left the road. There was no sign at the junction, but the path was well marked and easy to find: Someone had erected a small rock cairn at the turnoff, not unlike the cairns back at the ceremonial flat. I wondered if the cairn might be a Lemurian standing guard over the treasure.

The trail was an eighth of a mile long and contoured across a nearly vertical slope. The route was mostly level, though, and followed a narrow ledge, except near the end, where it scrambled down the rocks to the base of the falls.

As you approached on the trail, the falls were fed to you gradually. First you heard them, a gentle roar in the distance. Then you smelled the mist in the air (the sulphur essence was long gone). Then you caught a glimpse, then a wider glimpse. And finally, Ney Creek Falls were revealed in their full awesome majesty.

Ney Creek Falls

J. Herbert Gumble had been correct. In retrospect, perhaps it was better for me to wait twenty-eight years before witnessing the most exquisite of all waterfalls. Had I seen it in 1970, when my quest for the perfect waterfall was just starting, it would have diminished all the others I've collected over the years. One thing I've learned about waterfalls, though, is that each has its own mystique and unique beauty, and it's foolish to compare them.

I'd estimate the waterfall's height at 150 feet. Maybe a little less. It's not an immense height, but it's enough to be impressive. The water's ordeal began far overhead, in a vertical-sided rock chasm. The churning white fluid entered, then instantly dropped 30 feet into a little collecting pool to catch its breath for a split second. While in the upper collecting pool, the water somehow twisted ninety degrees. It then charged out in full force and fury, fanning out over a magnificent white rock face before dropping into a much larger collecting pool at the base of the plunge. There were places on the rock face where you could probably sit and enjoy a shower in late summer after the early-season flow slacked off. When Pat and I visited on the Fourth of July, however, the abundant, roaring water would have crushed anything that dared get in its way.

I looked for a route to the upper collecting pool. But to get there, I'd have had to scale a vertical, moss-covered rock face that contained no handholds that I could see. I'm sure it was possible, but not for me.

I was content to climb down to the edge of the lower collecting pool and let the mist wash over me as I stood beside my wife. I put my arm around Pat's waist and gave her a little squeeze. And she put her arm around my waist and gave me a little squeeze.

"Anna would love this," I said.

Pat agreed.

Our youngest daughter Anna, in addition to liking hot springs, had an absolute passion for waterfalls.

PART 5

ONE YEAR LATER, IN AUGUST 1999, PAT AND I RETURNED TO NEY SPRINGS, THIS time with our daughter Anna and her best friend Phaedra. My beloved spouse and I had spent a year talking the place up. Anna was anxious not only to see the waterfall but also to bathe in the cistern and visit the ceremonial flat with the stone circles. Not to mention seeing the rock cairns that might really be Lemurians. Her real desire was to see the monthly ceremony. Or better yet, to participate in the ceremony. At age seventeen, Anna's biggest regret in life was having been born thirty years too late for the hippie era.

"You didn't miss much," I liked to inform her when she inquired about what the world was like back then. In Anna's mind, Pat and I had squandered the greatest cultural revolution and spiritual advance ever to reveal itself to humankind.

As we drove to Ney Springs in 1999, my wife warned the girls about the smell. "Be prepared to hold your nose," she said. She was exaggerating, of course. But a year earlier we had been assaulted by sulphur, almost from the moment we stepped out of the car. This time, when we got out of the car, we smelled nothing. I sensed immediately that something was wrong. I began feeling uneasy. And a little worried. I'm not sure why I was worried about the lack of a smell from a hot spring, but I was.

Very.

"It sure is a pretty creek," said Anna. "But I don't smell a thing."

"You will," I tried to assure her. "Wait until we get to the ceremonial flat."

A year earlier the sulphurous aroma had been pungent at the flat. This time we could smell only pine needles, wild lilacs, and a rushing mountain stream. While these were wonderful aromas, they were not what we anticipated.

The whole aura at the ceremonial flat had changed. On our 1998 visit Pat and I had sensed the spirits of lots of people having fun. This time the place felt dead, abandoned. I looked around for some indication that everything was okay. But I found none. The stone circles had been scattered, and the cairns were all knocked over. From the vegetation around the scattered river cobbles that once formed the circles and cairns, it appeared as though the destruction had occurred gradually, through weathering over several years. Had I not been to the site a year earlier, I'd have guessed that it hadn't been used in a decade or more.

The devastation made me feel slightly ill in the pit of my stomach. I found myself worrying about the fate of the Lemurians, the protectors. Then I hastily reminded myself that there were no such things as Lemurians. At least according to J. Herbert Gumble.

Anna kept staring at Pat and me, as though we'd made up the story about the sulphur smell, the ceremonial flat, the hot spring, and the waterfall.

"For this you dragged us all the way to California?"

We insisted that the place had been very different a year earlier, but I don't think Anna or Phaedra believed us.

We walked up to the hot spring and still there was no sulphur smell. Feeling a sense of dread that I could not explain, I extended a finger and stuck it in the water. My worst fears were instantly realized. The water coming out of the pipe in the stone wall was as cold as a January night. So was the water in the cistern by the creek. The cistern water was green and slimy, and you'd have to have been insane to bathe in it. The row of boulders that created the beautiful pool in the creek had also vanished.

The Lemurians were not being protected. Something was definitely wrong.

"Oh well," I said, trying to sound nonchalant. "Let's hike up to the waterfall. That can't have possibly have gone anywhere."

"Unless the Lemurians took it," Anna joked.

The waterfall, much to my relief, remained unchanged. It was as gorgeous and awe inspiring as ever. Anna acknowledged that it was among the prettiest she'd ever seen.

Anna and Phaedra had a fine time wading in the collecting pool and enjoying the swirling mist. So the trip wasn't a total waste.

PART 6

ACCORDING TO MONTY ELLIOTT, A GEOLOGY PROFESSOR AT SOUTHERN OREGON University in Ashland, there's a logical, scientific explanation for the hot spring suddenly going cold. A record snowfall the previous winter had raised the water table and cooled everything off. The spring, he said, might or might not heat back up following the next dry winter. On further investigation I learned that it was the first time, dating back at least to the California Gold Rush of the 1850s, that Ney Springs had gone cold.

I heard an alternate explanation, from a New Age type in Grants Pass, where I live. She suggested that the hot spring had cooled because Mount Shasta was gathering heat into itself. According to my informant, the only reason the mountain would gather heat into itself was because an eruption was imminent.

I did not like this explanation.

I don't know the answer. All I know is that even though I remain about as unspiritual as a carnival barker, I can't help thinking that the cooling of the hot spring had to do with the unexplained destruction of the stone circles. And that the loss of that spiritual nexus will ultimately affect the stability of Mount Shasta. And that somehow, the Lemurians are involved.

Here's the strange part: Even though I don't believe in Lemurians, I keep finding myself thinking about them, pulling for them. I figured out the reason for that, too. It didn't occur to me until the trip to Ney Springs with Anna, but I don't just admire Mount Shasta as a beautiful mountain. It is *my* Power Source, or one of my Power Sources. It always has been. I just could never admit that I had a spiritual Power Source until it was threatened. If Mount Shasta ever ceased to be a Power Source, I would be diminished, northern California would be diminished, and the world would be diminished. I found myself praying for the recovery of the hot spring and that the Lemurians were safe and doing their job. And I never pray.

There is also a broader lesson that I learned from J. Herbert Gumble, the 1970 ceremony, my twenty-eight-year quest to find Ney Springs, the mysterious cooling of the spring, and the destruction of the stone circles. The lesson is this: Whatever your personal Power Source might be, you need to always protect the Lemurians who keep the power flowing. Even if you don't believe in them. Because you don't have to believe in them to protect them.

THE HIKE: *Ney Springs Falls Trail, Shasta-Trinity National Forest, Mount Shasta City, California.*

LENGTH *(one way): 0.25 mile.*

DIRECTIONS: *Take I-5 to the central Mount Shasta City exit. Turn west, away from town, toward the fish hatchery, then turn left (south), toward Lake Siskiyou (bear right at the fork). Just beyond where the road crosses the dam, turn left onto the paved Castle Lake Road, then immediately turn left again onto the first gravel road. Bear right at the junction a mile or so down. Just before the road crosses Ney Creek and is blocked by a gate, a primitive dirt road takes off uphill right. Follow it as far as you can, then park and walk. It's about 1 mile up the road to a 50-foot side trail, on the right, that leads to the hot springs. A second trail, this one a couple of hundred feet long, takes off directly opposite, on the left, and leads to the bathhouse foundation by the creek. The unmarked, 0.25-mile path to the waterfall is also on the left, up the road 0.25 mile beyond the hot spring.*

HIKE THREE
PANIC ON THE PACIFIC CREST

PART 1

THERE ARE TWO FUNDAMENTAL, ABSOLUTELY INVIOLATE RULES OF HIKING. All hikers know about them, even if they've never heard them articulated in so many words. They're like Ohm's Law or the Theory of Relativity. Without them, hiking would be prohibitively difficult and risky.
The rules are:

1. A mile is always a mile. Distances from point to point will never be 2 miles one day and half a mile the next. You may hike the same distance faster one time and more slowly the next. And time may appear to go by more quickly or more slowly. But when you come right down to it, a mile is always a mile. You can absolutely count on it.

2. A trail that is uphill in one direction will always be downhill in the opposite direction and vice versa. Although a trail may occasionally seem like it is uphill in both directions, this is a physical impossibility and contrary to the laws of physics.

There are other rules of hiking, of course, such as "always bring a jacket just in case." But those are more on the order of helpful hints. The two rules just described, Bernstein's Uniformity of Distance Rule and Bernstein's Uphill/Downhill Rule, are basic because they have to do with the predictability of the universe. You cannot go hiking in an unpredictable universe because you might never find your way home on a trail, for example, that was 1 mile long on the way in and suddenly turned into a thousand miles on the way back.

That would be a very bad trail.

There is an old saying, however, that appears to have some relevance to the two absolutely inviolate rules of hiking just described. It goes like this:

"It is the exception that proves the rule."

I admittedly have never understood that saying. It always seemed to me that it was not exceptions that proved the rule but lack of exceptions. I did, however, have an experience once with an apparent exception to the above-cited "inviolate rules of hiking." Whether the exception proved or disproved the rules, I cannot say. All I know is that ever since, I've never regarded the mundane constraints of distance and topography, which I'd always pretty much taken for granted, as quite so rigid and predictable.

It all began on a warm summer night in late July 1999, when I couldn't sleep. The reason I couldn't sleep was that I planned to hike 15 miles the next day and needed to be well rested. There is nothing more likely to ruin a night's sleep than the imperative of having to get a good night's sleep or else. I suppose that's an absolutely inviolate rule, too. The result was that hours after going to bed, I found myself staring at the ceiling and muttering over and over, "When am I ever gonna fall asleep?"

Normally I sleep pretty well the night before a hike, even a very challenging hike. Whether the cause of my sleeplessness that night was a full moon, anticipation, too much caffeine, poltergeists, or the fact that deep down, I really didn't want to go, I cannot say. While the hike was to be somewhat longer than my normal day-hike distance of 5 to 12 miles, that shouldn't have mattered. It wasn't that much longer.

As nearly as I could figure, the problem was this: There is a threshold—for me at least—where hiking stops being fun and starts being work. As much as I love hiking, the activity loses something when the only objective is to crank out the miles to meet a publisher's deadline, especially late in the season when I've been hiking every weekend for months. In other words, I was going on this hike not because I wanted to but because I had to.

I once talked to a forest service employee who boasted that he averaged 35 miles a day when he hiked. To me that's just nuts. Things would whiz by so fast, you wouldn't have time to see anything, let alone stop to smell the roses. Or the monkey flowers. Besides, there are only three or four trails that are 35 miles long in all of southern Oregon. On most southern Oregon trails, you'd end up back in Medford if you kept going for 35 miles.

The most I ever hiked in a day was 20 miles. I could hike 35 miles in a day if I wanted to. More than that, even. On a level trail, if I left at five o'clock in the morning and hiked as fast as I could with no breaks, meals, or pauses of any kind until eight that evening, I could cover 45 miles in a day. But why would anybody in his right mind do such a thing?

In retrospect, the most ironic part of the entire Sky Lakes debacle was a conversation I had with my spouse, the comely Patricia, over dinner the night before. We'd gone out to Balboa's Pizza Deli, where I'd ordered an Italian salad and a giant pizza slice. Pat had a salad and a pepperoni roll. It was all very greasy but extremely tasty. There is no more heavenly aroma than the smell of baking pizza.

"I don't even want to go on that stupid hike," I whined between bites. "It's too far and I'm not in the mood. Besides, I think I may be coming down with something."

That was a lie. I was not coming down with anything.

Pat normally had better things to do with her life than go hiking every single weekend in summer. She accompanied me once or twice a year but no more. But of course she was not the person in the family who got paid to write trail-hiking guides.

"Then don't go," she said with a shrug, without looking up from her plate.

"I have to. You know I have a deadline. Besides, I've hiked 15 miles in a day before. With a full pack, too. It's not that far. I can't understand why this stupid hike is bothering me so much. According to the map, it doesn't look that difficult."

"Then go," said Patricia. "But whatever you decide, stop worrying about it."

"I don't want to go. You know what I wish?"

"What do you wish," said Pat, rolling her eyes in exasperation.

"I wish I could make the hike somehow over with, without ever going on it. I wish I could snap my fingers and I'd already be done with it, with full recall and everything."

"Nice idea." Pat smiled, looking me in the eye for the first time in a while. You have to understand that one of my wife's many talents is that she is blessed with amazing spiritual insight that is often overwhelming in its simple logic. In that arena she is rarely wrong. "Except if you did that, you would only have to make it up somewhere else."

"What do you mean?" I inquired.

"Think about it. If through some miracle of wishful thinking you succeeded, for example, in compressing a 15-mile hike down to an inch, then somewhere else in your life, probably not very far away, an inch would be stretched into 15 miles to make up for it. That's how those things work."

"I guess you're right" I sighed, turning my attention back to my giant pizza slice and trying to take her advice and not think about the impending hike. Still, I continued to wish that the hike were over with.

My destination the next day was to be the Seven Lakes Basin, one of the highlights of Oregon's sprawling and majestic Sky Lakes Wilderness Area, which stretches 40 miles southward from Crater Lake National Park's south boundary to the 9,495-foot volcanic summit of Mount McLoughlin, southern Oregon's highest mountain. I needed to hike the route for a book I was writing on the trails of the southern Oregon Cascades. And I was up against an imminent contractual deadline with a book publisher (which happened to be Falcon Publishing). It was that weekend or never.

I'd been to the Seven Lakes Basin before, visiting three of the seven lakes by a much steeper but shorter route than the one I was to take the next day. It had been a spectacular hike that I'd thoroughly enjoyed. I'd never taken this alternate route, and I'd never been to lakes four through seven.

Now, you might be wondering why I chose to hike 7.5 miles into a high-mountain wilderness, and another 7.5 miles back, all in one day, rather than camp out. The answer is that although I've written numerous guidebooks to hiking trails, and although hiking ranks high among my great passions in life, I dislike camping out and go to great lengths to avoid it. Ninety-nine percent of my hikes are completed all in the same day. I hate the hassle of assembling all that gear, lugging a cumbersome backpack for mile after mile, and sleeping on the ground. I rarely get any sleep when I camp out.

I had an additional reason for not wanting to camp out in the Seven Lakes Basin. The basin, like all of southern Oregon, had experienced a record snowfall the previous winter (1998–99). As a result, even though it was late July, I wasn't sure I'd be able to make it all the way to my destination without being turned back by deep snow on the trail. The person I talked to at the forest service didn't know if the trail was passable or not.

In my mind it made more sense to hike the 15 miles all in one day, free from the constraints of a backpack, than it did to risk toting a pack for 5 or 6 miles, only to get turned back and be unable to camp out. I know it sounds illogical, but my objective was not necessarily to be logical. My objective was to avoid, if at all possible, carrying a backpack and camping out. Besides, as you will see, very little in this story is logical.

However, as the night before the hike wore sleeplessly on, I grew increasingly upset over the prospect of hiking 15 miles into a mountain wilderness on no sleep. I'd lie anxiously in bed with my eyes closed and wait and wait and wait to fall asleep. When I couldn't wait any longer, I'd open my eyes, look at the clock glowing mockingly at me in the dark, and see that another forty-five minutes had passed.

Then I'd get up, go to the bathroom, head to the kitchen, look vacantly into the refrigerator, plod back into the bedroom, and try again, even though I knew it would be a futile gesture.

On each of my forays into the bathroom, I did something besides use the toilet. Every time I went there, after one-thirty in the morning or so, I gulped down a couple of over-the-counter pills that I knew had a sedative effect. By 4:00 A.M. I had consumed enough medication to knock out an enraged rhino. The final count ended up at six melatonin tablets, two aspirins, eight Tylenols, and a Motrin. I was as far from falling asleep as bunny suits are from General Patton.

During that fateful 4:00 A.M. bathroom trip, I had the brilliant, drug-induced idea to drive to the trailhead instead of continuing my exercise in futility, and try to get a couple hours of sleep there. In my crazed illogic, I reasoned that two hours of driving would surely tire me out. Of course, I didn't think about the obvious fact that even though I wasn't able to sleep, that didn't mean I was alert enough to drive. After all, my kidneys had just been assigned the monstrous and time-consuming task of detoxifying my system of six melatonin tablets, two aspirins, eight Tylenols, and a Motrin. Until my kidneys completed their mission, in twelve to fifteen hours, I was legally and physically unfit to operate a motor vehicle.

After concluding, finally and irrevocably, that the single fitful hour between midnight and one o'clock was all the sleep I was going to get, I got dressed, brushed my teeth, threw many handfuls of cold water onto my face, and gathered the gear I'd assembled the night before, including my lunch in the refrigerator. At four-fifteen I pulled out of the driveway and headed off into the bleary night.

I do not drink coffee, by the way. It tends to keep me up at night.

The drive to the trailhead seemed to go by pretty quickly and I found myself surprisingly wide-awake. Listening to all-night talk radio shows about UFO's and conspiracy theories helped me stay reasonably alert. I didn't feel as though my driving was impaired, although in bright sunlight with traffic, it would probably have been a very different story. The first dim rays of morning peeked tentatively through the gaps in the mountains just as the road I was on started up into the mountains, east of Medford. It was a very nice time of day, a time I didn't often get to experience.

It took two hours to drive from my house to the Sevenmile Marsh Trailhead on the eastern edge of the Sky Lakes Wilderness. I followed the interstate from Grants Pass, where I live, to Medford, 25 miles away and southern Oregon's largest city. Then I drove the paved highway over the mountains toward Klamath Falls. Halfway to Klamath Falls, past Lake of the Woods and Mount McLoughlin, I turned north onto Westside Road, then followed a bunch of gravel logging roads deep into the forest to a beautiful little trailhead at a small campground.

I arrived at the trailhead at six-fifteen, exhausted from lack of sleep and groggy from a ton of medication. I parked the car, shut the engine off, put the seat back all the way down, laid my jacket across my eyes to keep the about-to-rise sun out of them, took a deep breath, and attempted one last time to get a little shut-eye.

Normally, when I try to sleep in the car, if I sleep at all, which I usually do, I doze off within a minute or two. This time I reclined in the car for about twenty minutes, only to discover that I was even more wide-awake than I'd been at home. I almost cried.

Surprised to find myself with a modicum of energy, and not knowing how long it would last, I reluctantly got out of the car, affixed my belly pack to my belly, put on my jacket, and shouldered by my funky old duct-tape-covered blanket canteen that was my constant companion on every hike. My belly pack contained a camera, film, insect repellent, sunscreen, toilet paper, a watch, a knife, and my lunch.

With a sigh of resignation, and no idea how far I'd get, I started reluctantly but doggedly down the trail.

PART 2

THE SEQUENCE OF TRAILS AND THE DISTANCES BETWEEN TRAIL JUNCTIONS ARE critical to this story. The route I started out on, from the Sevenmile Marsh Trailhead, was called the Seven Mile Trail. It headed east for 1.75 miles before dead-ending inside the Sky Lakes Wilderness at the junction with the Pacific Crest Trail. The Pacific Crest Trail runs for 1,800 miles from the Mexican border to the Canadian border. Of that, 47 miles lie inside the Sky

Lakes Wilderness. And of those miles, 3.25 were on my anticipated route. At the end of the 3.25 miles, I would leave the PCT and follow the Seven Lakes Trail for a 0.5 mile into the Seven Lakes Basin, past Grass Lake and Middle Lake. At Middle Lake, according to the map, the Lake Ivern Trail took off northward, passing North Lake before reaching Lake Ivern after 2 miles.

To summarize:

Seven Mile Trail	1.75 miles
Pacific Crest Trail	3.25 miles (1.5 miles to overlook, then 1.75 more miles)
Seven Lakes Trail	0.5 mile
Lake Ivern Trail	2.0 miles

Total: 7.5 miles each way, or 15 miles out and back

Some more numbers before getting on with the story: The elevation at the Sevenmile Marsh Trailhead was 5,800 feet above sea level. The highest point of my proposed route, 6,400 feet, came on the PCT, 1.5 miles past the Seven Mile–PCT junction and 2.25 miles from the trailhead, at the Middle Fork Rogue overlook. The elevation at the beginning of the Lake Ivern Trail was 6,100 feet; at Lake Ivern, 5,700 feet.

I had a topographic map with me so I knew what the elevations were, approximately how long each trail segment was, which trail segments would be uphill, and roughly how steep they were. The Seven Mile Trail had the steepest uphill gradient, followed by the 1.5 miles on the PCT from the Seven Mile junction to the overlook. Beyond the overlook, the path began a long, gentle descent into the Seven Lakes Basin. It continued to descend to Lake Ivern.

The point is that none of these gradients was particularly steep and all fell into the "easy" category. Only the latter portion of the Seven Mile Trail, the route's steepest segment, nudged slightly toward "moderate."

And by the way, the 1.5-mile distance from the Seven Mile–PCT junction to the Middle Fork overlook was only an estimate. It looked like 1.5 miles on the map, and I was pretty good at estimating such things. I knew from experience that while I occasionally underestimated map distances, I virtually never overestimated them. What looked like 1.5 miles on the map might turn out to be 2 miles but it would never turn out to be only 1 mile.

Based on the two inviolate rules of hiking described at the beginning of the story, there were two things, as I started the hike, of which I was absolutely certain:

1. Everything that was downhill in the "in" direction, if I followed the same route back, would be uphill in the "out" direction, and vice versa.

2. The 7.5 miles in, if I followed the same route back, would also total 7.5 miles out. At least that's how it had always been on past hikes. And that's how I expected it would always be.

Normally one mile takes me twenty to twenty-five minutes on level ground and thirty to thirty-five minutes on steep ground. If I am hiking up a mountain at high elevation, a mile can take an hour or more. But at this elevation and on these easy gradients, the length of time required to hike a mile was fairly predictable: twenty to twenty-five minutes. Barring injury, or the heretofore-unknown effects of the fatigue factor, the length of time required to hike 1 mile constituted yet another inviolate rule. Not absolutely inviolate but mostly inviolate.

Before starting out, I reminded myself of an interview I once watched on TV with Phil Simms, the old New York Giants football quarterback. After winning the Super Bowl, Simms admitted to Johnny Carson on the *Tonight Show* that he was so nervous the night before, he hadn't gotten any sleep whatsoever.

If Phil Simms could do it, I could do it.

Sure enough, like the railroads in Italy under Mussolini, I arrived at the Seven Mile–PCT junction in thirty-five minutes, precisely on schedule. I found it encouraging not only that I'd made good time, but also that the 1.75 miles seemed to go by quickly and with little or no fatigue or discomfort. With the hike's uphill portion more than 50 percent behind me and the steepest part over with, I figured the rest of the trip would be a piece of cake. Or at least a spoonful of peanut butter. As long as my stamina held up.

Much to my surprise, I actually enjoyed the Seven Mile Trail, even though I felt a little groggy and my hands and feet seemed slightly numb. For the first mile, the path held a fairly level contour through a majestic old-growth conifer forest on a hillside high above Sevenmile Marsh, a brilliant green, many-fingered meadow with a creek meandering down the middle.

Beyond the sweet-smelling meadow, the path got a little boring as it commenced a rocky climb, still in the deep woods, up the route's only moderately steep gradient.

Before long I was standing at the PCT junction, a nondescript, level spot still in the cool, shaded forest. A tiny wooden sign nailed to a tree announced that it was 6 miles south on the PCT to Devil's Peak and 12 miles north to Crater Lake National Park. The next side trail north, according to my map, lay 3 miles distant.

Beyond the junction, just as my map had predicted, the PCT began a very gradual uphill ascent, still in a balsam-scented old-growth forest of white fir, Shasta red fir, western white pine, and mountain hemlock.

It took me exactly twenty-five minutes to cover the 1.5 miles to the overlook, which was excellent time. Very excellent time. Almost too excellent, especially on an uphill grade. It actually seemed more like ten or fifteen minutes but my watch said twenty-five.

Maybe this won't be so hard after all, I thought as I stood at the overlook, gazing out at the panorama. I quickly dismissed and tried not to think about my wife's statement the night before, about compressed distances having to be made up somewhere else.

Approaching the overlook, the woods gave way to an airy, light-filled dwarf forest of lodgepole pine, stunted by the extremely sandy, nutrient-poor volcanic ash. At the overlook itself, the only vegetation consisted of a few scraggly manzanita bushes.

Man, what a view! A few feet beyond where I stood, the world abruptly fell off into Oregon's most magnificent glacial canyon, the Middle Fork of the Rogue River. The Middle Fork Glacier (as it had been named in retrospect, since it had no name while it actually existed—at least none that anybody is aware of) had started at Devil's Peak, a 7,700-foot, multicolored volcano that rose abruptly upward, just south of the Seven Lakes Basin. I'd climbed Devil's Peak the pervious summer, as part of the same book for which I was hiking this trail.

While the Middle Fork Glacier had been busy carving out the Seven Lakes Basin, it was also gouging imposing yellow cliffs into Devil's Peak's north face. On exiting the basin, the glacier dropped 2,000 feet over another series of cliffs into a 20-mile-long, flat-bottomed, steep-walled gorge, which it had also proudly carved and which remains as the glacier's legacy for hikers like myself to wonder at in awe, ten thousand years later.

I remember thinking, as I stood at the overlook admiring the view, that the hike's first 2.25 miles probably seemed to go by so quickly because I was still a little stoned from the sleep medication. I'd just sort of hiked and spaced and didn't waste time worrying about trivia like whether I was out of breath. In fact, I hadn't spent much time thinking at all during the hike thus far, except at the junction and the overlook. In hiking parlance that's called "focus," and it's considered good.

Shortly after departing the overlook, fatigue or no fatigue and grogginess or no grogginess, I was abruptly jolted back to reality and forced to think. What happened was that I was attacked by mosquitoes.

When I say *attacked*, I don't mean just that there were a lot of them. I mean I was deliberately and maliciously assaulted. It was the mosquito equivalent of Pearl Harbor. The Sky Lakes Wilderness had a reputation not only for great scenic beauty, but also as a mosquito haven of unparalleled magnitude. It probably has something to do with the profusion of lakes, ponds, puddles, and marshes.

To make matters worse, a spin-off effect of the record snowpack the previous winter was a record mosquito crop. Mosquitoes are at their most aggressive and voluminous right when the snow melts. Toward the end of summer, when many of the smaller puddles and ponds dry up, the population usually settles down to something reasonably bearable.

Normally I don't have much problem with mosquitoes. There's something in my blood that makes them stay away if there's anything or anyone the slightest bit more palatable around. On this day there apparently was not.

It started with a simple bite on my wrist as I walked through a marshy area between the overlook and the basin. I swatted the little guy away, only to discover three more of the bugs on my wrist. Then there were a hundred of them on my hands, forearms, and neck. Then a thousand. The only way to fight them off was to wave my arms wildly and swat at my face and neck. The instant I stopped, they moved in. It felt like a red-hot, multi-tipped branding iron.

Fortunately I had a small bottle of mosquito repellent in my belly pack. Industrial-strength DEET. But to retrieve it, I had to stop waving my arms for a second, which was all the incentive my tormentors needed to make my life unbearable. Eventually I gritted my teeth, hurriedly got out the repellent, and sprayed it on my arms.

Middle Lake

With the first spray, the swarm of bugs backed off about 4 inches and would come no closer. With the magic shield in place, I was able to observe the situation more closely. I swear there were a thousand mosquitoes per cubic foot of air space. It was incredible.

Oddly enough, on the way back a few hours later, I wasn't aware of any mosquitoes, or hardly any. The attack seemed to have coincided with the emergence of full sunlight into the basin, at around eight o'clock. Following the mosquito onslaught, the apparently accelerated rate of time passage and my level of alertness returned to normal. It's difficult to space out with a hundred million starving mosquitoes dive-bombing you all at once. Before long Grass Lake, with its wide surrounding meadow, came into view, then Middle Lake. I was still making very good time.

Middle Lake turned out to be one of the loveliest bodies of alpine water I'd ever seen, a perfectly transparent, eighteen-acre pool in the middle of the forest at the foot of a jagged cliff, with Devil's Peak soaring upward above the cliff.

I liked the Lake Ivern Trail best of all. Despite my fatigue, I also managed to locate North Lake half a mile down the Lake Ivern Trail in a magnificent little side basin with no trail access. The highlight of the Lake Ivern Trail, aside from North Lake and Lake Ivern, was a beautiful cold spring at the halfway point.

Lake Ivern was the smallest of the basin's seven lakes. It occupied a little bowl on a ledge above a tremendous gray rock drop-off called "Boston Bluff." The lake outlet, through a narrow V cut into some rock outcrops, afforded a view of the Middle Fork Canyon that was even better than the view at the overlook. Far in the distance I could see the mountains that surrounded Crater Lake. Some of the long-vanished glaciers on the mountainous upwelling in which Crater Lake is located once flowed into the Middle Fork Glacier.

At ten-thirty, four hours after setting out on my hike, I found myself perched contentedly on a boulder above Lake Ivern's outlet creek, watching the little stream tumble thousands of feet into the canyon. I also watched the lake and the mountains in the distance. And I felt the warm summer sun massage life into my shoulders like a pair of loving, giant hands.

As I sat looking at the scenery and eating a bagel with cream cheese, with M&M trail mix for dessert, taking an occasional gulp of the drinking water I'd collected in my canteen at the spring, it occurred to me that I was enjoying myself. In fact, I was amazingly contented. All I needed was about ten hours' sleep.

Oh well.

If the walk back to my car went only half as smoothly as the hike in, the day would go down in my personal annals as a glorious outing.

PART 3

SURE ENOUGH, THE RETURN HIKE SEEMED TO GO EXTREMELY WELL. FAR BETTER than I had any right to expect. At first, anyhow. Phil Simms and the Super Bowl notwithstanding, it is an inviolate rule of nature that lack of sleep eventually catches up with you. One lesson I learned on the day of my Seven Lakes hike was that fatigue is not the only symptom of sleep deprivation. Another symptom is insanity.

The walk back to Middle Lake from Lake Ivern took about as long as the hike in the opposite direction had taken, approximately an hour, even though the path now sloped ever so slightly upward instead of downward.

The half mile from Middle Lake to the PCT, and the 2.75 miles on the PCT back to the overlook, also passed by fairly smoothly. The only problem I encountered was that the slight uphill trend on those segments seemed exaggeratedly steep, most likely because I was just plain worn out from having hiked 10 miles. But heck, I'd been exhausted on the way back from hikes before. Lots of times. I'd been so tired I felt like a gangster who had run afoul of the Mafia and had his feet encased in concrete preparatory to being dumped in the river. I'd been so tired my peripheral nervous system, including my vision, had started to shut down.

The best thing to do in those situations, I'd learned, unless you're so sick or exhausted you can't go another step, is to just keep going and get it over with, the faster the better. I stop to rest on a hike only when I either arrive at someplace interesting or am out of breath and gasping for air. Being exhausted, for me, is not a reason to stop; it's a reason to keep going. Otherwise I run the risk of falling asleep in a grassy meadow somewhere and waking up freezing in the middle of the night.

My *keep-going-at-all-costs* attitude annoys many potential hiking partners, which is why I usually end up alone on my excursions.

What I did not realize, at the time, was that this was the most tired I'd ever been on a hike. I didn't realize it because fatigue was not my primary symptom. So I kept going, as always, motivated by the knowledge that once I reached the overlook the path would start downhill and life would become much, much easier. Arriving at the overlook would mean that I'd completed 12.75 of the 15 miles and was entering the home stretch. Most important, it would mean that it was smooth downhill sailing all the way to my car.

I was never so glad to see a place in my life as when I arrived at the overlook. After stopping briefly for a drink of water out of my canteen, I headed down the trail once again, back toward the junction with the Seven Mile Trail, back toward the blessed comfort of my car. For the first twenty minutes or so, the path looked and felt exactly as I remembered it from the way in, except in reverse. It ran slightly downhill, passed a stunted lodgepole pine forest near the beginning, then entered a dense, cool, relaxing old-growth conifer forest.

I remind the reader that on the way in, the 1.5 miles on the PCT from the Seven Mile Trail junction to the overlook had taken an inexplicably brief twenty-five minutes, despite a slight uphill climb. I expected that the return trip would take even less time because it was now downhill.

At least it would if the inviolate rules of hiking held true.

Twenty minutes after leaving the overlook, I passed a small clearing that I remembered as being very near the Seven Mile Trail junction. Excited about approaching the final leg of my trip, I speeded up my pace.

I didn't think much about it when the path leveled off, then started up a short, gentle rise. This was, after all, mountainous country, and a few ups and downs contrary to the general lay of the land were inevitable. I also didn't think much of it when I failed to arrive at the Seven Mile Trail junction after ten more minutes, which was five minutes longer than the trip in had taken. I figured I was probably walking a little more slowly after 12 miles, although it didn't feel like I was. Ten minutes after that, with the path still mostly uphill and still no Seven Mile junction in sight, I began to worry.

What ultimately did me in was a transient thought. Were it not for this thought, on which I immediately began obsessing, the whole strange experience might never have occurred. I might have arrived back at my car right on schedule.

The thought was this:

Maybe I already passed the Seven Mile junction and didn't see it.

My next thought was:

Shut up.

But it was too late. I was obsessing and would continue to obsess until I finally arrived at the junction, an event I hoped would take place very soon.

Logically, I knew the chances that I'd really passed up the Seven Mile junction were remote. The junction would be awfully hard to miss. I attempted repeatedly to reassure myself of that.

On the other hand (as the little obsessive demon in my brain kept reminding me), the junction marker was only a 3-inch by 12-inch wooden sign nailed to a tree. And if I had indeed passed up the Seven Mile Trail junction, it would not be the first time I'd overshot an important junction on a hike. I didn't do it very often, but it did happen on rare occasions. And there was no question that at that moment, I was not at my most alert.

Overshooting the Seven Mile junction would be a disaster of unthinkable magnitude. The next side trail on the PCT, the McKie Camp Trail, lay 3 miles farther down the path. According to the map, the terrain did not change very much between the overlook, the Seven Mile Trail junction, and the McKie Camp junction, so there would be few, if any, cues to verify my error. The only way I would know for sure that I'd passed up the Seven Mile Trail would be when I arrived at the McKie Camp junction. That would mean an extra 6 miles of hiking, 3 miles each way. The prospect of an un-anticipated extra 6 miles was so depressing, I could not allow myself to even entertain the remote possibility. I had to be sure.

Besides, if I'd been inattentive enough to miss the Seven Mile junction, what was to prevent me from also missing the McKie Camp junction? The next junction beyond the McKie Camp Trail lay an additional 6 miles away, 9 miles from the Seven Mile junction. I envisioned spending the rest of my life wandering aimlessly in the Sky Lakes, on the assumption that if I missed both trail junctions, my life expectancy would immediately drop to no more than a couple of days at best. If I didn't die of fatigue, thirst, or exposure, the mosquitoes would surely get me.

I obsessed on these thoughts for another fifteen minutes, alternating between attempting to ignore them and trying to decide whether to turn back and look for the Seven Mile junction or keep going forward. I almost turned around several times because nothing looked familiar and the path continued on its inexplicable and illogical uphill climb. But whenever I made up my mind to turn around, I would get a vague sense that the junction lay just around the next bend, only a few steps away. I'd breathe a sigh of relief, chuckle to myself about my imagination working overtime, and press on for a few more steps.

Finally, fifty-five minutes beyond the overlook, I ran out of reassurances. There was no question about it. I had to have passed the junction; the trail segment could not possibly take me twenty-five minutes in one direction and fifty-five minutes in the other. Not to mention, the terrain was sloping in the wrong direction. But there was still no way to tell for sure. No way whatsoever. I didn't want to hike an extra 6 miles, but I also didn't want to find myself back at the overlook feeling like a moron and having to hike the 1.5 miles all over again.

What I did was panic. What I did was start running. I have no idea why I started running, not to mention where I got the strength. Despite my exhaustion and the uphill grade, running seemed like the only solution. I ran and ran and ran, hoping at each curve in the trail that the junction would miraculously appear. I ran until I was gasping for air and my lungs felt as though I were breathing superheated sand. I ran until I was positive that if I took one more step, I would fall over and pass out. I ran until I couldn't think anymore. I ran until I didn't care anymore. And then I kept on running because I was afraid to stop.

I ran until I was struck by a flash of insight.

The insight was an extremely clear and distinct set of footprints going in the opposite direction on the trail. Each footprint contained a large, backward letter *N*. I hadn't noticed those footprints before.

They were my footprints. I could tell from the backwards *N*, which was not backward on my shoe sole.

I wear a fairly uncommon brand of hiking shoes because only one athletic shoe manufacturer makes an EEEE width that fits my EEEE foot. It was not the most popular brand of athletic shoe, and the chance that the imprints in the dirt belonged to somebody else was virtually zero. Not to mention, I hadn't seen a single other person on the entire hike, or another car at the trailhead. It meant I'd been there before, which meant I had not passed the Seven Mile junction.

That was when I stopped running.

Less than five minutes later, a full eighty minutes after leaving the overlook, I arrived at the Seven Mile junction. The marker was extremely obvious; nobody in his right mind could possibly miss it. I hadn't felt so happy and relieved on a trail since arriving at the summit of California's Mount Whitney, the highest mountain in the forty-eight contiguous states, thirty years earlier.

Once I turned off the PCT and onto the Seven Mile Trail, time, space, and slope direction returned to normal. It took me thirty-five minutes to get from the PCT junction to my car, which was exactly as long as it had taken me to get from my car to the PCT junction.

I slept for an hour and forty-five minutes in my car before heading home.

PART 4

I HAVE NO EXPLANATION FOR WHY IT TOOK FOUR HOURS TO GET FROM MY CAR TO Lake Ivern and five hours to get from Lake Ivern back to my car. I especially have no explanation for why that 1.5-mile segment from the overlook to the Seven Mile junction took an hour and twenty minutes even though I ran for twenty of them.

The only explanation I can think of is admittedly pretty lame. It is this: I guess my wife was right.

And by the way, there's yet another inviolate rule of hiking that I didn't mention before. I don't know if it's a rule with everybody or just with me. The rule is that no matter how miserable a hike is, no matter how many things go wrong (I once broke my foot on a hike), the bad stuff seems to fade the instant you get home. If it was a beautiful and worthy hike, you remember the beauty and worthiness. Mishaps are recalled merely as incidentals whose sole purpose is to make the story better when you describe the beauty and worthiness to friends.

In short, you remember the awe and not the pain.

Or at least I do.

That's how I remember my hike into the Seven Lakes Basin on the Seven Mile, Pacific Crest, Seven Lakes, and Lake Ivern Trails. That's why it was a memorable hike.

THE HIKE: *Seven Mile, Pacific Crest, Seven Lakes, and Lake Ivern Trails, Sky Lakes Wilderness, Winema National Forest, Oregon.*

LENGTH *(one way): 7.5 miles.*

DIRECTIONS: *Take OR 62 from Medford to OR 140, and turn right. At mile 48, past Lake of the Woods, turn left onto Westside Road. Proceed 17 miles, to where it becomes Sevenmile Road and swings sharply east. The gravel Forest Road 3300 takes off there. After 3 miles, FR 3300 arrives at a complex junction with a sign directing you to the Sevenmile Marsh Trailhead in 6 miles. Follow the gravel road (FR 3334) through old-growth forest to the trailhead and campground.*

HIKE FOUR
AGAINST BEARS AND MEN

PART 1

STOPPING FOR A DRINK AFTER A HIKE IS NOT SOMETHING I NORMALLY DO. I've done it perhaps five times in five hundred hikes. I have no explanation for why I picked that particular day to stop, a Saturday in October 1994, except that I wasn't anxious to get home. Mostly it just struck me as a good idea. I hadn't been in the Buckhorn Tavern, in the town of Yreka, California, since 1972.

When I decided to stop by the Buckhorn for a "quick one" consisting of club soda and lime water (I hadn't used alcohol since 1982), I'd just hiked to the tip of a remote glacier on the east side of Mount Shasta and had finished sooner than anticipated. While passing through Yreka on the way home, I got to thinking about the good old days when I'd first moved out west from Detroit, Michigan. I lived in Yreka, California's northernmost county seat, from 1970 to 1971, and again in 1972, after which I moved 80 miles up the interstate to Grants Pass, Oregon.

The thing about the Buckhorn is that even though I went there probably a hundred times during my two years in Yreka (in 1972 I did use alcohol), I had little idea of the interior decor. That's because they kept the place extremely dark—so dark you could barely see to walk across the room. Bright light is hard on your eyes when you're intoxicated. And bar patrons often don't want to know the fine details of whom they're talking to and what kind of joint they're in. That might explain why the Buckhorn was not only dark inside, but also darker than most other bars.

When I entered the Buckhorn, I found it just as dark as it had been twenty-two years earlier. And just as full of cigarette smoke. The main room consisted of a hardwood bar with bar stools, a long padded bench with tables along one wall, a dozen or so other tables, and hundreds of deer antlers mounted on the walls and above the bar mirror. Hence the name Buckhorn. The busy poker room in the back, which had a green-shaded bulb dangling from the ceiling over each table, was a little more brightly lit than the main room. But I rarely went into the poker room in the old days, except for a quick peek to see if there was anybody there I knew.

I was amazed at how little the Buckhorn had changed. It had changed so little that old Augie Atteberry, the Hoopa Indian game tracker, was still sitting at his usual table in the corner of the main room, drinking lemonade (a holdover, I presumed, from the days when local bars refused to sell alcohol to Native Americans) and smoking one cigar after another. A swirl of smoke over Augie's head glowed slightly in the dim light. Augie recognized me, even though we hadn't talked in twenty-two years and were never particularly close.

"Hey Bernstein. What the hell are you doing here?"

I ended up sitting with Augie through three drinks instead of my intended "quick one." I'd always liked Augie. The nice thing about nonalcoholic drinks is that you can have as many as you want.

Augie Atteberry was a tiny man, perhaps five-foot-three, with silver hair in a ponytail almost down to his waist. In 1994 he must have been pushing ninety, but he looked about the same as in the early 1970s. Of course, in the dim light of the Buckhorn, it was difficult to assess such things.

The ancient man wore a San Francisco Forty-Niners jacket, a black T-shirt with a Harley-Davidson logo, and a beaded necklace with an Indian motif that appeared to be some sort of religious amulet. He was, after all, a member of the Hoopa tribe.

"You still write them hiking books?" Augie asked. It pleased me that Augie was familiar with my books. He was one of the people who'd first gotten me interested in exploring the wonders and mysteries of the local backcountry.

"I sure do. Have you read any of them?"

"Looked through a couple," Augie said. "I wish we had more time to talk, because there are hundreds of fantastic trails I could tell you about that aren't on the map and most white folks never heard of. But as far as your books go, you do okay for a non-Indian."

"Thank you," I said. Coming from Augie, that was high praise.

"My only question is, how come almost all the hikes you write about are day hikes? Don't you like camping out?"

"It's because of my bad back," I explained, trying hard to look him in the eyes so he would know I was telling the truth, which I wasn't. "Nothing serious, just minor osteoarthritis. I have a terrible time sleeping outdoors."

Augie smiled a relaxed smile and took a puff on his cigar.

I would have done just about anything, at that moment, to avoid admitting the real reason I didn't like to go camping. I'd never admitted it to anybody. And the last person I wanted to tell was a rugged outdoors-type like Augie Atteberry. It was just too embarrassing, too threatening to my image as a self-sufficient, prepared-for-anything explorer of the wilderness. I really did have osteoarthritis, mind you. But it was very mild. Nothing a couple of Motrin tablets couldn't fix in twenty minutes. It did not keep me awake when I camped out.

"Ain't nothing wrong with your back," Augie announced.

"Yes there is," I insisted.

"If there is, it's all in your head," said Augie. "You don't look like a man with back problems."

"Trust me," I said. "I have a bad back."

"If you say so," said Augie. "But tell me this, you ever seen any bears on any of your hikes?"

When he said that, my osteoarthritis story collapsed like a house of cards in a hurricane. Augie knew. I could lie all I wanted but he knew. And he knew that I knew that he knew.

Here, then, is the truth, which I admitted for the first time ever to Augie Atteberry:

At the time of my encounter with Augie Atteberry in 1994, I had a much more compelling reason than back problems for avoiding camping out. The sad fact, I'm ashamed and embarrassed to admit, was that when I camped out, I was kept awake all night by constant worry about being eaten, or at least attacked, by bears.

As a trained naturalist, I knew that my fear of bears was not rational. And I realized that this fear put me in the same category as the child in the A. A. Milne poem who avoided stepping on the lines in the sidewalk because he was scared that a bear would suddenly jump up through a trapdoor.

Bears just aren't very aggressive. At least black bears aren't. That was the only kind of bear that lived in northern California and southern Oregon, where I did most of my hiking. Grizzly bears, of course, are another matter. Grizzlies, allegedly, will tear your arm off and eat your head as soon as look at you. Fortunately, the only grizzlies in the United States live in Alaska and Montana. Or at least it's fortunate for the rest of the United States. Or for me, anyhow.

Although I have since conquered my fear of black bears, I'm still afraid of grizzlies, despite having hiked in both Alaska and Montana. You're supposed to be afraid of grizzlies when you're in grizzly country.

The native black bears that inhabit the remote areas of nearly every state (except maybe Delaware and Hawaii) are much smaller than grizzlies, only three or four hundred pounds, maximum. Unlike their grizzly cousins, at the first sign of a human most black bears skedaddle like a cheating woman whose husband just pulled into the driveway. In my thirty years of hiking, I've never heard of anyone being seriously attacked or injured by a black bear, even when the bear was protecting a cub.

On the other hand, black bears are notorious for raiding campsites at night, foraging for Twinkies and trail mix. That, to me, was not a welcome prospect, despite repeated assurances from "experts" that the perpetrators would not harm me. Aggressive or not, I do not want bears peering into my tent while I'm trying to sleep. I guess I'm just modest.

When I did end up camping out in the wilderness, on an average of once every other year, of the twenty to thirty hikes I went on annually, I took (and still take) extraordinary anti-bear precautions. I locked my car and didn't leave food or edible-looking packages in plain view. I didn't bring food into the tent with me at night but instead hung it from a tree, out of reach of prowling beasts (although bears are amazingly intelligent and it would not surprise me if they eventually learned to untie suspension ropes).

It didn't help. I still worried and I still couldn't sleep.

There were no actual bear encounters during any of my hikes. They were all potential bears, possible bears, and imagined bears. With all the worrying I've done about bears over the years, and with all the hiking I do, you'd think I'd have run into dozens of the beasts.

"I've never seen a single bear on a hike," I confessed, in reply to Augie Atteberry's question. Actually I'd always thought that was strange, considering that nearly everybody I talked to about hiking, most of whom had been on far fewer hikes than I, regularly encountered the ursine pests.

"You're afraid of bears, aren't you," said Augie.

I nodded my head in sad assent. He had me. There was nothing else for me to do but capitulate.

"You need to get over it," said Augie. "The bears have been avoiding you because they know you don't want to see them. But one of these days, a bear is going to take offense at your attitude. That could be disastrous. Besides, you can't truly be in tune with nature if you are estranged from bears. It shuts out too much."

"I'd love to get over it," I said. "I keep telling myself that the fear is stupid. But it doesn't help."

"What you need to do," said Augie, setting his cigar in the ashtray and leaning forward so that his face was only a few inches from mine, "is subdue the spirit of the bear."

"Oh," I said, "is that all? And just how do I go about it?"

Subduing the spirit of a bear did not sound fun. It did not sound safe, either.

"The best way to explain it," said Augie, "is to compare it to a story in your Bible, the one where Jacob goes to see his brother Esau after many years. And yes, I've read the Bible. I could tell you a story from my tribe's folklore that also fits, but I like the Jacob story."

"I know that story," I said. "Jacob cheated his brother out of his birthright, then ran away and hid for twenty years. Then he finally had to face him."

"And Jacob," said Augie, picking up the narrative, "was scared to death about the meeting because Esau had sworn to kill him. Jacob realized that before he could face his brother, he must face himself. It says right there in the Bible that the night before Jacob was to see his brother, 'A man wrestled with him until the breaking of day.'"

Augie recited the rest of the passage:

> *Now when the man saw that he did not prevail over Jacob, he said,*
> *"Let me go."*
>
> *But Jacob said, " I will not let you go unless you bless me."*
>
> *And the man said, "What is your name?"*
>
> *And he said "Jacob."*
>
> *And the man said, "Your name shall no longer be Jacob but Israel,*
> *for you have struggled against God and men and have prevailed."*

"So what you're saying," I replied when Augie had finished, "is that all I have to do to capture the spirit of the bear, to secure the bear's blessing, is to struggle against bears and men and prevail? And I if I do, the bear will bless me and change my name?"

"Something like that."

"Seems to me, that's much easier said than done. Besides, I can't see myself ever pinning a bear in an all-night wrestling match, even if I could induce one to take me on, which is insane."

"I understand what you're saying, but remember this is a spiritual wrestling match. And don't worry. The opportunity will come. You'll see."

PART 2

IN MAY 1996, A YEAR-AND-A-HALF AFTER MY CONVERSATION WITH AUGIE ATTEBERRY in the Buckhorn Tavern, I had my second-ever bear encounter at a place called Frog Pond Meadow in the Red Buttes Wilderness, which straddles the Oregon-California state line. I'd just hiked in three miles from the trailhead. The bear, a smallish critter with nearly black fur, was standing smack in the middle of the meadow as I approached from the adjacent woods. I had the presence of mind to snap three or four photos before the thing got wind of me and sidled off to wherever bears sidle off to.

By the time that second encounter took place, I no longer had a problem with bears beyond a reasonable, healthy respect. That was because my initial face-to-face encounter, one year earlier, had cured me once and for all. The incident took place in March 1995, on a hiking trip to the Sycamore Canyon Wilderness of northern Arizona.

As the saying goes, "I remember it well."

I went to Sycamore Canyon for those two days in March mostly because of a rampant case of cabin fever. I always get cabin fever in spring. My annual bout with cabin fever begins when the snow closes the mountain high country in late November or early December and ends when the snow melts in May or June. Along about March or April, I start to get extremely restless. Most of the time I simply endure it. But if the early-spring weather in Oregon is particularly bad, and the snowmelt is particularly slow, I've been known to take off for a few days to warmer climates, usually within a day's drive. Maybe two days. Over the years I've ended up in or around Palm Springs, Tucson, Las Vegas, and Ensenada, Mexico. Not to mention Disneyland, Knott's Berry Farm, and the San Diego Zoo with the kids.

This time I decided to make a trip by myself to Arizona, to do some hiking in the Sycamore Canyon Wilderness. I'd seen much of the surrounding area, the Grand Canyon, Humphreys Peak (highest point in

Arizona), Montezuma's Castle National Monument, Wupatki National Monument, Tuzigoot National Monument, Walnut Canyon National Monument, and my favorite, Oak Creek Canyon, with its twisty road and intense red sandstone monoliths.

And always, in the middle of the map, like a big bleeding wound that demanded attention, miles from any paved road, was the sprawling, many-fingered, 56,000-acre Sycamore Canyon Wilderness, better known as the "Little Grand Canyon." If ever a place demanded that I hike its trails, calling to me like Bali Hai called to the sailors in *South Pacific*, this was it.

I spent the first night of my trip at a campground in Valley of Fire State Park, a few miles east of Las Vegas. Valley of Fire is a magnificent place, full of jumbled red rock formations leading down to the Colorado River. After a memorable sunset, I drove into Las Vegas for a couple of hours, then returned and slept like a baby in my tent, all night long, without a hint of back problems. I awoke to an awesome sunrise. The rocks grew redder and redder and redder until I literally feared they would catch fire.

I arrived in Flagstaff, Arizona, at around noon, saying hello to the Grand Canyon on the way past and touring Sunset Crater National Monument, which I'd never visited before.

I'd chosen for my hike the southernmost and supposedly easiest trail into the Sycamore Canyon Wilderness, which followed Sycamore Creek upstream from its confluence with the Verde River to a place called Parson's Springs. The path, called the Parson's Trail, was supposed to be Sycamore Canyon's most popular. I'd read that it afforded the best views of the canyon and boasted the most water, the most clearly defined canyon walls, and the easiest auto access.

I made the decision to backpack in and spend the night rather than stay in a motel or one of the hundreds of campgrounds in the region, because I'd been informed that the bears were still in hibernation, which meant I'd be able to relax and get some sleep rather than lying awake obsessing about potential nocturnal ursine visitors. Since I planned to do some exploring on side trails, a centrally located campsite seemed like an excellent idea.

I arrived at the Parson's Trailhead at about three in the afternoon. It was pretty easy to find. I was encouraged that all the dry washes crossed by the access road were dry and there was no indication of any impending storms, which is not always the case in March.

There were no other cars parked at the trailhead on that Wednesday afternoon, a fact that pleased me very much. It meant I could count on a little solitude. The trailhead sat on a sagebrush-covered flat, at the edge of a cliff with an impressive overlook of the lower canyon, with its pink rock walls. From the trailhead, I could see the first mile of the tree-lined Sycamore Creek, to where it made a right-angled turn to the left.

The path dropped 500 feet in a third of a mile from the trailhead. It was very dusty and exposed until I reached the bottom. Early on I passed through a gate, with a sign asking hikers to keep it closed. I presumed that the gate was to keep the cattle I'd seen grazing on the surrounding hills out of the protected wilderness. I was wrong. I later discovered that the gate's actual purpose was to prevent cattle grazing in the wilderness from wandering onto the surrounding lands.

Once the path reached the creek, it pretty much hugged the water's edge, except for occasional forays where it cut across open (usually sandy) areas or over rock outcrops when the creekside became too twisty or rough. As I hiked, the scenery grew more and more lovely and the canyon walls drew closer and higher.

After 1 mile, the trail crossed the creek through ankle-deep water, where the canyon veered sharply left. Soon after, it arrived at Summer Spring (great name!), a popular swimming hole in summer with a sandy beach, where the creek widened and deepened at the base of a vertical red cliff. At Summer Spring the path crossed the creek a second time.

I checked the skyline as I forded the creek, to make sure there were still no storm clouds that could cause a flash flood and either cut off my return trip or kill me. I wasn't too worried about flash floods. As long as I knew that the bears were safely sleeping, these other potential, but far-fetched, dangers didn't concern me too much.

In addition to both black and eastern cottonwoods along the creek, I observed (for starters) Mexican walnuts, Emory oaks, ponderosa pines, velvet mesquite, and Arizona sycamores. Mesquite was the most common tree, scraggly little things no bigger than a dogwood and covered with thorns. Not surprisingly, the stars of the show—the largest and showiest of the trees— were the sycamores. The Arizona sycamore looks much like the stately American sycamore found in urban front yards that's native to the eastern United States, except its habitat is completely different. The Arizona tree adores desert streams such as Sycamore Canyon, where summer heat is

intense and winters are extremely mild. Emory oak and Mexican walnut also love to hang out in such places.

I arrived at Parson's Springs after a leisurely two-hour stroll, which included four more stream crossings. The canyon widened out around the spring, which meant there was more potential grazing land than lower down. Parson's Springs turned out to be one of the most beautiful places I'd ever been: a small, emerald pool surrounded by reeds and sedges. It seemed to be a haven for hummingbirds and the happy songs of canyon wrens and hermit thrushes. Unlike Summer Spring, there was no sandy beach. To swim, you had to push your way through a sea of reeds.

For my night's lodging, I picked out a beautiful shady spot alongside the creek, a few hundred feet down from the spring. There I snacked on trail mix, set up my little dome tent beneath a large cottonwood, stowed my gear inside, and ventured out for a little more hiking before turning in for the night. I arrived at the spring at four forty-five in the afternoon, so there was still a little daylight left even though it was only March.

It was soon confirmed, as I erected my tent and ate my snack, that like many wilderness areas of the West, Sycamore Canyon is leased for cattle grazing. A bunch of cows filed past, amid a cacophony of mooing and bell clanging. Apparently they were heading for another grazing site not quite so close to this human intruder. I worried that they might decide to come back in the middle of the night, bringing their mooing and clanging with them, so I was as rude as I could possibly be, shouting and waving my arms. Each time I shouted, they speeded up their pace a little. The cows did not appear to want any more of my company than I wanted of theirs.

After getting settled and running off the cattle, I continued up Sycamore Creek for another 1.5 miles, to a large oxbow meander. It was quite a trek, past some beautiful hidden side canyons and fern grottoes. For the most part the trail was either very faint or nonexistent, but it would have been difficult to get lost. One of the side canyons, not far from Parson's Springs, led to what looked like a breathtaking and easily reached vista point on the lower flank of something called Black Mountain. I decided to return in the morning and spend a couple of hours checking out this off-trail route. When I returned to Parson's Springs from my side trip, an hour-and-a-half later, I saw no sign of the cows.

It was on the hike back to my campsite that things really got interesting. A quarter-mile from my tent, I came over a rise and observed a huge black bear sitting in a field. Actually it wasn't black; it was a light cinnamon bordering on strawberry blond. But since it was obviously not a grizzly, it had to be a black bear despite the color. The thing weighed at least five hundred pounds.

I knew this was not a grizzly bear for two reasons. First, it had no fatty hump on the back of its neck. Second, there are no grizzlies in Arizona. There's a third way to identify a grizzly bear. Grizzlies have fine silvery hairs growing amid their otherwise brown fur, which is where the name *grizzly* comes from. I did not get close enough to the Sycamore Canyon bear to check out such details.

Oh shit, I thought. *They lied to me. The bears aren't in hibernation.*

Or at least this one wasn't.

As far as I could tell, the bear wasn't doing much. It was just sitting there, puttering around, and enjoying life. Were I in its position, I'd probably be doing exactly the same thing on a warm afternoon in early spring.

On seeing this animal, the first bear I'd ever encountered on the trail in twenty-five years of hiking, I stopped, backed up a little until the bear was out of view (which meant I was out of its view), and, with my heart pounding, pondered what to do. Since the thing was practically in the middle of my intended route, there was no way around that did not involve an eyeball-to-eyeball confrontation. I waited several minutes but the animal seemed settled in where it was, with no inclination to move anytime soon.

Finally, struggling to remember everything I'd ever heard about fending off bears, and mustering every ounce of courage, I shouted at the top of my lungs. Despite its immense size, the startled beast took off like a whippet at a dog track, in the direction away from my voice.

Boy was I relieved.

It was not until several minutes later, as I resumed my hike back to the tent, that it occurred to me that during the five minutes in which I was aware of the bear and the bear was not aware of me, I'd had ample opportunity to get out my camera and take a picture. I could have taken a whole roll, in fact. But the thought had never entered my head.

Back at the tent I feasted on a dinner of canned beef stew and trail mix. Afterward I meticulously scoured my utensils in the creek, along with the empty stew can, to get rid of any food scent that might attract my ursine neighbor to come a-calling in the middle of the night. Then I sat for a while, puttered around, and generally enjoyed life. I did exactly what a human would be expected to do on a warm evening in early spring, by himself in the wilderness.

I tried not to think about the bear.

One thing I did, just before going to bed, was suspend my backpack with a nylon rope from a tree. Then I blew up my air mattress, unrolled my sleeping bag, and, as the shadow of night slowly moved from the canyon rim down across the valley, reluctantly crawled into my tent to try to get at least a little sleep.

I was not very hopeful. Usually my worry about bears is vague and unfocused. This time I had good reason to worry. Very good reason.

It did not help when, later that evening, the cows decided that they simply could not live without my scintillating company. Either that or I'd inadvertently camped in their favorite creekside overnight spot. With the usual clanging and mooing announcing their return, they plopped themselves (literally) not far from my tent.

The problem, I soon ascertained as I snuggled up in my sleeping bag, was that cows tended to moo constantly and for no apparent reason. For animals that just stand around and chew cud all day long, they sure seemed to have a lot to say. In any case, I already had enough on my mind. In addition to worrying about the bear, I had that hike in the morning, up the steep red cliff, not to mention the 3.7-mile trek, with backpack, back to my car. A couple of hours' restful sleep would make life after sunrise much, much easier.

The cattle and I soon settled into a routine. It would be a quiet, still, wilderness night. Then somebody would start mooing. Then somebody else would start mooing. Then somebody else and somebody else until my bovine neighbors had a full-scale cow-chorus going. I'd endure it for a while, then yell at them from inside my tent. I discovered that whenever I yelled, there would be instantaneous and total silence for twenty to thirty minutes.

PART 3

THE COWS EVENTUALLY SETTLED DOWN FOR WHAT I HOPED WOULD BE THE remainder of the night. But I still couldn't sleep and I was still obsessing about the bear. Was I ever. At about three o'clock, in the midst of my tossing, turning, and fretting, I noticed that my head had somehow penetrated the rear wall of my tent and that I was looking up at the stars. I could feel the gentle night breeze on my face. It was very pleasant and the stars were lovely, illuminating everything around me. Visibility was pretty good despite the darkness.

It wasn't until the next morning that I realized that my head could not possibly have penetrated the rear wall of the tent. At least not without inflicting major damage to the tent, if not to my head. There was no noticeable damage to either.

At the time, I recall reveling in the fresh air. At least I reveled until I saw a bear out of the corner of my eye. It was the same bear I'd seen in the field. I quickly tried to pull my head back inside, but it was apparently stuck. As I struggled, growing ever more terrified, the bear came closer and closer, walking on all fours with long, slow strides. It approached to within three or four feet of where I lay. Then it leaned over, breathed on me with warm, sour-smelling breath, looked me squarely in the face, and mooed. That was when I remembered the famous Bernstein anti-bear, anti-cow hollers that had been so effective the previous day. With sublime confidence, I opened my mouth and screamed:

"Get the hell out of here!"

The bear did not respond. It did not bat an eye. It was as though the animal had gone completely deaf. My magical holler was a dismal failure.

I was baffled and confused at this sudden impotence of the fabulous Bernstein vocal chords. For a minute. Then it occurred to me that I was sleeping and had only dreamed my yell. Fortunately, the dream yell had awakened me.

I yelled again, this time for real. Again there was no response. The bear just stood there and stared at me. I quickly determined that I only dreamed I had awakened and that my second yell was also a dream yell. The scenario repeated itself four or five more times.

The net result of my dream shouting was that I attracted two or three additional mooing bears, along with any number of cows, which were also mooing. By then I had figured out that the whole thing was a dream. But I was still plenty frightened. Or terrified, if you must know. Especially when the bear pulled me the rest of the way out of the tent. I was naked, of course, because that's how I always sleep. I lay on the ground curled up in a defensive ball, with my arms protecting my head, as the bear prodded, poked, dragged, growled, bit, and generally knocked me around like a Hacky Sack ball. I couldn't breathe and honestly feared I was about to die.

I had heard somewhere that if you dream that you die, you actually will die.

That's when I finally got pissed off. I didn't want to die. If there's one thing I fear more than bears, it's death. Spiritual battle or not, dream or not, this nonsense had gone on long enough. I jumped to my feet with an angry grimace on my face. And with my uncovered and unprotected genitalia flapping in the night breeze, I kicked the bear in the rear end.

This time the bear, not me, ended up curled into a defensive ball on the ground. It looked up at me and growled the most plaintive, chilling growl I have ever heard. Then the animal got up and limped off into the night. Apparently the other bears, and cows, went with it, because I slept soundly from then on.

When I awoke for real, it was daylight and both my head and body were securely inside the tent. I was very tired, more tired than I should have been on three hours' sleep, and I felt extremely drained. But I was happy that morning had finally arrived, happy to be in the wilderness, and looking forward to breakfast followed by a side hike up the beautiful red cliff to Black Mountain.

What a silly dream, I thought, chuckling inwardly as I went outside to relieve myself, enjoy the magnificent morning, bathe in the spring, and fix my meal.

As I walked around the camp, I made a discovery that stifled any further chuckling. The nocturnal bear, it seemed, had been very real indeed. It left tracks around my campsite and clawed at the tree where the rope holding my pack was anchored. There were also cow tracks all around the camp that had not been there when I went to bed.

Most of the tracks, both cow and bear, were concentrated around the rear of the tent, where I'd dreamed that my head had poked through the tent wall.

Suddenly I felt far less powerful and far more vulnerable than when I'd gone to bed. I could not be sure that my yells had all been dream yells or that my kick had been a dream kick. The fatigue I felt was the kind of drained exhaustion you might experience after a toe-to-toe confrontation or a terrifying run-in.

I felt like Jacob might have felt in the morning after wrestling all night with an angel. Or with a man. Or with God. Or with himself. Or after dreaming he had wrestled all night. But I did not feel blessed by the bear, and there was no evidence that my name had been changed.

PART 4

AFTER A BREAKFAST OF INSTANT OATMEAL, A WARM CARTON OF JUICE, AND YET more trail mix, before I folded my tent and rolled up my sleeping bag for the trip home, I made the hike across and up Sycamore Creek to the side creek leading to a red rock mesa.

The trek turned out to be glorious, if exhausting, gaining 600 feet in half a mile. The day was perfect: slightly cool with scattered clouds far in the distance. Despite the clouds, I still saw no evidence of an impending storm, or any buildup over the high peaks to the north.

My route zigzagged alongside and up a large gully. Patches of thin, wet soil, trapped in the crevices between the brilliant orange rock and boulders, teemed with wildflowers of every hue, tint, tone, and shade. Far overhead I could see the terrace that was my destination.

Near the beginning of the uphill part of the hike, the path crossed the only pure water, unpolluted by cattle, that I'd encountered on the entire trip, coursing down a lively side creek. While I couldn't imagine cattle venturing up the steep slope, I purified the water when I filled my canteen. Good hikers are supposed to always purify their water before drinking.

High overhead, the beautiful red shelf, like a dam made of bricks, beckoned me upward. As I drew closer, I could see from the stains on the rock that a lovely waterfall occasionally spilled over shelf's edge. On my March visit the flow had dwindled to an ooze down the blocky rock face.

Eventually, after climbing around brush clumps, steep boulder fields, isolated forest pockets, and sheer rock faces, I surmounted the bench. Looking around, I concluded that I'd chosen well. Scanning westward from the vista point, the entire Sycamore Canyon, 7 miles across and 20 miles long, spread out below me. To the south lay Clarkburg and the farmlands of the Verde Valley. Behind me lay the gentle, pine-covered, 6,000-foot summit of Black Mountain.

In the canyon below I could see the spot where my tent had been. A group of cows now lazed on the creekbank not far away. From the clouds now gathering on the horizon to the north, in the area around Humphreys Peak, which I could not see from the campsite, I felt the first breeze of what would prove to be a serious storm. I left, prudently, very soon after.

As to the symbolic significance of my psychic, or possibly real, confrontation with the bear: Unlike the biblical Jacob, neither my name nor my personality was profoundly altered by the experience. I didn't notice any effect, in fact, until the next time I camped out, which wasn't until two years later. I discovered that I wasn't nearly as worried about bears as I used to be.

I guess old Augie was right after all.

In retrospect I can see that as a result of the Sycamore Canyon experience, I somehow became more empathetic to the spirit of the bear, and to other sources of vague dread in my life.

On the other hand, I now seem to be afraid of cows.

THE HIKE: *Parson's Trail, Sycamore Canyon Wilderness, Clarkdale, Arizona.*

LENGTH *(one way): 3.7 miles, plus side trips.*

DIRECTIONS: *From I-40 at Flagstaff, go south on I-17 toward Phoenix. After 5 miles, at exit 337, take US 89A 46 miles through Oak Creek Canyon, Sedona, and Cottonwood. Just past Cottonwood, "Historic 89A" goes straight while 89A veers left. Historic 89A takes you through Clarkdale. In Clarkdale, follow signs to Tuzigoot National Monument. Immediately after the road to the monument crosses the bridge over the Verde River, turn left onto Sycamore Canyon Road, which is paved for 2 miles. At mile 5, you will start seeing signs saying you are on Road 131 and directing you to Sycamore Canyon. Proceed 11 miles from the turnoff, along the Verde River at first, then across some rolling desert country, and finally up a step rise to the Parson's Trailhead.*

The trailhead is located on a ridge 300 feet above the canyon. There is parking for 30 cars.

SPECIAL INFORMATION: *The access road is very rough in spots and crosses several dry washes with signs admonishing not to proceed if there is water in the washes. This is excellent advice, because you might find yourself stranded on the way back if the water rises, as it can easily do. My first Sycamore Canyon hike was in March 1996. Luckily I visited between winter storms so the dry washes, and the water level in the creek, did not present a problem. I was advised, however, that rain in the surrounding mountains can send down flash floods very quickly, which can be extremely dangerous even if it doesn't rain where you are.*

The best season to avoid flash floods is summer. The trailhead elevation, however, is only about 2,000 feet, and a low-elevation canyon in Arizona is the last place you want to be in summer. The temperature in Cottonwood, when I visited in August 2002, was 107, which is fairly typical. I suspect it was hotter in the canyon. When the trail through the canyon approaches the creek, the humidity jumps way up even though there is shade. Away from the creek, there is no shade and the solar radiation reflects off the sandy pathway, greatly magnifying the heat. Bring plenty of water whenever you visit: There are grazing cattle in the vicinity and the water in the creek can be kind of scummy.

HIKE FIVE
I HEAR FOOTPRINTS

PART 1

ON 99 PERCENT OF MY HIKES, NOTHING OUT OF THE ORDINARY HAPPENS, and I get no inexplicable, nagging feelings about anything. None whatsoever. I just go, have a good time, or sometimes a lousy one, and then come back. Still, I seem to have a sixth sense when hiking. Or a fourth sense, since my hikes usually do not involve touch or taste. While I don't receive sixth-sense (or fourth-sense) messages very often, they have definitely influenced a few of my outings.

The sixth sense is this: I know when something is watching me. I can tell when there is a mountain lion lurking deep in the underbrush or on an overhead rock, its eyes following my every movement. I can tell when there is a bear nearby. Or a camouflaged pot garden with booby traps. Or a deranged lunatic. Or family of bigfeet. I know when I've trespassed where I don't belong. I can't explain how I know. I just know. I'll be on a hike, happily minding my own business, when a thought, usually a fairly specific thought, pops into my head. The content varies, but the idea almost always involves something watching me, something that might attack at any minute.

Oddly enough, when I actually have seen a bear or mountain lion while hiking (three times in five hundred hikes over thirty years), the sighting was not preceded by any prescient warning. And when I've sensed a bigfoot or mountain lion lurking behind the trees, the beast, if there was one, has invariably chosen to remain behind the trees.

The truth, if you must know, is that I've never actually had one of my "feelings" verified. Except once, on the Bear Lake Trail in Everglades National Park in 1969. It was the very first time I ever had one of my premonitions; it was their premier appearance, their debut on the Bernstein stage. It was also one of only two occasions, of the twenty-five or thirty times I've "sensed danger" on a hike, when the feeling was strong enough to cause me to turn back without rationalization or excuse.

That hike in Everglades National Park in 1969 was the first in which I turned back solely because of an intuitive feeling that something bad was about to happen. There was just me, my runaway imagination, and a string of odd coincidences that began, innocently enough, with a brief, probably misunderstood conversation with a not-too-bright waitress in Marathon Key, Florida, who mistakenly served me grits for breakfast.

The Everglades trip began at my parents' house in Detroit. I was home from graduate school for the holidays with time on my hands. Back then, when I found myself with a few days to kill between semesters in school, I sometimes went on what I called "crazy trips." I'd jump in the car and drive as far as I could in forty-eight hours, and then come home. I'd done that in every direction but south.

Heading north, I once ended up on the only road that touches James Bay, an offshoot of Hudson Bay, in Moosonee, Ontario, right next to the village of Moose Factory.

Man, was I ever north.

Actually the road only went to Cochrane, Ontario, 180 miles from Moosonee. You had to take a train the rest of the way, which I did. Moosonee and Moose Factory were fascinating, if bleak, places that smelled of fish. And by the way, if you're wondering why it's called "Moose Factory," no, they do not manufacture moose there, except in the broadest sense (many moose are born in the vicinity). Back in the 1600s, when the town consisted of nothing but a lonely Hudson's Bay Company trading post—one of the first—the post operator was called a "factor." And the building was therefore a "factory," located on the Moose River.

None of this, obviously, had anything whatsoever to do with my trip to the Everglades. To make a long story somewhat less interminable, because it was a couple of days before Christmas back in 1969, the season of the year precluded another visit to Moosonee. I therefore headed in the opposite direction.

I'd always wanted to see Florida. In elementary school, classmates invariably went to Florida over winter break, returning with deep, off-season tans. Everybody but me. The Bernsteins never went anywhere, except to California in summer of 1954. When the movie *Where the Boys Are* came out in 1961, the lure of the Sunny South became even more irresistible. And it grew stronger yet when I enrolled in graduate school at the University of Michigan, studying natural history. My special interest, at the time, was the national parks and ecosystems around the United States. South Florida, the Keys, and the Everglades ranked high on my list of "wanna see" places.

With five days to kill and miserable weather settling into southern Michigan, the timing seemed perfect for a patented Bernstein Crazy Trip to check out South Florida. Especially the Keys and Everglades.

The first day of the journey proved uneventful. I left Detroit at 5:00 P.M., on December 20. It got light when I was somewhere in Tennessee and dark again as I entered Florida. There's not much daylight that time of year. I spent several hours sleeping in my car in a freeway rest area near Lake Worth, Florida. It's hard to imagine this, but when you drive the 1,200 miles from Detroit to Miami, one-third of the trip is inside Florida.

Most of day two was spent motoring down Florida's Atlantic coast, through Daytona Beach, St. Augustine (the oldest European-founded city in the United States), Cape Canaveral-Kennedy-Canaveral, Palm Beach (fantastic houses!), and Fort Lauderdale. Late in the day, after a wide loop around Miami, I headed out the spectacular Key West Highway. I loved the concept of driving a hundred miles straight into the warm ocean at Christmas. I loved the sunny, eighty-degree weather. I loved the water that looked like a giant, sparkling swimming pool. I loved the lack of surf. I loved the mangrove bushes with their stiltlike roots. I loved the strange pink birds and the hardwood trees that had not, and would never, lose their leaves just because it happened to be winter.

Key West was unbelievable. Despite the tropical sunshine, the moss-draped live oaks, the gnarled old banyan trees, and the majestic palms, the town's graceful elegance brought to mind a New England fishing village, or maybe the Hamptons on outer Long Island. I envied the charter-boat operators in the town harbor, lazing around in their Hawaiian shirts, their only activity being to haul rich people out to fish for marlin and sailfish.

What a life!

After taking in the sights of Key West, including the southernmost point in the southernmost city in the continental United States, I slept for a few hours on a white sand beach in a little state park on one of the Keys. These days you wouldn't do such a thing. Except, perhaps, if you were insane. The world, with a few notable exceptions such as the nuclear arms race, was much safer back then. Or at least I thought it was.

And by the way: Man, was I ever south!

The next morning, day three, I reluctantly dragged myself out of the soft sand and drove into the town of Marathon Key for breakfast, stopping at a small roadside cafe, the community's only eatery. I'd taken a washcloth bath and changed into clean clothes in the state park rest room, but I still felt pretty grubby. The restaurant appeared clean enough, except for twenty or thirty strips of flypaper dangling from the ceiling, which badly needed to be changed. Also, the place smelled of mildew and rancid grease. But I was starving, so I chose to overlook these shortcomings of ambience.

After I spent a few minutes examining the menu, a waitress in her forties, with stiff, bouffant hair, way too much makeup, and a food-stained, candy-striped apron approached to take my order. She had a thick southern accent that I could barely understand.

"Y'all wanna poo incognito?" she asked, readying her pen over the order pad. At least that's what it seemed to me like she said.

I placed my order without responding to her inquiry about pooing incognito. I ordered eggs over medium, toast, hash browns, and pork sausage. When my food arrived, a few minutes later, it was exactly as I had envisioned, except for a small deposit of revolting white slop near the edge, with butter melting on it.

"What's that stuff?" I inquired.

"Grits."

That was the only thing she said that I understood.

"I didn't order grits."

"Comes wi'the foo fanny."

"Oh, okay."

Then she said something that completely baffled me.

"Y'all watch out for Martians, now."

Having no idea what she actually said, and little hope of comprehending any possible clarification I might request, I just ate my breakfast and did not press for details. I did not eat the grits, although I did take a small taste, which I nearly spit out. Then I got in my car and headed for the Everglades, still puzzling over the waitress's remark.

I eventually decided, as I drove through the town of Homestead, that what I'd heard as "Martians" was probably a contraction of Marathonians, or some similar word, in the waitress's strange dialect. Marathonians, I assumed, were residents of Marathon Key. Even with that bit of insight, her statement made no sense. It did not explain why I should watch out for people from Marathon, if indeed that was what she'd said, which it probably wasn't.

PART 2

THE BEST WAY TO DESCRIBE HOW MY THIRD DAY IN FLORIDA "WENT BAD" IS TO jump forward thirty years, to New Year's Day 2000. That day was remarkably similar to my day in the Everglades in 1969. Except I was 3,000 miles away, on the Pacific coast rather than the Atlantic coast or Gulf of Mexico, and I was with my wife.

Not being party types, my wife and I chose to spend the final hours of the Second Millennium A.D, and the initial hours of the Third Millennium A.D., camping out on an ocean beach in northern California. We selected a secluded campground, accessible only by a 10-mile dirt road, nestled in the coastal dunes in Redwood National Park. It was the only campground I knew of in California located right in the dunes on the beach.

To our surprise, despite somewhat unsettled weather (light rain and a temperature in the midthirties), the campground was nearly full. We set up our tent, used an old watch to determine (roughly) the exact instant of the New Year, guzzled a jereboam (more like a quart, actually) of sparking cranberry juice at the stroke of midnight, then went to sleep.

We awoke at daybreak, around six-thirty. The initial image either of us saw by the first light of day in the year 2000 was a rainbow over the ocean! Having slept in our clothes, and coats, and mittens, and sleeping bags, and comforters, we didn't really have to get dressed, except for putting on our shoes. We went for a short walk on the beach, heated up a pot of cocoa on our camp stove, then took down the tent and departed.

It was during the walk on the beach that we first noticed the silence. Although the campground still appeared full, with tents and parked cars everywhere, we didn't hear a voice, see another person, or observe any sign of human movement. Not during our walk, not while making the cocoa, and not while folding up the tent or loading the car.

The dirt road out to the highway was completely deserted. So were the first 25 miles we drove on Highway 101, the region's principal and usually busiest thoroughfare. We didn't see another human or pass another moving vehicle, even when we went through a town. Pat and I speculated that on the stroke of midnight, humankind, for some reason, had ceased to exist. Except for us. It was not a bad fantasy. Of course, there was the slight problem that if humankind had indeed ceased to exist, it meant our children and grandchildren were gone. We concluded that maybe it was better if all humankind but us had not ceased to exist at the stroke of midnight but had somehow managed to endure.

The world's humanity, to our relief, rematerialized when we pulled into the parking lot of a small gambling casino outside Klamath, California. The casino advertised cheap breakfasts, which was precisely what we were after. The dark, smoky, noisy, jingling casino was crammed with hung-over revelers. After we left, there seemed to be lots of cars on the road.

The incident reminded me of the day, thirty years earlier, when I'd visited Everglades National Park for the first and only time.

Things seemed normal enough at the massive Everglades Visitor Center and Entrance Station, just inside the park, near Homestead. Far from being deserted, there were hundreds of cars, and people milling everywhere. As I pulled into a parking place, I must have inadvertently cut somebody off, a young man in a beat-up old Volkswagen Beetle. His car had been spray-painted black. The guy in the Volkswagen beeped his horn at me, then flipped me off. Not knowing what I'd done and with no desire to find out, I smiled politely, looked away, and continued parking my car while avoiding eye contact.

As I got out and walked toward the building, I heard somebody behind me shouting obscenities. It might have been the fellow in the Volkswagen, still angry about who-knows-what, or it might have been some road-weary parent chastising his kids. I didn't look around to find out. I figured if it was the guy in the Volkswagen, it was best for me to simply get lost in the crowd rather than confront him and get sucked into a pointless argument.

I'd caught a brief glimpse of the Volkswagen driver when he flipped me off. He was a fellow about my age, mid-twenties, with a black T-shirt. He looked very unkempt and unpleasant. Of course, after three days on the road, sleeping in my car and in the sand, I myself was hardly the epitome of kempt pleasantry. And I, too, had on a black T-shirt. I still wear black T-shirts.

I spent maybe ten minutes in the visitor center, then started down the road to Flamingo Village. I noted, as I departed the center, that the Volkswagen was parked four or five spaces from me.

It took me a while to realize that there were no other cars on the Flamingo Road. The first inkling came several miles down the highway when I pulled into a parking turnout with a short nature walk. I found it a little odd that I was the only visitor there on a weekend in December at ten in the morning. I didn't see any cars or people in the parking area or on the wooden boardwalk through the swamp, just lots of pink, white, and red birds, and an

Everglades viewing area

alligator. The same was true at the Mahogany Hammock turnout and a couple of other turnouts. It was only after Mahogany Hammock that it dawned on me that not only were there no other cars or people at the turnouts, there were none on the road, either. It was a very creepy revelation.

At first I attributed it to coincidence, or a momentary aberration. I compared the phenomenon to something I'd learned in elementary school science class years earlier: There are trillions of oxygen molecules in the air and they are in constant random movement around the room. It is theoretically possible that for a brief instant, they could all end up on the same side of the room, leaving the other side devoid of oxygen. Highly unlikely, but possible.

The lack of other cars or people evolved in my mind from curiosity to a slight, gnawing threat when I arrived back from the ten-minute hike at Mahogany Hammock, a turnout halfway between the park entrance and Flamingo Village. I found the dreaded black Volkswagen parked there. When I saw the car, my pulse rate took an abrupt lurch and adrenaline swept over my body. There was nobody in the vehicle, however, and I hadn't passed anybody on the trail, which made sense since it was a loop trail. It also made sense, I tried to reassure myself, that somebody who'd entered the park the same time I had and was driving the same main road, would stop at the same major turnout that I did.

Still, I couldn't help wondering what had happened to the rest of the teeming horde of sight-seeing humanity who'd also entered the park when I did. Among all of them, the guy in the Volkswagen was the only person I didn't care to see again. That, no doubt, explained why my imagination started running wild when I observed his vehicle in the Mahogany Hammock parking lot.

The Volkswagen, as it turned out, was only the starting point, the jump-off, the launch pad, the Cape Canaveral of the notorious Bernstein imagination.

Instead of bears, bigfeet, or psychopaths, my "intuition" that day revolved around Martians, no doubt influenced by the mumbling waitress in Marathon Key. It sounds ridiculous, but Martians were the most logical explanation I could come up with for the lack of other cars. I tried to think of other explanations but none seemed nearly as consistent or reasonable as the Martian Theory. Had the road had been closed due to a chemical spill or an escaped convict, which might also account for the sudden dearth of traffic, there would have been cars in the opposite direction, or police, or something.

Only Martians have been known to stop all traffic dead in its tracks in all directions. In fact, I always wondered how they managed that. Every time you hear about somebody seeing a flying saucer close up, invariably on a lonely country road at night, his or her car always mysteriously dies. And it invariably starts up again the instant the flying saucer leaves.

Of course my Martian Theory did have its holes. Presuming all the other cars but mine had mysteriously stalled because of magnetic rays emitted by a hovering flying saucer, there should have been stalled cars everywhere, with people running up and down the highway screaming in terror. And there should have been a flying saucer overhead.

Also, the Martian Theory did not account for the continued flawless functioning of my little powder-blue Plymouth Valiant. Why was my vehicle alone impervious to the alien rays while all the other cars were dropping like mosquitoes sprayed by insecticide? And above all, why was the black Volkswagen also impervious to Martian electronic interference?

Unless . . . unless the Volkswagen was actually a disguised "away" vehicle from the Martian mother ship. And the driver, the guy in the black T-shirt, was a Martian. And I alone had been singled out for abduction.

The story made perfect sense. Too perfect. Too ludicrously perfect. I tried to reassure myself that it was all nonsense, that there were no Martians, and that very soon I'd begin seeing traffic again. But my imagination, and my obsessive brain, would not be assuaged. Especially when I drove the final eighteen miles to my intended destination, the Bear Lake Trail, and still didn't see another car.

PART 3

BEFORE HEADING OUT BEAR LAKE ROAD, I STOPPED BY FLAMINGO VILLAGE, WHICH turned out to be one of the most beautiful places I'd ever been, before or since. It consisted of a vast lawn facing the ocean and dotted with palm trees, with mangrove swamp on either side and the intoxicating aroma of warm ocean air permeating everything. The only problem was that there wasn't much to do in Flamingo Village, unless you happened to own a sailboat, which I did not. Aside from that, the only activities I could find to do were (1) walking around and (2) browsing in the little store. I did both, ending up the proud owner of a brand-new Popsicle and a bunch of postcards.

I love Popsicles. Especially in December.

And yes, there were people in Flamingo Village. Lots of people: pasty-faced, Hawaiian-shirted tourists with Brownie cameras, and children frantically dashing every which way, basking in the momentary release from their automotive oubliettes. And, of course, there were lots of parked cars. And lots of boat trailers. But I never saw any cars, or any people, until I was in the actual parking lot. I never saw a car or a person on the highway. Not one. Except for the Volkswagen at Mahogany Hammock.

I was immensely relieved, on arriving at Flamingo Village, that the "no cars, no people" state of affairs had ended. I laughed to myself over the silliness of my Martian Theory. There had, obviously, been other cars on the road after all. I just hadn't noticed them.

I stayed in Flamingo perhaps twenty minutes, after which I drove back to the Bear Lake Road turnoff and followed the 2-mile, arrow-straight route to the trailhead at the road's end. Once I left the village, all the cars and people vanished again. Again, I tried to persuade myself that it was all my imagination. I passed no cars on the highway and no cars on Bear Lake Road. I didn't expect there to be cars on Bear Lake Road. At least, I reassured myself, there were no black Volkswagens at the trailhead. Or Martian spaceships.

I got out, locked my vehicle, and started hiking up the 1.6-mile trail, which began at a small, stagnant, brackish-smelling pond. The route traversed a dense, tropical hardwood forest of mahogany and buttonwood, full of strange little air plants, near the edge of the mangroves. It paralleled a canal teeming with squawking waterfowl, egrets, herons, flamingos, and bald eagles. Lengths of wooden boardwalk kept my feet dry through the swampy areas and minimized the chances of being attacked by alligators or poisonous water snakes.

At this point, except for a slight lingering worry about Martians and the guy in the black Volkswagen, I wasn't receiving any premonitions or intuitive feelings. In fact, I actually enjoyed the first few minutes of the walk.

My anxiety level rose slightly when I started hearing footsteps behind me. Or what sounded like footsteps. The noise was very faint at first. So faint, I didn't notice it for a while, and can't say precisely when it started. When I became aware of the noise, a quarter mile into the hike, I again attributed it to my overly active imagination and snickered at myself for my silliness. Besides, what with the birds, alligators, raccoons, squirrels, deer, pumas, bears, insects, cottonmouths, copperheads, and water moccasins, I was walking through a pretty busy and noisy place. Were something tailing me, or skulking alongside me in the woods, it should not have been a total surprise.

I stopped two or three times to look behind me. The trail was nearly straight, so if somebody or something were following me, I'd surely have seen them. Or it. Unless they ducked into the impenetrable underbrush at the last second. In that case I would not have seen them.

Or it.

What disturbed me most about the noise I kept hearing was that instead of pumas or crazed stalkers, my thoughts kept returning to Martians. That, obviously, was not very logical. In fact, it was pretty stupid. Exceedingly stupid. Why would a Martian be following me? It seemed to me that if Martians wanted to abduct or kill me, they would just do it, straight out. They wouldn't need to track me for miles and go to such lengths to keep out of sight.

Still, whatever was or wasn't going on, my intuition absolutely, positively insisted that Martians were somehow involved. The idea would not go away.

After a while the footsteps behind me began to grow louder. So loud that there was no mistaking that something—Martian, raccoon, another hiker, whatever—was making a noise to my rear. The noise speeded up when

I sped up, slowed down when I slowed down, and stopped when I stopped. I repeatedly checked myself to make sure there was nothing dangling from my shoes, jiggling in my pocket, or slapping against my back or legs.

It didn't help that the forest was exceptionally spooky, like something out of *The Wizard of Oz*. I could almost picture trees with faces on them cursing and throwing apples at me as I ran off screaming and terrified. I reminded myself that I'd hiked through spooky forests before. There was Washington's Olympic rain forest, for example, with its giant conifers, musty smells, light-starved understory, and moss-draped branches. The Olympic rain forest, however, despite the Hansel and Gretel imagery, hadn't evoked any spooky intuition. None whatsoever. Zero.

The Bear Lake Trail was feeling less safe by the minute. But I was determined to tough it out. If I turned back, I could never admit to anyone, not for the rest of my life ever, that I hadn't completed my only hike in the Everglades out of fear of Martians.

I pressed onward until the noise behind me started growing louder yet again. It now sounded like a two-hundred-pound Dutch peasant girl in wooden shoes and rustling skirts, walking perhaps ten steps to my rear. While the concept of a two-hundred-pound Dutch Martian in wooden shoes amused me, the circumstance did not.

Then I began hearing rustling in the bushes around me. Not occasional rustling but constant rustling, as though every animal in the neighborhood were tracking me, watching my every move, ready to pounce. Finally, when I heard a distinct growling noise in front of me, I stopped dead in my tracks.

The instant I stopped, the universe fell silent. I took two or three hesitant steps forward and the noise started up again. Including the growling.

It made my flesh crawl.

As an experiment, I turned around and walked a few steps back toward the car. And I was greeted with nothing but profound, blessed silence. When I started back toward Bear Lake, the noises commenced once again. I figured the lake was half a mile away at that point.

At the rate the noises were escalating, there was no telling where they would end up by the time I arrived at my destination. Reluctantly, I opted for the direction of quietude and peace of mind. I opted to get the hell out of there.

I told myself that I was tired, that it was getting late in the day, that the trail was way too long, and that it was not very interesting. None of those things was true.

The farther from Bear Lake I got, the more relaxed and relieved I felt. By the time I arrived back at the trailhead, I felt downright elated, if a little embarrassed.

A lot embarrassed.

As I was getting into my car, the black Volkswagen pulled into the parking lot. It frightened me for a second, especially when the driver got out and started walking toward me. Until I saw that he was smiling.

"Hey man," he said, "how was Bear Lake?"

"Fantastic," I lied. "Lots of wildlife."

With a polite nod, the Volkswagen guy walked past me and started up the trail.

The fellow did not look like a Martian. In fact, he didn't look threatening in any way. Still, I don't know why—call it intuition—but I was glad I was not sharing the path with him, which would have been the case had I continued to Bear Lake instead of turning back.

When I pulled back onto the Flamingo Highway and headed back toward Homestead, there was traffic all over the place, in both directions.

And the world was whole once again.

PART 4

FOLLOWING MY WHIRLWIND EVERGLADES TOUR, I SPENT THE NIGHT SLEEPING IN my car in another freeway rest area, this one near Jacksonville. My plan was to swing up through Georgia and South Carolina, make the drive through Great Smoky Mountain National Park, then head home. The Smokies would delay my arrival home by perhaps six or eight hours, which I considered time exceedingly well spent.

I did not plan to go hiking in the Smokies. I was too busy trying to figure out what the heck had happened on the Bear Lake hike and what all those strange noises and premonitions had been about. In retrospect, I was not 100 percent sure I'd really heard all those footsteps behind me. Or the other noises. While they'd sounded frighteningly real at the time, the whole business made no sense.

In fact, little about my Everglades trip made sense. Not my idiotic worry about Martians, not my fear of the guy in the black Volkswagen, not the inexplicable absence of cars, not the footsteps behind me. Nothing. I spent the entire drive to Jacksonville, and much of the night, rehashing the experience in my mind.

After a few hours of sleep, however, my adventure of the previous day seemed much more remote. I awoke to a new day, a day in which all the silliness and worry seemed to no longer matter. I was relieved and grateful that my preoccupation had dissipated and that my mind apparently had moved on to more elevating subjects.

Actually, when I woke up I wasn't thinking about much of anything. Not the Everglades and not the Smokies. All I thought about was filling my gut, then putting as much mileage as possible between my little Plymouth and the state of Florida, and as few miles as possible between my car and the Smokies.

I always thought about filling my gut when I got up in the morning. Breakfast is my favorite meal, especially a nice, greasy, fried-egg breakfast in a roadside cafe. One of my first acts of the day, at around seven o'clock, was to stop and eat. That was always a highlight during my Crazy Trips.

Unlike the previous day, I selected a nice, new, clean, mostly plastic restaurant at a freeway interchange. It was far superior to the place in Marathon Key. This establishment was spotless and smelled of butter and syrup rather than dead flies, rancid grease, and mildew. It boasted a charming little gift section that sold plaster figurines of kittens, puppies, and elves. It also sold Florida souvenirs, including the now highly illegal stuffed baby alligators wearing derby hats.

I ordered just about the same meal as I had in Marathon Key: eggs over medium, toast, hash browns, and sausage. This time I understood every word the waitress said. And there were no grits with the meal, although there were grits on the menu. Oh yes, and the food was much, much better.

To keep my mind occupied while eating, I decided to purchase that day's issue of the *Miami Herald*. I get bored pretty easily when I'm by myself, and I often read the local newspapers. I planned to save the paper and read it at lunch, also.

The first place I turned to was the sports page. For some reason, basketball and football scores fascinated me. They still do. They didn't fascinate me as much as baseball scores but it was late December, and beggars can't be choosers. After extracting every iota of relevant information from the sports page, which took about thirty seconds, I moved to the front page, which also had a marked paucity of attention-grabbing material. The lead story, as I recall, was about South Carolina senator Strom Thurmond, the same person who ran for president in 1948, marrying a twenty-three-year-old beauty pageant winner. It was what professional journalists call a "slow news day." (As I write this story in 2001, Mr. Thurmond is in his late nineties and still a senator from South Carolina. I don't know whether he's still married to the beauty pageant winner or not. She would be fifty-five.)

Page two of the first section of the *Miami Herald* was just as uninteresting as page one. Page three would have been even more boring, except for a small article near the bottom.

The headline said, KILLER ELUDES CAPTURE IN EVERGLADES. I read it only because I happened to have been in the Everglades the previous day. The tragic, frightening story had to do with a family—mother, father, and four-year-old daughter—who were robbed and shot to death while camping in a state park near Homestead. The alleged perpetrator had fled into the Everglades and apparently was still on the loose. They had a description of his car from an eyewitness.

His car was an old Volkswagen Beetle that had been spray-painted black.

The police had identified the alleged perpetrator from fingerprints at the crime scene. He was a notorious twenty-three-year-old drug dealer and habitual miscreant from Miami. His name was Henry Heath Mars.

Oh yes, I was later told by friends that Bear Lake is a very nice place. I plan to go back one of these days. The next time, I hope to make it all the way to the lake.

THE HIKE: *Bear Lake Trail, Everglades National Park, Florida.*

LENGTH *(one way): 1.6 miles.*

DIRECTIONS: *Take the main road (Highway 9053) from US 1 in Homestead, Florida, into Everglades National Park, toward Flamingo Village. One mile before Flamingo (38 miles from the park entrance), turn right onto Bear Lake Road. It's 2 miles to the Bear Lake Trailhead.*

HIKE SIX
DREAM TRAILS

I'S IMPOSSIBLE TO HIKE AS MUCH AS I DO WITHOUT HAVING IT INVADE YOUR dreams once in a while. While many of my hiking dreams involve places I've actually been, the best, most scenic, and most deeply moving all seem to involve fantasy locations that do not exist in reality. When I wake up from such dreams, I find myself longing for the places in them and hoping that somehow, somewhere, I will eventually find them.

My three most memorable dream hikes are all recurrent, which means I have the same dream over and over. For years these recurrent hiking dreams were a great mystery to me. While my success in attaching Freudian explanations to them has been marginal, I did eventually figure out one thing: The dreams are all basically quests or journeys. Logically, there is no more significant journey than the journey through life, and there is no more significant quest than the quest for the meaning of that life. I now believe that my recurring dreams—elemental, repetitive slices of my unconscious— all dealt with unanswered questions about how my life, my personal quest or journey, would turn out. Questions such as *who will I marry, who will my children be* and *how and when will I die?* I spent a lot of time wondering about those things when I was young. I still do, although many of these questions have since been answered.

PART 1: THE WATERFALL DREAM

IN THIS DREAM I AM WALKING ALONG A TRAIL THAT BEGINS IN A BEAUTIFUL autumn wood, near the rim of a deep, vertical-sided gorge with a river at the bottom. At the head of the gorge, a huge, Niagara-esque waterfall plunges over an undercut cliff. I'd estimate the height at around 100 feet and the width at maybe 500. After a few hundred feet along the rim, the path makes a long switchback down the cliff to the water's edge. It then parallels the river upstream to the base of the falls. A forest of sugar maple, red maple, beech, paper birch, eastern white pine, jack pine, tamarack, and balsam fir covers the level ground on the canyon rim.

Every time I ever had the dream, the beeches, birches, and maples were resplendent in autumn color. Which is as it should be in a dream. The conifers, obviously, were not in fall color (except for the tamaracks). But they were just as resplendent. When I reach the river, I can see that there is a beautiful blond woman, probably in her early twenties, by herself on the trail not too far ahead of me.

Understand that beautiful, young, blond females are not uncommon in my dreams. Heck, I can populate my dreams with anybody I want. Given a choice, say, between three-headed penguins and beautiful young women, why shouldn't I opt for the females?

I can never see the woman's face. But from the rear, she is a knockout. I assume, in the dream, that she is also a knockout from the front. And if she isn't, I can easily make her beautiful. It's not that difficult, a cheap card trick. Especially with the miracle of "garbage dump beauty" at my disposal.

Garbage dump beauty refers to the fact that perception of beauty, in a dream, does not necessarily have to match the actual visual image. In a dream there's nothing to prevent you from looking, for example, at a garbage dump and reacting emotionally as though you were looking at the Taj Mahal. That's one of the nice thing about dreams.

My dream woman is dressed casually, in jeans and a nylon windbreaker. Her long blond tresses billow behind her in the cool, moist breeze eternally kicked up by the falling water. It is the thickest hair I have ever seen. The air smells of balsam, river, mist, and autumn. Not to mention beautiful young female humans.

The greatest aromas in the world.

In the dream I find myself with an overwhelming urge to catch up to the woman and talk with her. I continue following her down the trail, drawing ever closer, but I never quite overtake her.

In real life, during the years when I was having this dream, I was painfully shy around beautiful young female humans. I still am, for the most part.

I have brilliantly dubbed this dream the "Waterfall Dream."

I first had the Waterfall Dream when I was six or seven. At the time I didn't have a clue which tree species populated the dream forest near the waterfall. I didn't learn to identify trees until I enrolled in forestry school while in my midtwenties. But since I continued to have the dream after learning to identify trees, I have taken the liberty of doing so here. Not that I ever stopped to identify the trees while the dream was in progress. It was only after waking up that I reasoned that since I lived in Michigan, the trees in my dream had to be Michigan trees. More precisely, they had to be tree species of the mature upland forests in Michigan's Upper Peninsula, where the state's most spectacular waterfalls were located.

Of course physical location, in a dream, is as meaningless a concept as beauty. Although I lived in Michigan, the actual setting for the Waterfall Dream was not Michigan at all. It was the deep recesses of my sleeping brain. But the dream was inspired by Michigan, which was virtually all I knew for the first two decades of my life.

Eventually the dream trail reaches the base of the falls. Then it goes behind the falls. I loved when it went behind the falls, into a magical, dank-smelling little chamber with a deafening wall of crashing water on one side and sandy yellow sandstone on the opposite. If you were to step into the waterfall's tumbling torrent, you'd be killed instantly. There is sufficient space to walk most of the way behind the falls but not out the other side.

The fact that there is no far exit is my ace in the hole in my attempt to catch up with the young woman. Since she'll be forced to turn around, all I need to do is wait, secure in the knowledge that when we finally speak, there will be no more romantic setting anywhere on heaven or earth.

The romantic aspect began to creep in when I was twelve or thirteen. Before that, I had a juvenile crush on the young woman, the kind a child feels for a kindergarten teacher. But no matter how old I was, it was always the same woman, always in her early twenties, always wearing the same clothes and always just out of reach.

While I often approached to within a couple of feet of the woman, so close I could smell the dampness and sweetness of her lush hair, I invariably woke up before we had a chance to talk. In fact, I never made any effort to speak with her.

I was always disappointed when I woke up before speaking with the woman. On the other hand, I was exceedingly grateful that I never ran into her during any of my other recurring dreams, especially the one where I was naked on the school bus. I never initiated a conversation, probably, for the same reason that I rarely initiate conversations with beautiful women in real life: I didn't want to risk rejection. I can think of no greater rejection than being rebuffed by a woman you invented. Especially when the invention is a sweet, gentle person who is herself extremely shy.

Oh yes, I almost forgot. There's one more thing you need to know about the Waterfall Dream. One reason I find the waterfall so extraordinarily beautiful is that the plunging water of the falls is not white, as is the case with most waterfalls. It's gold: clear, liquid gold with sun sparkles dancing on the surface. Pure gold. Real gold. Such a color, as far as I knew, was only possible in a dream.

I never was able to make much headway in interpreting the Waterfall Dream. The waterfall might have symbolized birth and renewal, or ceaseless, irreversible rush of my life. A more important question was, who was the woman? The embodiment of my personal hopes and aspirations, perhaps?

While I had no absolute answers, I did know this: Whatever she symbolized, it was essential in my life, for reasons I was never able to articulate, that I eventually muster the nerve to speak to her.

Anyhow, the kite string of my life slowly, then more rapidly, played out, as it always does. And the Waterfall Dream of my childhood and youth went the way of Puff the Magic Dragon. I grew up, started college in 1960, graduated in 1964, enrolled in graduate school in 1968, and earned a master of science in forestry in 1972. From 1964 to 1967, I worked full time as a welfare social worker. During my first year in graduate school, I managed to land an excellent part-time job as a social worker in a mental hospital.

While employed at the mental hospital, at age twenty-five, a particularly convivial coworker introduced me to the woman I would marry. The coworker was named David Gebow and he was the hospital's gym teacher, or "recreation therapist." The initial encounter with my future bride took place at a party at David's house in Detroit, on a dismal January weekend. A young woman showed up who, David informed me, worked with his fiancé.

David introduced the woman as Patricia O'Leary. She was the most beautiful human being, by any conceivable definition of the word, that I have ever had the pleasure of speaking to, before or since. In addition to being kind, selfless, and intelligent, she was in her early twenties, knockout gorgeous, and had the thickest blond hair I had ever seen.

And she was painfully shy.

Because of our mutual shyness, we didn't talk much at the party. But somehow, toward the end of the evening, I got up the nerve to ask her out. To my amazement, she accepted.

Upper Tahquamenon Falls

We drove up to Ann Arbor, where the University of Michigan is located and where I happened to live, on our first date. Ann Arbor is 40 miles from Detroit. We had a fantastic time touring the campus and visiting some of my favorite "secret places." I took her to a grassy opening atop an old glacial moraine I knew about, from which you could see the entire city and campus, with the Huron River meandering through it all. Patricia was very impressed. Or at least she said she was impressed.

I did not kiss Pat on our first date. And I nearly didn't kiss her on our second date. As I said, I'm pretty shy. Since she was too, she didn't exactly send out obvious signals. Of course, agreeing to the first and second dates was a pretty obvious signal. But that never occurred to me.

On my second date with Patricia, I picked her up early in the morning and we drove 300 miles to the Upper Peninsula. It was October, the height of the color season, and the drive was awesome. We ended up in the aptly named town of Paradise, then decided to take a quick swing through Tahquamenon Falls State Park, which neither of us had seen before. I'd heard it was a pretty nifty place.

We parked at the parking area in the beautiful autumn woods, stopped briefly at the rest rooms, then started down the trail to the base of the Upper Falls. We'd walked maybe a hundred feet down the path, to where the route dropped over a cliff into the gorge, when I suddenly stopped short.

As you've probably guessed, it was the dream trail of my childhood, down to the most-minute detail. And Patricia, beautiful Patricia, was my real-life dream girl, the one I was always too shy to talk to, the one whose face I could never see.

It was worth the wait.

I held Pat's hand as we walked down the trail together. I wasn't sure whether to run because I was excited, or go slowly and savor every step. I ended up doing a little of both. Poor Pat didn't know what to make of this. She probably thought I was nuts. It would not be the last time she'd think that. And even though we'd only known each other a couple of weeks, it was not the first time, either.

I did not tell Pat about the Waterfall Dream until afterward. I thought the unfolding drama would go better if I didn't.

To make a long story short, the very first time I kissed the lovely Patricia, the person who was to become my wife, we were behind the falls, at the spot where you can go no farther, the spot where in my dream, I always woke up. Our loving, lingering kiss lasted nearly five minutes. Then we kissed again.

While it was a memorable kiss, it later occurred to me that in the dream, all I ever wanted was to talk to the woman. There was never anything about a kiss. Still, I didn't complain.

And by the way, if you ever get a chance to visit Tahquamenon Falls, don't miss it. Not only are the forests, gorge, and waterfall magnificent, especially in autumn, but the water in the Tahquamenon River is very rich in tannin and therefore the color of tea. Where the water crashes over the escarpment, when the sun hits it right, it looks for all the world like pure liquid gold.

(*Note:* The last time I visited Tahquamenon Falls, in 1991, the Upper Falls Trail followed a wooden walkway to a vista point. You could no longer walk up to or behind the falls.)

PART 2: THE VOLCANO DREAM

I STARTED HAVING THE VOLCANO DREAM IN MY LATE TEENS, WHILE THE WATERFALL Dream was still in full swing. As I said, I have many recurring dreams, and some have hung around for decades. The "Naked on the School Bus" dream lasted well into my forties.

In the Volcano Dream I am hiking up the side of, you guessed it, a volcano. The mountain is about as big as Mount Shasta, the immense solitary peak that dominates the California Far North. And no, I won't try to identify the trees for you.

Oh, okay. If you insist. Mountain hemlock, subalpine fir, Alaska cedar, lodgepole pine, Pacific silver fir, and noble fir, with white-bark pine at the highest elevations. These species are found from northern California to southeast Alaska.

Unlike the Waterfall Dream, which always commenced in a parking lot, it is never clear where I began the volcano hike. I just find myself hiking up a mountain. In the hike's lower portions, I am following a path through a spectacular wildflower meadow. The meadow has more flowers per square foot, and more different flower species, than I've ever seen in a real mountain meadow. And I've seen lots of mountain meadows. The flowers in my dream meadow are always in full bloom. How could it be otherwise?

Perhaps half a mile away, maybe less, on my left, the meadow plummets to a massive glacier: white, looming, and cut by mighty crevasses that a bus could fall into, never to be seen again. Beside and in front of the glacier, immense mounds of fresh gravel have been bulldozed up by the giant ice sheet as they eat into and devour the mountain beneath.

From my vantage point in the meadow, I see that the glacier begins high up the mountain, in an area of glistening snowfields where several glaciers merge. Above that, the main summit rises—barren, rocky, foreboding, and probably insurmountable. By me, anyhow. I make no pretense of climbing the mountain. I am just out for a walk. Even down in the meadow, the elevation makes for a pretty stiff workout. I find myself huffing, puffing, dragging my feet, and stopping to catch my breath every few yards.

I always suspected that the Volcano Dream was touched off by my visit to Mount Shasta, and nearby Lassen Volcanic National Park in 1966, during my first trip to the West Coast. I was smitten by the two peaks from the moment I laid eyes on them. It is no coincidence that I ended up living within a couple of hours' drive of both.

It is not surprising that I would dream about volcanoes, which possess extreme potential for symbolism. Long before my first trip west, I had spent many hours eagerly reading about volcanoes, including Shasta and Lassen, and staring longingly at photos of them. I'd also eagerly read about Mount Ararat in Turkey, Africa's Mount Cameroon, Hawaii's Mauna Loa, Krakatoa West of Java, and Siberia's Klyuchevskaya.

As it turns out, the sweet-smelling, perfume-scented meadow in the Volcano Dream is the easy part of the hike. At the meadow's upper end, the path dead-ends at the base of a steep, treeless, gravelly ridge that radiates off the summit. My destination is the crest of the ridge, from which I hope to peer back down on glacier and meadow, and across to another glacier on the other side. The air is clear, cool, and invigorating. Despite my fatigue, I am happy.

There is a woman with me in the Volcano Dream. Unlike the lady in the Waterfall Dream, we are hiking together and obviously good friends. She walks mostly at my side and we are talking, joking, laughing, and enjoying each other's company. The only similarity to the waterfall girl is that I can never quite see her face and have no idea who she is. She can't be Patricia, my wife, because she's brunette, not blond, and she looks nothing like Patricia. The girl could be just a friend. Or a future second wife. Or just a dream dalliance. You never know in dreams.

My companion is short, in her early twenties, and has a round face, a quick wit, and a ready smile. As with the person in the Waterfall Dream, I know she is beautiful even though I can't see her face. Beautiful by any and every definition of the word.

The girl and I hike and hike and climb and climb until we finally reach the top of the barren ridge. Occasionally, as we climb, I reach down to give her a hand up. And occasionally, she reaches down to give me a hand up. It's all very egalitarian. She is probably in slightly better shape than I am.

Finally, sweaty and panting, we stand on the rocky crest atop a lingering summer snowfield and survey the scene that has just revealed itself on the other side, ready to be bowled over by the majestic high-mountain wilderness panorama.

To our amazement, or to my amazement at least, there is a rather large building on the other side of the ridge, with dozens of parked cars in front, accessible by a road that, had we known about it, could have saved us miles of walking. The building looks like one of those ornate, rustic old national park lodges from the 1920s, constructed from logs and immense roof timbers, at a time when you used to take the train to national parks and stay for weeks at a time. Back when the pace of the world was much slower and more relaxed.

My reaction on seeing the building (and I mention this with some embarrassment) is not disappointment but delighted surprise. I know this violates every acceptable hiking and wilderness ethic. But think about it: You are approaching the summit of a world-class mountain toting a huge backpack, with every motion painful and laborious. What could be better than to reach the top and discover a warm, comfortable hotel (or better yet, a Tibetan monastery) with overstuffed sofas and a big-screen TV in the lobby, rooms with clean, soft beds and hot baths, and a really good restaurant? And maybe a masseuse, thrown in for good measure?

I had the Volcano Dream for about fifteen years, from my late teens to my early thirties. Then it gradually faded away and I forgot about it. And naturally the wheel of my life, the carousel of time, continued to turn. I married Patricia O'Leary and we moved to Grants Pass, Oregon, in the Pacific Northwest, where I landed a job as a forester and eventually started writing guidebooks to hiking trails. Along the way, or should I say *along the path*, Pat and I were blessed with three beautiful daughters. Sara was born in 1973 and Anna showed up in 1982. When I married Pat in 1971, she came with a wonderful, ready-made three-year-old named Jennifer, by way of a first brief marriage. During Pat's and my wedding in the Reno Court-house, Jennifer sat between us on the floor playing with Barbie dolls.

In 1997, some twenty years after I stopped having the Volcano Dream, my daughter Sara had just graduated from Portland State University and was living and working in Portland. She'd landed a job in Savannah, Georgia, which is about as far from Oregon as you can get. Before she left, I wanted to get in some "quality time" with her, if you'll pardon the hackneyed expression. We'd always been close, and Sara loved the outdoors as much as I did.

Over a long summer weekend, I drove up to Portland and absconded with my daughter. Our first stop was the home of an old professor of mine from the University of Michigan, who had retired to an island in Washington's Puget Sound. Then we toured the Olympic Peninsula and checked out Mount Rainier National Park, both places neither of us had been before.

We found Professor Ross Tocher, who lived on Stretch Island, near Bremerton, happy and endlessly busy, as always. After spending the night at Ross's house, we circled the Olympic Peninsula and visited Olympic National Park, which is pretty much unavoidable when you circle the Olympic Peninsula. The highlight of the second day was the drive to Hurricane Ridge, a high-mountain aerie and visitor center offering one of the most spectacular vistas on this or any other planet. From the visitor center, the ridge drops down to a huge black river canyon, then ascends to Mount Olympus, Home of the Gods and the park's high point. At 7,965 feet Olympus isn't all that high. But in an area receiving hundreds of inches of rain a year, the glaciers on Olympus are spectacular. The same torrential rainfall is responsible for the rain forests on the park's west side, which we also visited.

We spent the second night in a motel in Port Angeles, then drove to Mount Rainier National Park on the third day.

I'd heard a lot about Mount Rainier, and had seen many photos of Washington's highest peak, but I'd never been there prior to 1997. Rainier stands 300 feet higher than Shasta and falls only 95 feet short of California's Mount Whitney as the highest mountain in America's lower forty-eight. Rainier is heavily glaciated for the same reason that Mount Olympus is heavily glaciated, only more so because Rainier is nearly twice as high (they call it "Rainier" but it should be "Snowier"). The glaciation on Rainier is

Nisqually Glacier/Mount Rainier

much more extensive than on Mount Shasta, which receives much less rainfall and is located in a slightly warmer climate.

By the time we pulled into Mount Rainier's Paradise Visitor Center, Sara and I were tired and grumpy from too much driving and riding. That's the main reason we decided to go for a short hike, a 2-mile walk from the visitor center to McClure Rock, a spot that supposedly offered an outstanding view of the Nisqually Glacier, the Cowlitz Glacier, and the Rainier summit.

The visitor center was a circular building of tan brick in a style that had been considered modern but utilitarian in the 1960s, when it was constructed. The snack bar reminded me of the hot dog concession at Tiger Stadium, back in Detroit when I was a child. Both places were plagued by long lines and not nearly enough tables. Most people either took their food outside or ate standing up.

Our trail began in the vast Paradise Park meadow, immediately adjacent to the visitor center. The meadow turned out to be a stunner of memorable proportions. I'd never seen so many wildflowers in my life, all in the shadow of the mountain, on a ridge overlooking the Nisqually Glacier. I'd never smelled so many wildflowers, either. The only flies in the ointment, or massive gnat swarms in the ointment, were the hundreds of hikers also out enjoying the summer weather, the scenery, and one of the world's most incredible natural botanical displays.

Sara didn't say much during the hike. Sometimes she gets that way when she's tired. And sometimes she gets that way when she isn't. I didn't blame her for being tired. I was tired myself. Even with her bad mood, I figured it would be a good memory for her. I was reminded of a trip to Cape Cod when Sara was thirteen. At the time she hated being trapped with her parents and cut off from friends for two solid weeks. She spent the entire trip loudly making her mother and I aware of her displeasure. But she later insisted that the trip was a good memory and that she'd had a wonderful time.

At the upper end of the meadow, the trail steepened as it made its way up McClure Rock. But the going still wasn't that difficult. It took half an hour to get from the visitor center to the vista point. Sara mumbled that it was "real nice," and probably meant it, but I found her lack of enthusiasm irritating.

It wasn't until we were standing side by side on a lingering snowfield on the top of McClure Rock, with our backs to Rainier, glaciers to our left and right, Paradise Park in the middle, and the visitor center at the far end of Paradise Park, that it dawned on me. This was my Volcano Dream! And the faceless female with me in the Volcano Dream was none other than grumpy old Sara, my firstborn child.

It took me until McClure Rock to notice this because when we'd first arrived at the visitor center in the car, we hadn't bothered to drive the last quarter-mile to the road's end. Had we done so, we would have seen Paradise Lodge, one of the most beautiful, well-restored national park lodges from the 1920s. Paradise Lodge is famous for the massive log beams in its ceiling.

I didn't see Paradise Lodge until I was standing atop McClure Rock, looking back. The layout was not exactly the same as in my Volcano Dream. Unlike Tahquamenon Falls, which duplicated my dream to the minutest detail, I had the lodge in the wrong place. It should have been on the other side of McClure Rock, between the main summit and the Cowlitz Glacier. And the real-life Sara didn't play her role quite the way she should have. But children rarely do.

Despite these discrepancies, there was no question in my mind, none whatsoever. This was the Volcano Dream.

(*Note:* I've also had many memorable hikes with Jennifer, my oldest daughter, and with Anna, my youngest. I just thought I should mention that.)

PART 3: THE CHINESE WALL DREAM

WHEN I WAS ABOUT FIFTY, YET ANOTHER RECURRING DREAM EMERGED. AS WITH the other two, it involved a hike to a location known only in the recesses of my unconscious. I called it the "Big Cliff Dream" for the same reason that I called the two others the "Waterfall Dream" and the "Volcano Dream": The dream involved a big cliff.

Coincidentally, I knew a kid in high school named "Big Cliff": Clifford Imerman. My dream had nothing whatsoever to do with him.

The Big Cliff Dream is less complex and more "otherworldy" than the other two dreams, a brief snippet rather than an unfolding story. In it, I am driving in a pickup truck along a dirt road through a grassy meadow dotted with orange rock outcrops. In the near distance a huge, endless cliff rises abruptly skyward. The cliff is also composed of orange rock. A light dusting of snow adorns my dream cliff's upper portion, creating a stunning contrast with the orange, the intense blue of the sky, and the green meadow.

The grass in the meadow is the deepest, brightest emerald green I have ever seen. The meadow is dotted with clusters of insect-eating members of the pitcher plant family called "cobra plants." In real life I have seen cobra plants many times in the wet meadows and bogs on areas of rare serpentinite rock in southwest Oregon. There are also lady's slipper orchids and Mendocino gentians in the meadow, both highly endangered, along with the less endangered but exceedingly beautiful western tiger lily and western azalea. Needless to say, the flowers are in full bloom, despite the snow on the clifftop. Flowers are always in bloom in my dreams.

The only trees are a few scraggly, stunted, weirdly contorted Jeffrey pines at the meadow edges and along the top of the cliff. The entire meadow smells of Jeffery pine, which has a distinctive aroma that puts me in mind of pineapples.

I find myself intrigued by the row of clownlike Jeffrey pines peering down at me from the clifftop. I want to peer down from the clifftop, too. In real life I often look up at cliffs and think about how much nicer my world would be if I were looking down from the top rather than up from the bottom. If at all possible, I try to find a way to the top. At one point in my life, I attempted to divide all of humanity into "looking down from the top" people and "looking up from the bottom" people.

I feel an urgency about my desire to surmount the cliff. A lot of urgency. An urgency that goes well beyond merely wanting to examine the stunted trees and check out the view. The urgency is a matter of life and death.

The dirt road dead-ends at a beautiful little creek that runs through the meadow. I park, spend a few minutes getting ready for the hike, then gingerly hop from rock to rock as I make my way to the creek's far side. Across the creek there is a trail, which I begin following. The trail leads through the meadow and over some low hills and rubble to the base of the cliff.

As I walk, at a fairly brisk pace, I look for the path to begin ascending the cliff. But it never does. I find this disappointing, even maddening. I keep walking, trying not to panic and reassuring myself that there is no hurry; I will reach the top eventually. The path starts up a few times, then invariably, just when I think I'm making headway, ducks back down to more horizontal and amenable terrain.

In fairness to my subconscious, I've been on lots of trails up cliffs and mountains that took their sweet time reaching their objective and did so only after numerous false starts. The Union Peak Trail in Crater Lake National Park comes to mind. This path completely passes the mountain, then doubles back in the opposite direction, passing the mountain again before making a final push to the summit.

As with my other recurring hiking dreams, I have a female companion in the Big Cliff Dream. Unlike the other dreams, where the woman always does the same things and acts the same way, this woman is extremely inconsistent. Sometimes she's with me from the start, sometimes she joins me in the middle, and sometimes she deserts me in the middle. Sometimes she is friendly and reassuring and we are walking side by side, sometimes she is angry and critical, sometimes she refuses to talk to me, and sometimes she stays far ahead of me as I try in vain to catch up.

Sometimes I love and enjoy this person and sometimes I find myself feeling annoyance or even hatred when she arrives.

The main thing this particular woman has in common with the females of my other dreams is that I can't see her face. From the back she looks a little like the Volcano Dream lady. She looks nothing like the woman in the Waterfall Dream. Nothing whatsoever.

The woman in the Big Cliff Dream is not in her twenties but her forties. Since I'm in my fifties in the dream, that's still pretty young. The person is short and a little overweight but basically attractive. She has a bouncy, confident gait that some might find amusing. She loves to laugh and make jokes but her conversations can also be very intense. She sympathizes with my setbacks and praises my accomplishments. But she is also likely to become enraged over an innocent remark and storm off in a huff.

I have an alternate name for the Big Cliff Dream, by the way. Sometimes I call it the Chinese Wall Dream. That's because the trail follows the base of a structure that reminds me of a geologic formation I've seen pictures of in the Bob Marshall Wilderness of central Montana— just south of Glacier National Park, about 50 miles from a town by the name of Paradise. The Bob Marshall is one of the oldest and largest units of the U.S. Wilderness Preservation System. Bob Marshall was a forest service employee and writer who conceived the primitive area and wilderness systems in the 1930s.

The dominant geologic feature of the Bob Marshall Wilderness is a 22-mile-long, 1,000-foot-high escarpment that must have reminded somebody of the Great Wall of China. It is called the "Chinese Wall." I've never been to the Chinese Wall in either the Bob Marshall Wilderness or China. But I've seen photos of both, and there is definitely a resemblance.

Aside from the presence of a tremendous cliff that seemed to go on for miles and miles, from one horizon to the other, the Big Cliff Dream did not appear to be based on central Montana, about which I knew very little. Instead, it's an idealized version of a place much closer to my Oregon home, the Kalmiopsis Wilderness.

The Kalmiopsis is a huge tract of extremely wild country in Oregon's extreme southwest corner. I've been hiking in the Kalmiopsis dozens of times. The area boasts two main features. One is an exceedingly rare member of the heath/blueberry family called the kalmiopsis plant, a dwarf rhododendron maybe 8 inches high. The entire earthly range of the kalmiopsis plant is limited to perhaps fifteen clonal clusters, all within the Kalmiopsis Wilderness.

The area's other main feature is a rare and fascinating rock called serpentinite. Serpentinite is the primary rock type of the oceanic subfloor. On land, serpentinite is found only on the leading edges of continents, on the side of the forward drift. The theory is that the serpentinite was bulldozed up from the ocean by the advancing continent. Serpentinite is greenish black in color. On exposure to air, which doesn't happen very often since most serpentinite is underwater, the rock weathers to an extremely rough textured buff-orange color.

An odd feature of serpentinite is that most common plant species won't grow on it or are stunted by it. Yet, several rare and endangered plants, such as the kalmiopsis plant, grow only on serpentinite. Jeffrey pine, which is fairly common in California, grows in Oregon only on serpentinite.

The location of the Big Cliff Dream could have been just about anyplace in the mid-to-upper-elevation serpentinite areas of the Kalmiopsis Wilderness. Except, of course, there no cliffs in the Kalmiopsis that look anything like Montana's Chinese Wall. At least none that I'm aware of.

An old wives' tale says that if you die in a dream, you will wake up dead. You know what I mean. It's the perfect old wives' tale because it's absolutely unprovable. If you were to die during a dream in which you died, nobody would ever know. Of course if you dreamed you died, then woke up in fine fettle and perfect health, that would definitely disprove the myth. But still, I've never met anybody who had the dream and lived to tell about it. Or who had the dream and did not live to tell about it.

As far as I can recall, I have never dreamed that I died. Whether or not that is the reason I remain very much alive, I cannot say. All I know is, I hope I never have the Death Dream. And if I do, I hope the old wives are dead wrong.

I used to have my own unproven superstition about dreams, my personal old wives' tale that I made up myself, even though I am not an old wife. The superstition was based on my observation that whenever I have to go to the bathroom while sleeping, just as the pressure on my bladder is about to wake me up, I invariably dream I'm in the middle of some extremely crowded place, searching frantically for a rest room. When I finally find one, I grunt and strain trying to relieve myself but nothing ever comes out. Then, just when my bladder is about to burst, I wake up, laugh at the foolishness of my dream, and drag myself out of bed to the toilet.

Aside from the discomfort of bladder pressure, I like going-to-the-bathroom dreams because they have virtually no Freudian significance or deeper meaning. Their only meaning is that I have to go to the bathroom.

My superstition about bathroom dreams, which weaseled its way into my cranium and refused to leave, was this: If I ever *was* able to successfully urinate in a dream, I would wake up to discover that I had wet the bed. As long as I continued, in my dream, to grunt and strain in futility, I was okay.

Then one day, in my early fifties, the unthinkable happened. I dreamed I snuck into a private girls' school to use the toilet. I was being chased by security guards, so I had to work fast. To my consternation the commodes in the girls' john, the only rest room I could find, were all 3 inches high. After the usual grunting and straining, and with amazingly accurate aim, I succeeded in relieving myself. Did I ever!

It was a momentous event—the first time in nearly half a century of attempting to pee in my dreams that anything ever came out. In the dream, however, I was more concerned with the pursuing security guards than with stopping to admire my accomplishment. I hurriedly zipped my pants, then climbed out a window that opened onto a formal sculpture garden. With six security guards chasing me, I discover, to my horror, that I still had to go to the bathroom.

When I woke up, expecting to find myself drenched in warm, pungent fluid, I discovered, to my profound relief, that my bed, and my body, were as dry as a Saharan bone. So much for old wives' tales.

And yes, in case you were wondering, this bit of information is relevant to the story. At least the part about the Death Dream is relevant. The part about going to the bathroom was included only for illustrative purposes.

The primary difference between the Big Cliff Dream and the other two dreams is that in the Big Cliff Dream, I actually figured out who the woman was without the dream ever coming true.

The woman is my mother. Even though I can't see her face, we had precisely the relationship depicted in the dream. And I react to the woman exactly as I reacted to my mother. Sara looks very much like my mother and not at all like her own.

The thing is, my mother passed away in 1975. She died of breast cancer, and of rampaging infections from psoriasis, way too many cigarettes, depression over my father's death ten years earlier, and not giving a damn whether she lived or died. It was the slowest, most hideous, most painful death I have ever seen.

In my dream, my mother is well and whole. She is her predictably unpredictable, often volatile self. And that is as it should be. I could not face having to relive her hideous final illness in my dreams.

What, you might ask, is the significance of encountering my deceased mother on the trail over and over again? I wrestled with that question for years before coming up with an answer. Or at least a possible answer.

The significance is this: I have always believed that I will die on a trail. I now believe that it will not be just any trail, it will be this trail. It's like the Death Dream of the old wives' tale. Were I ever to dream that I make it to the top of the cliff, I am convinced that I would not wake up. The same is true, I believe, if I were to somehow locate the site in reality.

And no, I have no plans to avoid hiking in the Kalmiopsis or Bob Marshall Wilderness Areas. After watching my mother gradually shrivel up and die over ten years, I can think of no better way to exit this dimension and ascend to the next plane of existence than from a landmark such as the Chinese Wall in the Bob Marshall Wilderness.

Finally, there is this: If the Big Cliff Dream is indeed a vision of how my life will end, and if there is a consistency to these recurrent dreams, then the Waterfall Dream and the Volcano Dream must be taken into account when interpreting the Big Cliff Dream. When I do that, one thing becomes absolutely clear: Whenever, wherever, and however my death occurs, it will be in Paradise. Or near paradise.

(*Note:* I just hope my mother has the good sense not to overstay her welcome when I reach my destination. As much as I love her, she does tend to get on my nerves.)

TRAIL 1: *Upper Falls Trail, Tahquamenon Falls State Park, Michigan.*

LENGTH *(one way): 0.75 mile.*

DIRECTIONS: *Take I-75 north to the Mackinac Bridge and cross over to the Michigan Upper Peninsula. Eight miles beyond the bridge, go left on MI 123 and continue for 55 miles to the town of Paradise, on Lake Superior's Whitefish Bay. Stay on MI 123 past Paradise for 8 miles, to Tahquamenon Falls State Park and the Upper Falls parking area, visitor center, and trailhead.*

TRAIL 2: *McClure Rock Trail, Mount Rainier National Park, Washington.*

LENGTH *(one way): 2 miles.*

DIRECTIONS: *From I-5 south of Tacoma, Washington, take WA 512 East to WA 7 South. Proceed 24 miles to WA 706 East. Follow 706 for 25 miles to Mount Rainier National Park. The McClure Rock Trail begins at the Paradise Visitor Center.*

TRAIL 3: *Unknown*

LENGTH *(one way): Unknown*

DIRECTIONS: *Unknown*

HIKE SEVEN
CRYPTOZOOLOGY

PART 1

THEY'RE OUT THERE AND THEY'RE WATCHING US," I REPEATED FOR THE hundredth time as Brian Boothby and I hiked through a particularly dense and spooky stretch of woods.

"You're crazy," said Brian, also for the hundredth time.

"I'm not crazy, we are going to see one and I'm going to get me a photo."

"You're not going to photograph a bigfoot," Brian reiterated in exasperation. "You wanna know why? Because *there's no such thing as bigfoot!*"

Brian's cynicism, and the strength of his reaction, was one reason I kept bringing up the possibility of a bigfoot sighting. I enjoyed getting a rise out of him. Not that I didn't very much hope to encounter a bigfoot. But I realized that the chances were pretty slim. I would never admit that to Brian, though.

As we talked, Brian and I rounded a bend on the Stuart Fork Trail, on which we were hiking, and started up a short, steep, rocky segment where the path briefly veered away from the fast-flowing river. The calming shade that had covered the initial 3 miles was replaced, for several hundred yards, by rocks and brush. The pungent aroma of snowbrush permeated the air.

I liked Brian as a hiking companion because we rarely agreed on anything and invariably ended up in intense, albeit mostly good-natured debate. It made the miles go by faster. About the only thing we agreed on was that we both liked to hike. Brian was a mailman in Medford, Oregon, and walked 7 miles a day on his route so he was in astonishingly good condition for our anticipated 50-mile, three-day outing. Much better condition than I.

"I'll find me a bigfoot one of these days," I reassured my companion. "I've figured out exactly where to look. How hard can it be?"

"Hard enough so that nobody's ever done it before. At least not that they've been able to conclusively prove."

"A minor consideration," I said with a grin. "The trouble with you, Boothby, is that you have a closed mind. Even if you stepped on a bigfoot's toe, or a bigfoot stepped on your toe, your subconscious would probably register the animal only as a very large dog."

"And the trouble with you, Bernstein, is that you're a idiot."

One benefit to being a hiking fanatic and living in southwest Oregon is easy access to the heart of the area sometimes referred to as "Bigfoot Country." While the elusive, often sighted but never verified man-ape has been reported throughout northern California and the Pacific Northwest, more encounters have occurred in or near California's Siskiyou, Trinity Alps, and Russian Wilderness Areas than all other locations combined. The Trinity Alps Wilderness, the third largest federal wilderness area in the United States outside Alaska, was precisely where Brian and I happened to be hiking.

The Stuart Fork Trail was prime bigfoot habitat. That was one reason I'd chosen it for our hike. Another reason was a desire to visit Emerald and Sapphire Lakes, supposedly the two most exquisitely beautiful alpine glacial lakes in the world. Maybe in the universe. Emerald Lake lay at mile 14 of the Stuart Fork Trail's 16 miles. Sapphire Lake adorned mile 15.

"Get out of here with your 'prime bigfoot habitat,'" said Brian, sounding annoyed. "There's no such thing as prime bigfoot habitat because there's no such thing as bigfoot. An animal can't have a habitat if it doesn't exist."

"A habitat of the mind," I suggested. I liked that concept. Then I explained once again to Brian my theory about bigfoot habitat:

During my hundreds of hikes in California, Oregon, and Washington, I told him, I have developed an ability to sense when a bigfoot is nearby; when they're "out there watching us." At least I'm pretty sure I have. I realize that my innate sense is probably untestable and that even though a hundred bigfeet may be hiding behind the trees only a few feet away, and probably are, that doesn't mean one will ever actually step out in front of me, extend its hand, and say hello. It would be nice, but you have to be realistic about such things.

I always try to be realistic.

Nevertheless, I am convinced, based on the frequency and strength of my intuitive feelings, that I know where bigfeet live and where they don't. In fact, I have been able to map this out. I am certain that there is not a single bigfoot anywhere in the Mount Shasta, Yolla Bolly–Middle Eel, Castle Crags, Snow Mountain, Sky Lakes, or Mountain Lakes Wilderness Areas, which all lie within a hundred miles of the Trinity Alps.

The Marble Mountain, Kalmiopsis, and Red Buttes Wilderness Areas, also within a hundred miles of the Trinity Alps, are "iffy" as far as the presence of bigfeet. The habitat is there: dense coastal forest, lots of rainfall, and tens of thousands of acres of remote, rugged backcountry often with few trails. But I've rarely had that unexplainable "feeling" in the Marbles, Kalmiopsis, or Red Buttes.

There are three northern California wilderness areas where I am positive that the fabled beasts are never far away. I have never—not once—crossed the boundary of the Siskiyou, Russian, or Trinity Alps Wilderness Areas without being dogged at some point by the notion that someone or something was watching me. And I've hiked in those places scores of times.

The all-time favorite bigfoot hangout, according my readings on the subject, is purported to be not the Trinity Alps, Siskiyou, or Russian Wilderness, but a place called Bluff Creek, and adjacent Blue Creek, just south of the Siskiyou Wilderness. That's where the most sightings have occurred. The only undebunked photos of bigfoot to date, the famous 1967 Roger Patterson film, were taken on a logging road on Bluff Creek.

Well . . . some people consider them undebunked.

As an enthusiastic bigfoot stalker, I'd been to Bluff Creek many times. Sadly, in twenty-five years I'd never encountered so much as an EEE bootprint.

"If you've been in 'prime bigfoot habitat' that many times," said Brian, who had been listening attentively and making negative comments every couple of minutes, "you should have seen dozens of them by now. Hundreds. You should have invited a family of bigfeet home for dinner by now."

"You'd think so," I explained. "Except for the Prime Rule of Bigfoot Hunting."

"Okay, I'll bite, what is the 'Prime Rule of Bigfoot Hunting'?"

"The Prime Rule of Bigfoot Hunting," I explained, "is that if you purposely look for a bigfoot, you will never find one. To see bigfeet, you have to be patient and hope they decide to come to you. That's how it has been with every person who's ever seen a bigfoot. Or any other unverified mammal. And that's how it will probably be with me. Or with you and me."

"So we're screwed," said Brian. "Darn the luck."

"Not really," I said. "We are in prime bigfoot habitat and I'm well prepared, just in case one of them chooses to honor us."

"Don't hold your breath," Brian muttered.

I did not mention that I just made up the Prime Rule while we were talking.

Four miles from the trailhead, in the middle of an immense old-growth stand with trees so massive that virtually no sunlight penetrated to the forest floor, we arrived at our first landmark, the side trail to Alpine Lake. Our plan was to hike the 3 miles to Alpine Lake, take a few photos, return to the main trail before dark, and walk for 2 or 3 more miles before setting up camp for the night. It was only two in the afternoon so there was plenty of daylight left, even though, according to the topographic map, the Alpine Lake Trail was extremely steep. Because of the steepness, and because we planned to return in just three hours, we hid our backpacks in the underbrush behind some trees and took off barebacked down the side trail. It was an eighth of a mile to where the path forded the Stuart Fork.

"In case you're interested," I said, looking around at the ancient trees, which were even bigger near the river, "there are bigfeet right here."

There were, too. I was positive.

Brian grunted but didn't say anything. I guess he'd given up arguing with me. For a while.

Since it was late June, the river was high with spring runoff. It looked to be about 50 feet wide and, we guessed, 3 or 4 feet at the deepest, although you can never tell for sure. The river was extremely fast and a little intimidating. We debated whether to cross or not. Brian decided to give it a try.

"The worst that can happen is that I get washed a few hundred feet downstream," he explained.

"That's not the worst that can happen," I noted.

"If we get into trouble, one of your bigfoot friends can come and rescue us."

Brian made it across with relative ease, or at least without mishap, although he seemed to be straining against the current at the deepest part. The water there came a little above his waist.

Then I started across. I'm a couple of inches taller than Brian, and stockier, so I should have had an easier time. I'd have made it across, too, but when I got to the part where Brian was straining against the current, I began worrying about the $600 camera around my neck. Were I to lose my balance, I would probably not be injured. But I could not risk losing or damaging my precious Nikon. I turned around and returned from whence I'd come.

Brian was annoyed about having to cross the river a second time but there wasn't much he could do about it.

I plan to visit Alpine Lake one of these years. It's supposed to be very pretty.

Back on the Stuart Fork Trail, after we'd retrieved our backpacks, resumed our trek, and mentally adjusted to the fact that Alpine Lake would not be part of our itinerary and that our hike would now cover only 44 miles instead of 50, we started discussing bigfoot again. This time Brian brought it up.

"So tell me," he said, "have you ever *almost* seen a bigfoot? Like the rear end disappearing into the brush, or rustling bushes and a quick glimpse? Or a fresh track, maybe. Lots of people supposedly see tracks. Have you seen anything like that? Anything at all?"

"Not really," I admitted. "The closest I ever came, and it wasn't very close, was in 1979 when my oldest daughter, Jennifer, was eleven, and I made the mistake of repeating to her some of what I'd read about the fabled giant. She'd been studying the controversy in school. Jenny got all excited, like a kid listening to ghost stories at camp, and begged me to take her Bluff Creek. You sure you want to hear this story?"

"Go for it," said Brian. Brian seemed to enjoy my hiking stories, of which I had many. The stories made the time go by even faster than arguing about bigfoot. He enjoyed my hiking guidebooks, also, partly because he got them for free, often with him posing in a couple of the photos and his name in the acknowledgments.

"Pleeeeease, Daddy," Jenny had exhorted. "Take me to find a bigfoot."

How could I refuse?

It occurred to me, as Jenny and I planned the excursion, that she probably hadn't thought through what she'd do if she actually ran into a bigfoot. But I figured such an occurrence was highly unlikely, so I didn't press the issue. Jennifer invited her best girlfriend, Mickey, to accompany us.

Now it happened that there was a charming little forest service campground on Highway 96, located in a narrow rock canyon where Bluff Creek dramatically spewed its guts into the Klamath River, between the tiny village of Somesbar and the Hoopa Indian Reservation. We spent the night at that campground. The girls stayed in a tent and I slept in the back of my canopy-covered pickup.

The 40-mile drive from Happy Camp, down 96 paralleling the Klamath, may be the most scenic paved road in a state famous for scenic roads. At the village of Somesbar, you are faced with the enviable but perplexing choice of either continuing on 96, past Bluff Creek and through the Hoopa Reservation to the coast, or turning off onto the even more beautiful and dramatic canyon of the Salmon River.

Shortly after going to bed at the Bluff Creek Campground, the girls began screaming. I scrambled out of my cozy little compartment, went to see what was wrong, and discovered that the kids had gotten into a *what-would-we-do-if-a-bigfoot-came-into-our-tent-in-the-middle-of-the-night* discussion. I managed to calm them down with assurances that bigfeet are deathly afraid of tents and eleven-year-old girls. But I couldn't resist letting out a few well-timed growls and howling noises during the night. It was pretty much expected. Had I not growled and howled, I'd have been drummed out of the Daddy Corps.

The next day we drove every inch of Bluff Creek and Blue Creek Roads. If there were bigfeet there, as there may well have been, they remained hidden.

At one point, while were driving around the upper end of Bluff Creek Road, Jenny asked if I really believed in bigfoot or if I was just humoring her.

"Of course I believe in bigfoot," I informed my daughter. I did not mention that the truth was much more complex and fuzzy, as the truth about one's beliefs often is.

"I thought you were a staunch, die-hard bigfoot booster," Brian interjected. "All of a sudden there is 'complexity'? Answer the girl's question. Either you believe in bigfoot or you don't."

"I believe, I believe." I replied. "But more than that, I am fascinated by the concept of a giant, almost human, or better than human, animal who somehow manages to remain hidden from a civilization that arrogantly likes to believe it knows everything. And I would give anything to see one. From a safe distance, of course."

Brian and I were now almost 8 miles from the trailhead and approaching Morris Meadow. This meant that very shortly, the valley would widen out and Sawtooth Ridge, a highlight of the Trinity Alps, would appear. I was anxious to see Sawtooth Ridge and Morris Meadow. Not as anxious as I was to see Emerald and Sapphire Lakes, but pretty anxious nevertheless.

"Even though I believe in bigfoot," I explained to Brian, "I am aware that it's all highly theoretical and that most bigfoot reports turn out to be hoaxes."

"All bigfoot reports are hoaxes," Brian corrected.

I told Brian about a news story I once read, about a motorist who swore he saw a bigfoot while driving along Interstate 5, near Siskiyou Summit. The beast was reportedly sitting on a rock, waving at passing cars. Oddly, only the one driver saw it. And, of course, many of the outsized footprints from which the animal gets its name were made by pranksters tramping around the woods wearing home-fabricated gorilla mukluks.

Still, there is a core in all the silliness that can't be completely discounted.

"No there isn't," said Brian.

"Yes there is," I insisted.

Here, for the record, is why I have never quite been able to rule out the existence of bigfoot, or any of the other unverified mammals of northern California and the Pacific Northwest: Having hiked hundreds of miles of trail, to the heart of the largest and most remote wilderness areas, I know that the paths visit only a minute fraction of the total area, which is covered with jagged mountains and dense, giant forests nourished by frequent coastal storms.

Could fifty or so large, herbaceous, highly intelligent primates who didn't want to be discovered successfully hide out there? Hell, if they played their cards right, they could hide out in a single valley and never be discovered. For example, the North Fork of the New River, in the western Trinity Alps—the two-thirds of the wilderness where hardly anybody ever goes—drains fifteen thousand acres, has no trail access, requires a 30-mile drive up a logging road and a 10-mile hike just to reach the edge of the drainage, and is visited, on average, by less than one person every five years. If that.

And that's just one example among many.

"And that's why you believe in bigfoot?" said Brian. "It seems to me you're basing your belief solely on the fact that you can't disprove a negative; that you can never prove something's nonexistence, only its existence."

"I'm just saying it's possible. Actually, it's like Santa Claus. The poet in me definitely believes in the spirit of bigfoot. And the scientist in me would love to find proof of the reality of bigfoot. But the realist in me knows that if somebody ever captured a live bigfoot, it would be a disaster both for the spirit of bigfoot and for the real live animal."

"On that, I agree," said Brian.

Brian is not always as cynical as he would lead you to believe. That's another reason I like to take him along on these excursions.

PART 2

I DESCRIBED TO BRIAN MY "BIGFOOT FANTASY" AS WE HIKED.

I've imagined it a million times: I'm by myself, deep within one of the immense wilderness areas that occupy much of the California Far North, on a trail hardly anybody ever goes on, near a beautiful high-mountain lake. Actually the pictures in my mind happen to be of Big Elk Lake, in northern California's Marble Mountain Wilderness. I've been there a couple of times and it's very pretty and remote. It's one of few places in the Marbles where I've definitely sensed the presence of bigfoot. More important, you can see the lake, and the meadow that rings the lake, from a mile away as you approach on the trail.

The oddest thing about Big Elk Lake is that it's smaller than nearby Little Elk Lake. But that has nothing to do with the story.

In my fantasy, it's morning and the world is fresh and dewy, as the world often is in the wilderness at that time of day in summer. After camping out the previous night, I begin hiking very early, just after daybreak, and have already been on the trail for an hour as I pass through a stretch of gloomy, light-starved forest, and my imagination starts to run wild. Runaway imagination is not unprecedented for me, and the tendency at least partially explains why I ended up a writer.

On this particular day I sense that the massive, five-hundred-year-old, balsam-scented Shasta red firs are following me with their eyes, or with the arboreal equivalent of eyes, whatever that might be. However the trees are accomplishing it, I know they are watching me, that they are very much aware of me, and that I am an unwelcome intruder in their domain.

Then the path breaks out of the woods. I find myself high above a medium-sized but exceptionally beautiful lake basin, looking down on a brilliant, sapphire-blue glacial lake, possibly Big Elk Lake, its water glistening in the morning sun. A rich yellow-green meadow, the color intensified by morning dew, surrounds the lake.

I expect to feel relief at my emergence from the woods into the light, where I am free from the prying tree-eyes. But I do not. The beauty of the scene is overshadowed by a persistent sense of unease—a feeling that something still isn't quite right. It's exactly the same feeling I had while in the woods, the same feeling I get whenever I sense that there are bigfeet nearby.

It seems to me that the smell of the air, which had been fresh and sweet with morning, is slightly off. I should be smelling trees, grass, soil, pine sap, wildflowers, and dew. And indeed, I smell all of those things. Yet I also sense, ever so slightly, the essence of sweaty armpits, not my own. At least that is the best comparison I can make. The aroma hangs faintly like a speck of spinach on an otherwise pearly-white front tooth.

Then I notice a large, furry animal sitting in the grass by the lake at the edge of some rock outcrops. At first I think it's a bear. Seeing a bear in a meadow in the Marble Mountains is not unprecedented. In fact, it's pretty common. If it is a bear, though, it's an awfully big one. One of the largest I've ever seen. I reach for my camera, which is belted around my waist inside a fanny pack that also contains my lunch, toilet paper, and insect repellent.

When the huge beast suddenly stands up and walks on two feet, my heart begins pounding in my chest like a body-and-fender man throwing a tantrum. That is definitely not a bear walk. Bears walk on two feet only for short distances and always with a sort of hobbling lope, steadied by their forepaws occasionally touching the ground, as though the upright position is extremely uncomfortable.

This particular animal just strolls across the meadow with bipedal confidence, its arms swinging at its sides.

I find myself hyperventilating. This is it! Finally.

Silently, crouching down, my hands trembling slightly, I point my camera at the animal, put the machine into the "telephoto" mode, and begin snapping. Within days I'll be sought by every magazine and news organization in the world.

I'll be a millionaire!

PART 3

"SO IT'S ALL ABOUT MONEY," SAID BRIAN, WHEN I'D FINISHED THE STORY. "IT FIGURES."

"Hey, somebody's got to pay for all this camera equipment. The quickest way to recoup the expense is to photograph an unverified mammal and sell it to the national media. Especially the tabloids."

"That's the third time you've used the phrase *unverified mammal*," said Brian. "Are there other nonexistent animals besides bigfoot we need to worry about? Six-foot-tall chipmunks, maybe, that speak Spanish?"

"Now you're talking," I laughed. "A shot like that would be worth way more than a plain old bigfoot. And yes, there are other unverified mammals in the California Far North."

"And do you believe in them, too?"

"Why not? Like I said, humans don't know everything."

"So what are some other unverified mammals, aside from giant chipmunks?"

"The only one I'm aware of is the California grizzly."

"The California grizzly isn't unverified, it's extinct."

"That's where you're wrong," I announced. "Or at least you might be wrong."

The authenticated facts, I explained, accepted by nearly everybody, are that the California grizzly was hunted to extinction following the Gold Rush of the 1850s and '60s. The miners thought the bears were a nuisance, probably because, unlike black bears, grizzlies tended to kill people who messed with them.

By 1890, following thirty years of methodical and merciless slaughter, the California grizzly was no more. The last known of its species had been dubbed "Old Reelfoot," due to an unfortunate encounter with a leghold trap. Old Reelfoot roamed the Siskiyou Mountains around Ashland, Oregon, along the California line, for forty years. In 1890 he was shot dead by a seventeen-year-old hunter who became an instant hero for his deed. Old Reelfoot was stuffed, then displayed for many years in the county museum in Jacksonville, Oregon. The mountain that rises directly above Ashland is called "Grizzly Peak" in honor of Old Reelfoot. And the Ashland High School athletic teams are named the "Grizzlies," also in his honor.

The thing is, in the bars and coffee shops of the most remote communities of the California Far North, in places like Somesbar, Happy Camp, and Willow Creek, especially around the Hoopa Reservation, there are those who aren't so sure the California grizzly is extinct.

A guy named Augie Atteberry informed me of the Native American view of the California grizzly, in no uncertain terms, in 1971. At the time Augie was playing low-ball poker in a tavern in Yreka, California's second northernmost county seat, after Crescent City. Among Augie's many noteworthy accomplishments, he was a Hoopa Indian game tracker.

"That stuff about there being no more grizzlies is crap," Augie announced one night while taking an immense puff off his big, acrid cigar. "My people, the Hoopa, Karuk, and Yurok, go a lot farther back into the woods than you white folks. We see grizzly all the time."

Given a choice, I'd rather meet a bigfoot than a grizzly. Bigfeet don't generally attack.

"You're not going to meet a bigfoot *or* a grizzly," Brian reminded me.

PART 4

AS BRIAN AND I ENTERED MORRIS MEADOW, WE WERE TREATED TO OUR FIRST glimpse of Sawtooth Ridge, a jagged row of spires that abruptly rose 3,000 feet above the meadow to the north and east, forcing the valley of the Stuart Fork into a ninety-degree turn. On looking at the ridge, I decided that *sawtooth* was not the best description. *Tiger-tooth* would be more accurate, although the white rock spires mostly reminded me of marimbas. With a large enough mallet, you could have played songs on them.

The magnificent white ice-cream cone mountain that dominated the valley's west side, opposite Sawtooth Ridge, was called "Sawtooth Mountain." I guess any formation with a jagged top was a candidate for the name back in the days when the area's only visitors were loggers carrying whipsaws. They were not a very creative bunch.

In the distance to the northwest, between Sawtooth Mountain and Sawtooth Ridge, we could see where the valley veered westward north of the meadow and ended up at Emerald and Sapphire Lakes, 6 miles from where we stood.

Suffice it to say, Morris Meadow exceeded all expectations and I was happy to be there. So, apparently, was Brian. So were a lot of other people who suddenly materialized. We hadn't passed that many people on the trail, in the 8 miles from the trailhead, but in the meadow, humans carrying backpacks swarmed everywhere we looked.

A hundred yards or so into the meadow, the path we'd been following for so long disappeared in the waist-high grass. We found that rather odd, considering the trail's high usage. Actually the route broke into several faint waytrails, which braided in and out of each other as we made our way across the grassy expanse. We were briefly concerned about losing the trail, until we figured out that it didn't matter which path we took. They all converged again at the far end.

All I knew was that I was actually in Morris Meadow, a place I'd wanted to visit for twenty years. And each step took me closer to Emerald and Sapphire Lakes, which I'd also wanted to visit for twenty years. I actually forgot about bigfoot for a while as I allowed the meadow's beauty to overwhelm my senses.

On the meadow's far side, 9 miles from the trailhead, the true path reasserted itself at a spot where a dense stand of giant Shasta red fir ventured out across the flat. In contrast to the open meadow's sunny glare, the forest was dark, silent, and musty smelling. Beneath the cathedral trees lay a low, green underbrush of ferns, salal, huckleberry, trillium, and vanilla leaf.

The shadow of Sawtooth Peak was starting to move across the valley but at six o'clock on a June evening it was a long way from nightfall. It gets dark around nine o'clock at that time of year. Still, it was a little darker in the woods than it would have been at noon. But only a little.

Because we were tired and it was getting late, Brian and I began keeping an eye out for a suitable locale to put up our tent, build a campfire, and turn in for the night.

The instant we entered the woods, I set what may have been the all-time record for neck-tingling, free-floating paranoia and the sensation of creatures peering at me. The psychic alarms, sirens, whistles, and buzzers were intensified by the stark contrast with the overwhelming joy I'd felt at the meadow. Once in the woods, my skin tingled, my brain set off so many radar blips I couldn't keep track of them all, and the pit of my stomach quivered like a can of paint on a mixing machine.

"There are bigfeet around," I kept whispering.

"Leave me alone," Brian kept whispering back.

"I'm not kidding. There are bigfeet around."

"Okay, there are bigfeet around. You better get your camera out."

"Good idea," I whispered.

We walked the next quarter-mile in silence. I had my camera out of its case and around my neck, poised and ready, just in case. Not that there was enough light for a decent photo. Any shot I took, I knew, would default to the "flash" mode, which meant I had to be within 15 feet of whatever I was photographing. While I desperately wanted to gaze upon my long-sought bigfoot, I wasn't sure I wanted to get quite that close. In all my fantasizing, I had never considered lighting and focus. I always pictured the encounter in full sunlight, out in the open, with no tricky camera adjustments. I'd just aim and shoot.

Adjusting my backpack shoulder straps, and my determination, I took a deep breath and pressed ahead, keeping one hand on the camera. The sound of my breathing, and Brian's, was the only audible noise in the eerie jungle-forest. The duff litter on the trail surface absorbed the impact of our footsteps while the trees and foliage absorbed all the other sounds except for an occasional songbird far overhead.

A few minutes later, as we rounded a curve in the path . . .

Sheesh! What the hell is that?

I stopped walking. Goose bumps rose on my forearms. My heart pounded in my chest. I'd have said something to Brian but I couldn't talk. Brian saw it too, obviously, because he also stopped walking. He glanced at me with just as puzzled a look as I undoubtedly had. Then we both stared at the animal that walked silently along the trail, magnificent, sleek, and eerie, perhaps 20 feet ahead of us, moving in the same direction we were going.

I'd never seen anything like it before in my life. I'd never heard of anything like it before in my life.

No, it was not a bigfoot.

I hadn't the faintest idea what it was.

My first thought, after several seconds of confused and frantic flipping through the Rolodex in my mind that contained every fact I ever knew about mammals, was that it was a cougar. Except it was black, like a jaguar or panther. Cougars are a light tan.

Even if the animal had been a cougar, which it clearly was not, seeing one on a trail was highly unusual. Many lifelong devotees of hiking and hunting in the region have never seen a cougar in the wild. I'd been a little more lucky. I once saw a mother and two cubs walk across the logging road on which I was driving, at the edge of the Salmon-Huckleberry Wilderness Area, near Mount Hood, in north-central Oregon.

But this was not a cougar. It was the wrong color. It was very much the wrong color. It was as black as india ink. It wasn't a black panther or a jaguar, either. The shape of its head was more cougarish than pantherish. Besides, there are no black panthers in California or anywhere else in North America. Unless you count jaguarundis, which live in Texas. But jaguarundis are much smaller than the creature Brian and I were seeing, and Texas was 2,000 miles away.

Saying nothing and keeping as quiet as possible, Brian and I watched the animal pad gracefully and silently along the path for about ten seconds, which can be a very long time. I moved my camera up to my eye, then hesitated for a second. It occurred to me that if I took a flash shot, it would frighten the animal away. On the other hand, the beast was at the very edge of my 15-foot range, and if I was going to get a photo, now was the time.

Slowly and firmly, I squeezed the button. And the flash went off. And the shutter snapped.

And almost instantly, the animal disappeared. Most likely it simply slipped off into the underbrush. My perception, and Brian's, however, was that it had vanished.

The good news was that as soon as the animal vanished, my sense of a mysterious presence watching us also vanished. Nevertheless we walked for another full mile, this time at Brian's insistence, before stopping for the night. Brian said he wanted to make sure we were far, far away from the prowling jungle carnivore we'd just seen.

Whatever it was.

The camping spot we picked seemed unthreatening, innocuous, and immensely comfortable. We spent the night alongside the Stuart Fork, on a tree-shaded flat by a swimming hole. The primary topic of conversation as we relaxed, swam, and cooked dinner was the strange animal we'd seen.

"It was a black panther," Brian insisted.

"That's impossible," I countered. "I'm a trained naturalist and I've taken university classes in mammalogy. I know for a fact that there are no black panthers in California."

"It was a black panther," Brian insisted.

And so the argument raged.

PART 5

WHEN I FIRST MOVED WEST, IN 1970, ONE OF MY FIRST EMPLOYERS WAS THE California Department of Fish and Game office in Yreka, California. One of my "duties" was to be dropped off in wilderness areas by a helicopter and hike out remote creeks in search of salmon-spawning habitat. I didn't find any uncharted salmon-spawning habitat during the entire project. I did manage to fall over a cliff once, though, 5 miles up a creek with no trail access. I hobbled out to the Klamath River Road covered with lacerations and with a badly sprained ankle.

Another task that summer was to snorkel the entire length of the California Salmon River counting summer steelhead.

Some job.

It was during my days in the office, that summer, that I fell passionately in love with a photograph of Emerald and Sapphire Lakes, taken from the top of Sawtooth Ridge. The photo adorned the cover of a map and lake-guide pamphlet to the Salmon-Trinity Primitive Area. An employee who'd recently retired from the very office where I worked had written the pamphlet.

"That's one gorgeous couple of lakes," I exclaimed, ungrammatically, on seeing the photo.

"You ought to see them in person," said my supervisor.

I helped myself to an entire set of the lake-guide pamphlets, which have never been reprinted. My pilfered set is extremely valuable, and the source of much of the background information contained in my many hiking trail guidebooks.

Emerald Lake covers forty-two acres and Sapphire Lake, twenty-eight. Both are set in a deeply cut, perfectly formed alpine glacial basin. The basin, according to the photograph, appears to have been carved into the white granite mountains by a giant ice cream scoop. Above Sapphire Lake lies another twelve-acre pool called Mirror Lake. And above Mirror Lake, an active (though very small) glacier clings to a ledge halfway up a black-and-white-striped rock headwall. And above the glacier, Thompson Peak, the highest point in the Trinity Alps, tops out at 9,002 feet. Thompson Peak contains the only glaciers in the United States west of the Sierra Nevada–Cascades chain and south of Washington's Olympic Peninsula.

A year prior to my Stuart Fork hike, I had actually seen Emerald and Sapphire Lakes, from five miles away on the top of Sawtooth Ridge. Immediately beyond my aerie the trail dropped 3,000 feet in 2 miles, meeting the Stuart Fork between Morris Meadows and Emerald Lake. I'd hiked with my wife to Caribou Lake, largest in Trinity Alps, and had taken the 1-mile side trip to the crest of Sawtooth Ridge.

Sapphire Lake

While seeing the two lakes from a distance had been exhilarating, it only made me crave greater intimacy with the two heavenly objects of my lust and unrequited affection. There would be no peace until I actually stuck a toe into their coveted waters.

The morning after Brian and I saw the black cougar, we slept until seven o'clock, downed a leisurely breakfast of granola and reconstituted powdered milk, and continued up the trail, leaving our tent and gear at the camp. We arrived at Emerald Lake two hours later.

Approaching the lake, the trail alongside the upper end of the Stuart Fork was extremely steep and rocky. Hiking it was like climbing an endless stairway to heaven.

The lakes exceeded all expectations. It was a place I never wanted to leave. After following the Emerald Lake shore for a quarter mile, the path started steeply uphill, moving from crevice to crevice until reaching a point 500 feet above the lake. Then, as the trail surmounted a ledge, Sapphire Lake appeared. If Emerald Lake was beautiful, Sapphire Lake was indescribable. The water was bluer and the white rock walls on either side were even steeper and higher. Because it was springtime, dozens of waterfalls rained over the smooth cliffs from the lingering snowfields above. There were no campsites that we could see: The entire area was solid rock, with very little vegetation except for a few well-placed wildflowers.

At the far end of Sapphire Lake, the bench on which Mirror Lake supposedly perched rose from the water. Theoretically a trail around Sapphire Lake leads to Mirror Lake. Several people we talked to told us they'd made the hike. But Brian and I saw no way around that didn't involve scaling the adjacent cliffs. As nearly as we could figure, reaching Mirror Lake required either a boat or excellent swimming skills. There is no trail shown on the map.

PART 6

ONE OF THE FIRST THINGS I DID WHEN I ARRIVED HOME WAS PHONE THE headquarters of Shasta-Trinity National Forest, in Redding, California, which is in charge of the Trinity Alps Wilderness, and talk to their resident wildlife biologist. I had several questions for him, including one about black cougars. Or black panthers.

"As far as I know," the wildlife biologist replied, "North American cougars, *Felis concolor*, are all a light tan. Black panthers, of course, live only in South America. There's a Florida panther but it's very small and more of a reddish brown. The only black mammal I can think of that's native to the Trinity Alps is the skunk."

The animal we saw definitely was not a skunk.

I spent the winter repeating the story to friends, or anybody else who would listen, about the fulfillment of my twenty-year quest, the magnificent lakes, and the strange and beautiful animal that was either a black panther or a very odd-looking cougar.

The photo I took of the cougar/panther turned out to be inconclusive. It showed an indistinct black form against an indistinct black background. It was not the stuff from which million-dollar deals with tabloid newspapers are made. I couldn't even get the photo printed in my hometown newspaper, which would have paid me ten bucks had they used it. They said it was too dark and blurry.

Oh well. Maybe next time.

PART 7

I FIRST MET DAVID ROBBINS AT A BOOK SIGNING IN A SMALL BOOKSTORE IN GRANTS Pass, Oregon, where I live, two years after my hike to Emerald and Sapphire Lakes. I was signing copies of my newly published volume on the Trinity Alps Wilderness and he was signing copies of his latest novel. It was "Local Authors' Day" and four other writers also busily scrawled their signatures and chatted among themselves between customers.

David is a talented but underrated novelist. Unfortunately he became stuck, early in his career, writing formulaic adventure series and has never been able to wriggle out of it. At the time I met him, he had two series going, cranking out a complete (if short) novel every month. Despite having written more than two hundred books, he had neither wealth nor creative fulfillment to show for his efforts.

David and I quickly discovered that we had several things in common. One was that we were both bursting with brilliant and original ideas for deep and meaningful novels that we couldn't sell. The reason we couldn't sell them, we both believed, was that we'd been locked into our respective genres by the tunnel vision of the publishing world.

As it happened, one of David's book series was called, "The Adventures of the Mountain Man." With my knowledge of the local wilderness, he thought I might be a good source of background information. We hit it off well enough that he invited me to meet him for coffee a few days later.

I don't drink coffee but I didn't mention that. I debated saying to him, *Why don't we meet for herbal tea?* but decided that might sound a little effete to a guy who wrote books about mountain men.

Our rendezvous took place at Denny's Restaurant, up by the freeway interchange. We sat in a booth, amid the aroma of bacon, eggs, coffee, and herbal tea. We were soon ensconced in a fascinating and wide-ranging conversation.

Ninety minutes into the discussion, as I was starting to think about leaving, David asked whether I believed in bigfoot. I told him what I tell everybody, what I had told Brian, that believing in bigfoot is sort of like believing in God. You can't prove it absolutely but you can never quite rule it out. And just when you think you can rule it out, something unexplainable happens.

That was when David told me something I hadn't known before.

"I'm a member of the International Society of Cryptozoology," he said.

"Our purpose is to study undocumented and unverified animals. Bigfoot is one of the animals that interest us."

"I can see where it would," I replied. "Bigfoot interests a lot of people."

"There are actually a couple of dozen species we're trying to gather information on," David explained. "Not just bigfoot. We're interested in animals that have been sighted by hikers or hunters, or sometimes loggers, but which no wildlife biologist or 'official' type has ever seen. Animals nobody has ever captured, killed, or photographed. Most are little subspecies of field mice and stuff like that. They're almost all nocturnal."

"That makes sense," I said. "I've always wondered how scientists ever became aware of the existence of something like the ringtail, for example. Ringtails are completely nocturnal, very timid, and there aren't very many of them. I've sure never seen one. All I have is the word of biologists. What else is on your society's list?"

"Let's see. There's the California grizzly, and the . . ."

"What about black cougars?"

David leaned forward with considerable interest, looking a little skeptical, but also excited.

"What do you know about black cougars?" he inquired.

"Are they on your list?"

"Absolutely. Reports of black cougars are considered more plausible than bigfoot reports, even though they don't occur nearly as often. The animals seem to be confined entirely to the Trinity Alps Wilderness, where they're sighted once every four or five years, usually by backpackers traveling cross-country, away from the established trails. No forest service worker or scientist has ever seen one, and most don't even know about them. We think they are genetic aberrations from normal parents, like a reverse albino. But they could be a distinct variety or subspecies. Nobody knows for sure because we haven't seen enough of them."

"Well then," I said, "do I have a story for you."

PART 8

THE EVENING FOLLOWING MY MEETING AT DENNY'S WITH DAVID ROBBINS, I excitedly called Brian Boothby to tell him what I'd just learned about black cougars. I figured he'd be extremely interested.

"You're crazy, Bernstein," said Brian after listening to my narrative. "I don't remember seeing any cougars. And believe me, I wouldn't forget something like that. Next you'll be telling me we saw a bigfoot on the hike."

THE HIKE: *Stuart Fork Trail, Trinity Alps Wilderness, Shasta-Trinity National Forest, Trinity Center, California.*

LENGTH *(one way): 15 miles (Sapphire Lake).*

DIRECTIONS: *Take CA 3 north from Weaverville to Trinity Alps Road near the Stuart Fork Bridge. Follow Trinity Alps Road 3 miles to the Stuart Fork Trailhead.*

HIKE EIGHT
MAD DEER

PART 1

SUPPOSE I SHOULD HAVE TAKEN IT AS AN OMEN WHEN BRIAN BOOTHBY AND I saw a rattlesnake at the turnoff to the Deer Creek Trail. We were in the center of northern California's Trinity Alps Wilderness, where the Deer Creek Trail branched off from the Stuart Fork Trail, 8 miles from the Stuart Fork Trailhead where we had hiked from the previous day.

Actually, we barely noticed the snake. It wasn't very impressive. It was just a shy baby that warned us well in advance and did its best to get out of our way. The little guy, or gal, quickly slithered off into the tall grass as we approached. We didn't pause or walk a wide arc around it or anything. We just kept on hiking up the trail.

I was too busy making puns and wisecracks about the name of the trail we'd just turned onto to worry about bad omens or infant rattlers. It was called the Deer Creek Trail, although the name registered in my mind as the "Dear Creak Trail." The trail led to Deer Creek Valley, Deer Creek Camp, Deer Creek Lake, Deer Creek Mountain, and Deer Creek Pass. Not to mention Deer Creek.

Since deer are about the most harmless animal ever to tread the surface of the globe (with the possible exception of possums, chipmunks, and three-toed sloths), Brian and I were looking forward to a pleasant and uneventful couple of days on the Deer Creek Trail. What could possibly happen on a path named for such a benign, passive, and boring creature as the ordinary, everyday, run-of-the-mill, dime-a-dozen, seen-one-seen-them-all, Pacific Northwest Columbian black-tailed deer?

Yuck.

What I did not mention to Brian was that although the rest of the world seemed smitten with the notion of adorable little Bambis, I found them slightly annoying. Their passivity, their lack of backbone, somehow struck a nerve.

Every time I saw a deer flee in terror, as they invariably did, I felt a wave of disgust. I knew my reaction made no sense; that deer are wise to flee and merely acting out their genetic programming. As nearly as I could figure, my hostility had to do with the passivity I sometimes saw in own personality. The deer represented a reflection of what I most disliked in myself. It was all very Freudian.

I did not reveal these insights about deer to Brian because I was too passive.

Brian and I started up the Deer Creek Trail at about four in the afternoon. At that time of year, the end of June, it didn't get dark until after nine. So we had plenty of daylight left. The only fly in the ointment of our itinerary was that we were both extremely tired after lugging backpacks for two days and 24 miles.

Our destination that evening was Deer Creek Camp, where we planned to spend the night. Most of the day had been taken up visiting Emerald and Sapphire Lakes, 15 miles from the Stuart Fork Trailhead and two of the most beautiful high-mountain lakes on the planet. No matter how the day might end, it had already gone down in my personal history as one of the most memorable.

According to the forest service map, the route ahead of us on the Deer Creek Trail was fairly daunting. Deer Creek Camp lay 4 miles distant. Beyond that it was 2 miles, with a 2,000-foot elevation gain, to Deer Lake and Deer Creek Pass, then 4 miles over Stonewall Pass and Little Stonewall Pass, then a final 6 miles to the Stonewall Pass Trailhead. The latter was one of the least used in the wilderness. We had dropped off a car there on our way to the Stuart Fork Trailhead. All three passes exceeded 7,500 hundred feet in elevation, and the trail's total length came to 16 miles.

Almost from the first step, the Deer Creek Trail felt uncomfortable. For one thing, there was that rattlesnake at the trailhead. For another, there were the people. Or the lack thereof. The Stuart Fork Trail had been among the most popular paths in the Trinity Alps. Hiking the Stuart Fork was like hiking the Haj in Mecca. Among California wilderness aficionados, the Stuart Fork Trail is legendary. As a result, it is not exactly a haven for seekers of solitude. You run into people every few minutes, most of them talkative and friendly, as someone in the middle of a once-in-a-lifetime outing ought to be.

The sense of spooky loneliness evoked by the Deer Creek Trail, on the other hand, wasn't just because we had the place entirely to ourselves. I'd been the only hiker on hundreds of trails and felt perfectly comfortable. Deer

Creek was different. It felt as though we were trespassing; as though everyone but us had the good sense to stay away.

"I don't like this place," I said to Brian.

"Neither do I," Brian admitted. "But that's probably because we're tired. I'm sure we'll feel better after we stop for the night."

"I hope so," I said.

Something else that distinguished the Deer Creek Trail from the Stuart Fork Trail was the lack of trees. To be sure, meadows and open areas dotted many of the region's valleys. But they invariably alternated with forest stands, and it was the forests, not the meadows, that usually dominated. Deer Creek Valley had no forests. Not even an occasional clump of pines. Also, the meadows along Deer Creek were dry and bleak. Cured-out grass and low, spine-laden bushes extended from the creek to the craggy peaks on either side of the valley. The sickening-sweet smell of snowbrush permeated the atmosphere. On our late-June visit, the grass should have been a brilliant, emerald green, as it had been on the Stuart Fork, one valley away.

The trail itself wasn't that bad. Even though the general trend was uphill, the rise was reasonably manageable. As we walked, I identified for Brian the wildflower and brush species. Despite the bleakness of the landscape, when you looked closely the area turned out to be fairly diverse. In addition to grass and snowbrush, I pointed out Indian paintbrush, low delphinium, lupine, oxeye daisy, green manzanita, whitethorn ceanothus, and a couple of dozen other species.

"I'm impressed," said Brian. "I'll bet we've seen just about every brush and wildflower species there is."

"Except for one," I replied. "We haven't seen any deerbrush."

PART 2

DEER CREEK CAMP HAD TO BE THE LONELIEST AND MOST BEAUTIFUL PLACE I'D ever experienced. Even cynical old Brian was impressed. The approach started half a mile away, where the creek, the valley, the trail, and the defining ridge all made a ninety-degree turn southward. Prior to the turn, these landmarks had all been oriented east to west. All Brian and I could see, during our initial eastward march, was Sawtooth Ridge to the north, and an unnamed mountain slope to the south. Not that those were bad things to see. On the contrary. Upon making the southward bend, however, the quality of the vista instantly ratcheted up several hundred degrees.

What happened at the turn was that Deer Creek's dramatic head popped into view, like the opening curtain at a Broadway play. Three glorious mountains, one white, one black, and one red, stood lined up in a row at the valley head like the monkeys who see, hear, and speak no evil. The white summit, composed of granite, was 8,400-foot Gibson Peak, one of the highest in the Trinity Alps. The black schist mountain, in the center, was Deer Creek Mountain, while the mountain of red serpentinite was Siligo Peak.

Deer Creek Pass, the highest point on our route, lay in the gap between Gibson Peak and Deer Creek Mountain. The pass was approximately 2 miles distant and 2,000 feet higher in elevation. It did not comfort us that we could see large patches of snow high up on the mountainside, level with the pass over which we were to hike. We couldn't tell whether there was snow on the pass itself or not.

"Be sure to get a photo," Brian instructed as the three mountains began glowing red in the low-angled, late-afternoon light. I quickly complied. Twenty minutes later our little valley was wrapped in shadow, even though it wouldn't be fully dark for another two and a half hours.

"This is going to be some shot," I commented as I pointed my Nikon at the peaks and fiddled with the lens settings. "Maybe the best of the whole trip."

Deer Creek Camp consisted of a large, open flat on the valley bottom, with a stone fire ring and room for a couple of tents. The first thing Brian and I did, after I took the photo, was sit down for a few minutes for a well-deserved rest. Or, I should say, we collapsed in exhaustion. It took us nearly forty-five minutes to get up the energy to put up the tent and make dinner. There was no hurry, though.

Actually, we made separate dinners. I dined on canned beef stew, trail mix, and a cold Pop-Tart. Brian treated himself to freeze-dried beef stroganoff.

While we cooked dinner on my little propane stove, I noticed a deer—a tiny, passive-looking doe, wandering around outside the camp, maybe 500 feet away. At the time I thought it was kind of charming . . . and perfectly appropriate considering the name of the place.

I didn't dislike does as much as bucks.

Gibson Peak, Deer Creek Mountain, and Siligo Peak from Deer Creek Camp

"Wow," I said, "look at the deer." Brian liked deer.

"Cool," said Brian. "I like deer."

As we ate dinner, the animal gradually moved in closer to us, almost to the edge of the campsite area.

"It's probably hungry," I said.

"Probably," said Brian. "I read somewhere that you're not supposed to feed deer human food or it could poison them."

"I read the same thing," I said. That was when I noticed that there were now three deer outside our camp and that they had all moved in a little closer. I smiled, reminded myself not to feed them, and continued eating beef stew out of a can.

The next time I looked up, in response to a rustling in the bushes nearby, there were twenty deer at the edge of the camp, including four immense bucks. They were all staring at us. Even though the gallery of animal-eyes sent a shiver down my neck, I was willing to give them the benefit of the doubt. These were deer, for heaven's sake, the world's most unthreatening mammal.

"Shoo!" I hollered, waving my arms in the air.

The deer scattered. If anything, they scattered a little too quickly. One instant, there were dozens of deer milling around. The next instant, there were none.

"Good riddance," I said to Brian. "They were starting to bug me."

After dinner, Brian took a quick, soapless bath in the creek to relax, clean up, and cool off. I did the same thing when he was done. Brian used the creek to wash off the shirt he'd worn that day, which was drenched with perspiration. He figured to wear it the next day, too. We saw no deer the entire time.

To dry the shirt, Brian stretched a clothesline between a bush and a dwarf, solitary pine tree that had somehow found its way into the camp. He draped the shirt over the clothesline, hoping it (the shirt, not the clothesline) would be dry by morning. By now the shadow of the adjacent mountain ridge had worked its way completely across the valley. It was about eight-thirty, which meant we had perhaps half an hour of daylight left.

After getting dressed again, Brian and I sat around the fire ring, continuing to nibble on trail mix and dessert foods. As we sat, a large buck with massive, six-pronged antlers suddenly appeared. This time it was inside the camp. It was the first deer we'd seen in a while and the first one to actually enter the camp. The animal made a beeline for Brian's shirt, which it began chewing on.

I thought the deer munching on Brian's shirt was funny. Brian did not.

"It probably wants salt," I explained. "Deer have a huge craving for salt. It's like cocaine to them."

"Well, it can't have *my* salt," Brian said as the animal continued dining on his shirt. And to the deer, Brian yelled, "Scram! Get outta here!" It did not have the same effect as when I'd shooed the animals off a while earlier. Brian's words went completely unheeded. Finally he picked up a small stick and tossed it at the preoccupied beast, hitting it lightly on its flank.

The deer took off, all right. But it took Brian's shirt with it. We looked all over for the shirt that evening, and searched again briefly the next morning. We never did find it.

After returning to camp following the attempt to locate Brian's shirt, we tried to spend the last few minutes of daylight relaxing, chatting, and enjoying the remoteness and beauty of our campsite. We kept reminding each other how lucky we were to be camping out in such a wonderful place. But all the deer had returned. All twenty of them. At least that was how many

I counted. They were hard to tell apart and constantly milling around, so an accurate census was difficult. For all I knew, there were fifty deer. Or a thousand. They kept walking, silently, around and around the campsite, like the army of Joshua surrounding Jericho before sounding the trumpets and moving in for the kill.

As unlikely as it sounded, we both sensed an intent in the deer that made us uncomfortable. I tried to tell myself, and Brian, that the animals were just deer, doing the things that deer do. All they probably wanted was salt, which we did not have. Perhaps they also wanted food, which we could not give them in any quantity. Actually I was rationalizing, trying to explain their behavior to make the situation a little less frightening.

The truth was, this was decidedly not normal deer behavior.

As the deer circled and recircled our camp, their ring grew gradually smaller and tighter. They'd move increasingly close until they were at the very edge of the 50-foot-diameter area that made up the campsite. Then one of us, Brian or myself, would holler at them to go away and they'd back off a couple of hundred feet. A few minutes later they'd be circling again and the noose would again draw tighter and tighter and tighter.

And then it was time for Brian and me to turn in for the night.

PART 3

DESPITE FEELING, PHYSICALLY, AS THOUGH WE'D BOTH JUST COMPLETED THE Boston Marathon twice with the flu and a fever, neither Brian nor I slept very well. It was the second consecutive night of not sleeping well. Neither of us sleeps very well in tents, even under the best of circumstances. We went to bed shortly past dark, after shooing the animals off several more times. It was a warm night, so I stripped down to my underpants and T-shirt. Brian, a little more formal than I, brought pajamas. I have never worn pajamas at home or anywhere else.

Immediately before I sealed us into the little two-person nylon dome tent for the night (which happened to belong to Brian), I urinated on the ground, 15 feet away, near some bitter cherry bushes. It was the closest thing the site offered to a rest room. While I was at it, I yelled at the deer to go away. Periodic yelling at the deer had become part of our routine, almost a habit. I couldn't see them in the dark but I could hear rustling in the bushes, not far away. I hoped they would eventually decide to go to bed and leave us alone. Or wander off and haunt some other hapless campers.

More likely, Brian and I figured as we lay inside the tent, the deer would either (1) circle all night, (2) start nosing around the camp looking for food as soon as we disappeared into the tent, or (3) turn into demons and murder us when the moon rose. And no, we weren't being paranoid; we were being perfectly rational. It did not strike either of us as likely that our tormentors would give up simply because it got dark.

Obviously, none of these imagined scenarios was very relaxing or conducive to sleep. I didn't know about Brian but I just had to get some sleep. The idea of toting my backpack over three snow-covered, 7,500-foot passes without having slept for two consecutive nights was as terrifying as any imagined worst-case deer scenario.

As I prepared to turn in for the night, I felt like a prisoner in a North Korean POW camp about to be "interviewed" by a brain washing inquisitor who relied on sleep deprivation and terror to break down his subject and force a confession.

Not that I had anything to confess. Except perhaps my long-suppressed feelings about deer.

After I returned to the tent from my last trip to the bitter cherry bush, Brian went outside and urinated. Then he, too, climbed inside and zippered the door shut.

Then we were alone, just Brian, and me, and the warm wilderness night. And twenty demented and unpredictable deer. My down mummy sleeping bag, which offered protection against the elements to thirty below zero, proved way too hot. I tried crawling inside it, briefly, but found myself, after a few minutes, sweating like a wrung-out sponge. That was unacceptable. Sweating was bad, not only because it made it harder to sleep, but because I did not want to excite the deer with the possibility that there was salt to be had inside the tent.

Brian also lay on top of his sleeping bag rather than climbing inside.

"Maybe the deer will regard our pee the way they do coyote or cougar pee," I suggested. Coyotes and cougars are territorial predators that mark off the ground within their domain with urine. Other animals, especially non-predatory animals such as deer, show the utmost respect for predator urine . . . if they know what's good for them. We hoped the deer would respect our territorial urine line.

Fat chance.

Not only did the deer disregard our line, but we observed the next morning that every spot where Brian and I had relieved ourselves had been pawed at and disturbed. One metaphysical explanation for the deer's lack of respect for our pee line was that they, or we, had become inexplicably confused as to the established order of the universe, wherein humans are the predators and deer are the prey.

More likely, the deer had eaten the urine for its salt content. Those fellows sure did fancy their salt.

For a long time after going to bed, Brian and I didn't hear or see anything except occasional rustling in the bushes, which could just as easily have been a breeze as a deer. Lying on top of my sleeping bag and looking up through a small mosquito-netting window in the ceiling, I could see an intense splash of stars across the universe, a splash that humans call the "Milky Way," an exceptionally mundane name for the spiral arm of a celestial galaxy. Our celestial galaxy. The window was my favorite feature of the tent. In addition to allowing us to see the sky, it enabled us to smell the occasional mountain breezes that wandered past.

Brian and I gabbed for a while about the day's activities, our wives, and our jobs. I could blackmail Brian with the information he has confided to me on various hikes while lying exhausted and drained in a tent just before going to sleep. And he could blackmail me. Not that either of us ever would.

We did not mention the deer, as we chatted, possibly on the theory that if we refused to acknowledge them, the problem would disappear. Besides, talking about it would only make us more on edge than we already were.

For a while the strategy seemed to work. At one point early in the evening, I came within a hair of dozing off. Then the moon came up. It was a bright, full moon, almost the intensity of daylight. The kind of moon that drives lunatics and vampires to the full fury of their insanity. The kind of moon we definitely could live without.

I don't know if it was the rising moon that touched off the deer or not. They were pretty nuts to begin with. All I know is that with the moonrise, anything that moved outside the tent was projected in shadow on the feeble layer of nylon that separated and protected us from all outside threat.

I first noticed the moving shadows when a gentle breeze shook the scraggly pine tree. Looking up at the tent wall through the darkness, the shadowy motion resembled the claw hands of a witch grasping at our tiny shelter. The sight made my stomach lurch for a second and triggered a brief squirt of adrenaline, until I figured out what it was.

"Look at that," I said to Brian, trying to make a joke. "It looks like the claw hands of a witch grasping at our tent."

"Shut up," said Brian.

A while later, when the rustling noises outside began increasing in frequency and volume, I attributed it to the wind. Until I saw the shadow of a deer on the side of the tent, projected to twice the size of a grizzly bear. This time there was no question: That was definitely not a tree branch.

Sweat or no sweat, I climbed into my sleeping bag and pulled it up over my head. I did not mention to Brian what I'd seen. I hadn't heard from him in a while, and if he was asleep I saw no reason to disturb him. On glimpsing the deer shadow, however, I knew that my night's sleep was pretty much shot.

"Did you see that?" Brian whispered. I guess he knew I wasn't asleep.

"Yeah. Our friends are back."

"Get the hell out of here!" Brian hollered at them. And the shadow dutifully trotted off.

But not for long.

A few minutes later the shadow returned with reinforcements. As they had done during dinner, they began circling our camp in an endless procession, drawing gradually closer. Also, as was the case at dinner, hollering caused them to back off at first; then they gradually got used to it and ignored our invectives. After a while the circle around our tent was so tight, we could hear deer flanks brush against the nylon in a soft *swoosh*.

This went on for hours. It felt as though it went on for a decade. We debated packing up and leaving but decided against it. While we might have found our way out of the valley and up to Deer Creek Lake by the light of the full moon, the tent, as frail as it was, represented our only defense against the midnight marauders. Once outside the tent, there was nothing to prevent the deer from following us wherever we went.

Brian and I kept reassuring ourselves that they were only deer and that deer never, absolutely never, attack humans. But it was scant solace. By now we weren't sure if they were deer or not.

Around 2:00 A.M., lying huddled in my sleeping bag, watching the shadows go around and around and around, I reached my limit. Rage, fatigue, frustration, and confusion welled up inside me like a tsunami in a tsuitcase.

"GET THE HELL OUT OF HERE!" I screamed, jumping out of my sleeping bag and rising to my knees. Half crying, I began pounding on the side of the tent. "GET OUT, GET OUT, GET OUT!" I must have yelled for ten minutes. Once I started, I couldn't stop. It all came rushing out. I was vaguely aware of Brian trying to calm me down. But it was just too much. In the last remaining logical corner of my brain, I rationalized that if I screamed and flailed long enough, I'd tire myself out and fall asleep even if the deer didn't go away.

Fortunately Brian's tent was pretty strong. I came close to knocking it over or ripping it. But in the end, no harm was done. I only wished my pounding made a little more noise. It made virtually none.

The one thing I did not do was go outside the tent. I might have been temporarily berserk but I wasn't that berserk.

Still, I managed to freak out poor Brian, who already had enough on his mind. He was forced to choose between staying inside the tent with an out-of-control lunatic or taking his chances with the devil deer.

"Feel better?" he asked, when I finally calmed down.

"I guess," I whispered.

I couldn't say whether the deer ever returned that night or not. They sure didn't hang around during my little outburst. When it was all over, I fell asleep within ten minutes. According to Brian, who was awake much longer than I, they did not return.

I was glad to have helped out.

Brian and I didn't talk much that morning. We woke up at around seven, gobbled down a very quick breakfast, packed our belongings, looked around one last time for the shirt, and departed. Or I should say, got the hell out. Half an hour after waking up, we started up the steep trail to Deer Creek Lake and Deer Creek Pass. I was still pretty tired and not looking forward to the great expenditure of energy I knew would be required that day, but I was now confident that I'd make it.

After a while we reached a point high above the valley, beside a beautiful spot where Deer Creek cascaded down the gray rock face. Pausing for the first time to look back, we could see Deer Creek Camp below us in the distance.

I'd estimate that there were a hundred deer milling around the spot where we'd camped. That was interesting to me because deer are not normally herding animals. From our vantage point, they looked more like buffalo on the Great Plains. It was probably my imagination but it seemed to me as though the deer were doing a dance, presumably in celebration of having driven out the two intruders into their domain who had refused to give them salt or food.

Okay, maybe there were only fifty deer.

PART 4

DEER CREEK LAKE WAS AS LOVELY AS ANTICIPATED; A SHALLOW, CLEAR TEN-ACRE pool in a small, smooth, treeless basin surrounded by the three jagged, multicolored peaks. What I liked most about Deer Creek Lake was that it lacked the mystical aura, the feeling of otherworldliness that we'd felt in Deer Creek Valley. The universe, to my great relief, felt normal again.

The reason the otherworldly feeling vanished was that there were actually people at Deer Creek Lake. A bunch of them. They were there because the side trail from Long Canyon joined the Deer Creek Trail just over the pass. It was only a 6-mile stroll from the Long Canyon Trailhead to Deer Creek Lake. Brian and I had hiked 14 miles to reach Deer Lake, not counting our 16-mile side-trip to Emerald and Sapphire Lakes.

Despite the easier access to Deer Lake provided by the Long Canyon Trail, I was surprised to encounter so much humanity in the middle of nowhere. I just wished some of them had shown up at Deer Creek Camp the previous night.

Nobody to whom Brian and I spoke at Deer Creek Lake had been to Deer Creek Camp or had the slightest intention of ever going there. I got the impression that the other hikers thought we were a little screwy for taking the route we took, which they (correctly) regarded as a godforsaken trail to nowhere.

"Not coming in by way of Deer Creek Camp was a wise decision," I commented to a tanned, athletic-looking couple in their fifties as we spent ten minutes sharing the experiences of our respective trips and exchanging information. Brian and I did not mention the crazed deer. We figured nobody would believe us.

To make a long story short, we managed to negotiate all three passes, scrambling in the snow at each one, and arrived at the Stonewall Pass Trailhead without further incident, happy but exhausted. Or exhausted but happy. Especially exhausted. All in all, it had been a memorable three days.

Only three days.

Eight years after my big Trinity Alps adventure with Brian, I hiked the Long Canyon Trail to Deer Lake. It's a very scenic route, although not as scenic at the Deer Creek Trail.

A few days after the Deer Creek Trail hike, I anxiously picked up my six boxes of slides from the photo processor. Soon after, alone in the living room with the shades drawn, I projected them onto the wall. The Emerald and Sapphire Lake shots were sublime, as were the Echo Lake and Siligo Meadow photos. The Deer Creek Lake shots were delightful.

The only photos that did not live up to expectations were the Deer Creek Camp shots. The first time through, I forgot to look for the slide that Brian and I had predicted would be the best of the entire trip. I had to back up and look at the Deer Creek Camp slides a second time before figuring out which photo it was. It didn't look anything like what we'd seen in person. The photo failed to capture the dramatic steepness of the mountain rise at the valley head. The glorious late-afternoon colors of the three mountains were all washed out. Also, I couldn't find any shots with deer in them.

None of that surprised me. I reassured myself that it was not the first time an anticipated "great photo" did not turn out as expected.

I phoned the Shasta-Trinity National Forest headquarters, in Redding, California, which is in charge of the Trinity Alps Wilderness, and spoke with their resident wildlife biologist about the Stuart Fork and Deer Creek Trails. To my question about unusual deer behavior at Deer Creek Camp, the guy replied, "If you saw deer at Deer Creek Camp, I'd be very surprised. I've camped at Deer Creek Camp a couple of times and have never seen a single deer. Neither has anybody else that I know of. Apparently, there used to be lots of deer in Deer Creek Valley. That's how it got its name, obviously. But they vanished fifty years ago when an organized gang of poachers shot them all. They massacred over two hundred deer in a few hours, right at Deer Creek Camp. Or so the story goes. Nobody has seen a single deer in Deer Creek Valley since then."

PART 5

ONE FINAL THOUGHT: AS FRIGHTENING AS THE EXPERIENCE ON DEER CREEK WAS, I came away feeling very differently about deer. I no longer regard them as quite so passive and timid. It's like the meek Casper Milquetoast who finally reaches his breaking point and tells off his domineering boss.

You invariably find yourself saying, "Go get 'em, Casper!"

Even if you happen to be the boss.

THE HIKE: *Deer Creek Trail, Trinity Alps Wilderness, Shasta-Trinity National Forest, Trinity Center, California.*

LENGTH *(one way): 16 miles (plus an 8-mile hike to the trailhead).*

DIRECTIONS: *From Weaverville, California, on US 299, take CA 3 North to Trinity Alps Road near the Stuart Fork Bridge. Follow Trinity Alps Road 3 miles west to the Stuart Fork Trailhead. Hike the Stuart Fork Trail 8 miles to the junction with the Deer Creek Trail.*

HIKE NINE
ON BEYOND BIGFOOT

PART 1

THINGS FIRST STARTED TO GO WRONG ON THE BIG TRIP OF 1971 IN EL PASO, when we rented a room in a little motel. From the outside the place looked reasonably nice, if modest: a nondescript, white clapboard accommodation at the edge of town with perhaps twenty rooms. We were amazed at how inexpensive the rooms were, so we grabbed one without first inspecting what would be our home for the next several hours. After that, my wife and I always looked at the room before we shelled out any money.

We were in Texas, in September 1971, as part of an automobile trip from California to Michigan. Back then my family consisted of myself; my wife, Patricia; and our three-year-old daughter, Jennifer. We were headed for Ann Arbor, where I had a one-semester teaching fellowship. Since all I needed to complete my master's was three credits and a thesis, one semester was plenty. I'd started my M.S. in 1968, then gotten sidetracked and moved to California in 1970. I was delighted at the unexpected opportunity to complete the program.

Obviously, since we ended up in Texas, we took the scenic route from California to Michigan. But we had plenty of time so we figured what the heck. We had driven from California across Nevada, then down Utah to the Grand Canyon, then across to Albuquerque, then down to El Paso. From El Paso we planned to visit Big Bend National Park, in West Texas, then head east and north.

The lodging in El Paso must have been some sort of flophouse or welfare motel, even though it appeared halfway decent from the outside. The actual room was not halfway decent. It was not a quarter of the way decent. There was no functioning air-conditioning (in a city where 110 degrees is common in summer, with nighttime lows in the 70s and 80s), the furnishings were run-down, broken, and frayed, and the room wasn't as nearly clean as it might have been. But we could have lived with that. We only saw one cockroach, after all, and it wasn't very big. What we could not live with were the drunks shouting, laughing, and cursing in Spanish in the parking lot all night long.

Not that the language they happened to speak made any difference. Loud noises are annoying in any language when you're trying to sleep.

We even might have been able to tolerate the noise, just as we managed to live with the room's low standards and buggy visitor. What really upset us was the three or four times during the night when drunken revelers loudly tried our doorknob. That especially freaked out Jennifer, who spent most of the night crying.

My main preoccupation during that long, frightening night was the wish that I had thought to bring the contents of our cartop box into the room. The box contained belongings intended to sustain us for the next eight months. Under the circumstances, I was not about to go outside and unload the box. I figured that would only call attention to it.

After a night of cowering and sweltering, morning finally came. To our relief, the cartop box was unmolested, as were we. Exhausted and grumpy, we bade a quick good-bye and good riddance to the motel in El Paso and hit the road.

I didn't know it then, but things were about to get much worse, even life threatening. For me, anyhow. Not for Pat or Jenny, thank goodness. To fully grasp the significance of my brush with death in Big Bend National Park all those years ago, you have to understand about Category Four animals.

At the time I'd never seen a Category Four animal. Or a Category Three or Category Two animal. At least none that I was 100 percent sure of. I'd seen plenty of Category One animals, though. Everybody has seen Category One animals.

Here's the thing: Bigfoot, the man-ape of rumor and legend that supposedly roams the remote forests of northern California and the Pacific Northwest, is only a Category Two animal.

Everybody loves bigfoot so it's a good place to start. I love bigfoot. Of all the cryptozoological critters creeping around in the backwoods, bigfoot attracts by far the most interest. How could humans not be intrigued by a species of 9-foot-tall beast that has managed to elude biological confirmation despite the concerted efforts of modern technology and a small army of bigfoot hunters?

From the bigfeet's point of view, I suspect they enjoy being just out of reach. Tantalizingly out of reach. I also suspect they're just as intrigued with us as we are with them. That's why they can't quite bring themselves to remain completely hidden.

Bigfoot is the best known among several unverified mammals in the remote backcountry of the rain-drenched coastal mountains of northern California and the Pacific Northwest. The California grizzly is another. And the black cougar. Over the entire United States, the list of unverified mammals is quite long. If you include places like the Brazilian interior or the jungles of Papua New Guinea in the South Pacific, there may be almost as many unverified animals in the world as there are verified ones.

In fact, I'll go you one better. Or three better, as you will see. I contend that there are animals so elusive, so rare, that there aren't even legends or rumors about them. Carrying this theory to its logical conclusion, I have come up with four possible categories of animals:

1. Real documented and verified animals, such as squirrels, bunnies, horses, three-toed sloths, gnus, tigers, ringtail cats, and meadow voles.

2. Nondocumented animals sighted from time to time but never officially verified, such as bigfoot. Some supposedly extinct animals may fall into this category.

3. Undocumented animals that nobody has ever seen or reported so there are no rumors or legends about them. For there to be rumors and legends, somebody, somewhere would have to have caught a glimpse of one. I suspect there are many animals in this category. Especially in the Brazilian interior and the jungles of Papua–New Guinea.

4. Imaginary animals that have no existence in reality but that can, under certain circumstances, be very, very real.

At the time of my adventure in Big Bend National Park, I believed in Category Two, Three, and Four animals but had no proof. I believe in many things for which I have no proof. And I don't believe in a lot of things for which I do have proof. Category Two, Three, and Four animals do not readily lend themselves to proof. Especially Category Four animals.

I'm not sure whether the animal I saw in that remote desert canyon in Big Bend belonged to Category Three or Category Four. But it surely was not in Category One or Two. Not by a long shot.

My wife, Patricia, does not believe in Category Three or Category Four animals. She doesn't much believe in Category Two animals, either. Although she likes the idea of fantastic creatures roaming the planet, unbeknownst to humans, she has trouble with the reality.

She informed me of this in no uncertain terms once, when I thought I might have seen a Category Three animal in 1970, shortly after we first moved out west.

Pat and I had a friend, back then, who lived 8 miles up French Creek Road in northern California's Scott Valley, at the edge of what is now the small but exquisite Russian Wilderness Area. The road to our friend's house was notorious for being extremely dark and spooky at night. After only a few weeks of living in her little rented cabin, the young single mother couldn't wait to move out. She was positive the place was haunted.

One incident that prompted her to leave—in addition to finding bear claw scratches all over her doorknobs and window edges every morning—occurred at dusk, while I was driving her into town. These types of incidents often occur at dusk. We were headed down the gravel road alongside the creek, not far from her cabin. There were no other houses in the vicinity, just miles and miles of forest stretching to the mountaintops.

That was when we passed a small mammal, about the size of a coyote. Except it wasn't a coyote. And it wasn't a bobcat. And it wasn't a cougar. And it wasn't a fox. And it wasn't a dog. And it wasn't a cat. And it wasn't a raccoon. And it wasn't a ringtail cat. And it wasn't a beaver or a porcupine or a baby deer.

It looked kind of like a black weasel, except with long, loping coyote legs.

"It was either a dog or a bobcat," Patricia declared on hearing the story, in an annoyingly dismissive tone of voice. "Either that or it's some species you don't know about. But I can't imagine that nobody else knows about it either."

As much as I respect my wife, I think she was wrong. Besides, she wasn't even in the car with us at the time.

None of my prior or subsequent experiences with questionable animals, not the French Creek whatever, not the black cougar I once saw in the Trinity Alps Wilderness, was nearly as strange as the animal in Texas that saved my life.

You have to understand that Texas is a mighty strange place anyhow, as far as animals go. As far as other things go, too. There are any number of mammals whose entire range in the United States is limited to the Lone Star State and environs. Texas is home to such bizarre and beautiful beasts as the javelina, the jaguarundi, and the armadillo. The javelina is a small, wild pig that roams in packs in the desert mountains of southwest Texas and southern New Mexico and Arizona. They can be very aggressive, and you don't want to mess with them. The jaguarundi is a miniature jaguar the size of a bobcat and one of the most beautiful animals in North America. And everybody knows what an armadillo looks like.

Suffice it to say, it was no surprise that I should have a first-class "odd animal" experience in Big Bend National Park, in the West Texas desert near the Mexican border. The Big Bend country, home to javelina, jaguarundi, and armadillo, is a land of barren, sunbaked high mountains and low desert along the Rio Grande. The lower elevations boast narrow, steep-walled canyons with one face in the United States and the other in Mexico. In the park's center, an upwelling called the Chisos Mountains soars to 7,825 feet at Mount Emory. The ancient volcanic peaks form a ring around an upland depression called the Chisos Basin. Most of the park's amenities are located in the Chisos Basin because the climate is considerably more tolerable there than in the surrounding low desert.

The rugged, 4.5-mile Pinnacles and Mount Emory Trails explore the park's highest elevations, beginning at the Chisos Basin ranger station. A 1-mile side trail branching from the Pinnacles Trail climbs Mount Emory's barren, rocky summit.

The Pinnacles Trail, and the Laguna Meadows Trail from the same trailhead, are part of the South Rim Trail Complex, which many consider the definitive Texas hike. While my hike up Mount Emory covered only 9 miles out and back, the South Rim Trail Complex offers a spectacular 12- to 15-mile loop with vistas purportedly even better than those from atop Mount Emory. The South Rim is an immense escarpment that plummets abruptly to the low desert and Mexico.

Despite the Chisos Mountains' high elevations, scattered forest patches, and occasional winter snow, the searing Chihuahuan Desert is never far away. The region, both upland and lowland, is a land of intense heat and precious little shade. Water is found only at the Rio Grande and a few widely scattered wells, springs, and creeks, most of which dry up in summer. No matter what the elevation, because of the water situation, it is not advisable to wander too far off the established routes.

I hiked the Pinnacles and Mount Emory Trails to the summit of Mount Emory in 1971. The Texans were right. It was a fantastic, memorable hike. Probably the best hike in the state except for the South Rim itself, 3 miles down the path.

I also managed to wander "too far" off the established route during my Big Bend hiking excursion. Trust me, it was a bad idea. A very bad idea.

PART 2

EVEN WITHOUT THE PROBLEMS AT THE MOTEL IN EL PASO THE PREVIOUS NIGHT, THE drive to Big Bend would have been exhausting. It was 300 desert miles, in temperatures over a hundred degrees. At least, I consoled myself, I didn't have to worry about the engine overheating in my little green 1970 Volkswagen squareback, the car with the homemade plywood box on the roof. Volkswagen engines in those days were air-cooled and located in the rear.

Jenny overheating was a different story. The car, like the motel room, was not air-conditioned. After sleeping most of the morning, Jenny became understandably bored, hot, and cranky as the seemingly endless day wore on and on. Her displeasure was expressed in constant whining, crying, and fussing. We tried to be patient, and we stopped frequently, but we were pretty cranky ourselves.

We all looked forward to the next day, when I would go hiking while everyone else relaxed and slept in, in the cool mountain heights of the Chisos Basin Campground.

By midafternoon we were on a highway along the Rio Grande between Presidio and Terlingua, still 60 miles from the park boundary. I noticed that the car was driving funny, kind of bumpy and wobbly. I pulled over and got out to take a look. As I stepped out of the car, the front tire fell off! It just plopped down on the pavement, with the car abruptly coming to rest on the brake rotor.

Pat and I spent the next twenty minutes hyperventilating and commenting on how lucky we were to have pulled over when we did. I managed to get the tire back on, but one of the four lug studs was bent and another had broken off. In a gas station in Terlingua, the home of the annual National Chili Cookoff, where nobody spoke English, they managed to get the one lug screw unbent enough to accept the nut. But for the four years that I drove the car after that, there were only three studs on the front driver's-side wheel. Tire salesmen and repair people would invariably inform me of the missing stud, admonishing that the situation was extremely unsafe. Nobody ever offered to fix it, though.

We entered Big Bend National Park, finally, at around three that afternoon and quickly discovered that all the places we wanted to go were still at least an hour away. Our first stop was a side trip to Santa Elena Canyon, one of the country's most beautiful and unheralded scenic sites. As you approach, across the low, fiery desert, a huge cliff slowly rises in the distance. After a while, you notice a notch in the cliff. The notch is Santa Elena Canyon, a vertical-walled chasm cut at right angles into the escarpment. The left side of the notch is Mexico and the right side is Texas. The Rio Grande flows through Santa Elena Canyon, then makes a ninety-degree turn and follows the escarpment base.

After miles and miles of driving, we pulled up to the Santa Elena parking area and made the short hike into the canyon, which you can follow for perhaps a quarter mile. The contrast between the hot, arid Chihuahuan Desert, which smelled mostly of creosote bush and death, and the canyon's shady coolness, was memorable, like driving endlessly across the freeways and factories of New Jersey, then emerging from the Lincoln Tunnel and finding yourself in the skyscraper canyons of Midtown Manhattan.

Jenny didn't want to leave Santa Elena Canyon. She wanted to go swimming, which she did. We all did. We were careful not to cross the midline of the river when we went swimming, which could have been accomplished fairly easily. The water was only about waist-deep. But you can never tell when the Border Patrol might be watching.

Reluctantly dragging ourselves away from Santa Elena's cool luxury, we arrived at the Chisos Basin Campground at around six. It was a sunny, pleasant evening, much cooler at 5,400 feet than in the low desert. The drive from the low, flat desert up into the stark, chocolate-brown Chisos Mountains was curvaceous and beautiful.

No matter how you enter the Chisos Basin, you cross over a mountain pass. That's because it's a basin. Actually, aside from a little more brush and grass, scattered small trees (Rocky Mountain juniper, Arizona cypress, and ponderosa pine), cottonwoods along the creeks, Douglas-fir in the most shaded, moist areas, and quaking aspen in the coldest spots, the vegetation in the mountains wasn't too much different from the vegetation in the low desert, where sagebrush, grass, agave, and cactus predominated.

Road into Chisos Mountains

The campground, surrounded by jagged peaks and ridges, had room for a couple of hundred people, but only ten or fifteen slots were occupied. We set up our tent, then Pat cooked dinner on the Coleman stove. We had deli potato salad and steak, both of which we'd purchased at the supermarket in Terlingua.

As at the gas station, nobody had spoken English in the supermarket. We did, however, manage to ascertain that in West Texas they are very proud of their steaks, which is the major industry. These were supposed to be exceptionally good steaks, even for West Texas.

And indeed they were. Pat and I have since gone semivegetarian, but that has nothing to do with this story. Suffice it to say, that long-ago meal in Big Bend, grilled outdoors in the Chisos Basin Campground, may have been the tastiest chunk of meat I ever consumed. Jennifer still enjoys a good, rare steak. As I write this, in my cholesterol-conscious senescence, I haven't eaten steak in years. But I salivate just thinking about that steak we had in Big Bend.

The starry night at 5,400 feet was just about perfect, neither too warm nor too cold. After the experience with the motel, and the terrifying tire incident, we all slept as though we'd been bitten by the tsetse fly, confident that everything bad that could happen had already happened and that there would be only smooth sailing from there to Detroit.

PART 3

I WOKE UP AT SIX-THIRTY TO A SPECTACULAR SUNRISE AND THE COOL, SWEET aroma of morning dew. As my wife and stepdaughter slept in the tent, I showered in the campground bathhouse, filled my all-important two-quart blanket canteen (which I still use now, thirty years later), and got dressed. Then I crawled briefly back into the tent and kissed Pat and Jenny good-bye, instructing them not to worry and to enjoy their morning of leisure and relaxation.

I expected to be gone maybe five hours on the 9-mile hike. My normal pace on moderate-to-steep grades is 1 mile per half hour. I figured ascending Mount Emory would slow me down a little but that I'd make up the time on the way back. Having made my initial forays, the first of hundreds, into California's Marble Mountains and Trinity Alps only weeks before, and having just completed an eight-month stint with the California Fish and Game Department, I considered myself in decent physical condition. Not fantastic but decent.

It was nearly a quarter mile from the campground to the trailhead, located near the store and ranger station. I debated driving there but figured Pat might need the car. So I walked to the trailhead, which added about six minutes to my total hiking time.

Once at the trailhead, I started briskly down the path, filled with joy and elation at the beauty of the scenery, the respite from the long, boring days of driving, and the goodness of a world that allowed me to witness such wonders.

The first thing to go wrong was that I missed the turnoff to the Pinnacles Trail. The path from the Chisos Basin Trailhead is called the Laguna Meadows Trail, with the Pinnacles Trail breaking off to the left soon after. Both the Laguna Meadows Trail and the Pinnacles Trail will get you to the Mount Emory turnoff, but Laguna Meadows does it in 8.5 miles as opposed to 3.5 miles for the Pinnacles Trail.

After hiking nearly a mile, crossing two dry washes, and starting up a series of steep, rocky switchbacks with no junction in sight, I decided to backtrack to the trailhead. According to the map, the Pinnacles Trail turnoff was less than a quarter-mile from the trailhead. I have no idea how I'd managed to miss the turnoff the first time around, but on the second pass it was right there, as plain as the nose of my face. Which is pretty plain.

Having wasted forty minutes, and now feeling slightly rushed and annoyed instead of joyous and relaxed, I started up the correct path. The scenery was predictably splendid. The park pamphlet's description of the Pinnacles Trail—"somewhat less steep but more exposed than the Laguna Meadows Trail"—proved reasonably accurate. The Laguna Meadows Trail skirted the west face of Mount Emory but did not climb the summit. The Pinnacles Trail made its way around the peak's east side, crossing Pinnacles Pass between Mount Emory and Toll Mountain. A 1-mile side trail took hikers from the pass to the top of the mountain.

The Pinnacles Trail was not only extremely scenic but also very crowded and hot. So was the Laguna Meadows Trail. The park brochure described both pathways as congenitally "crowded" and "hot." Still, one always hopes for an unexplained aberration.

As I walked, I passed other hikers every few hundred feet. Most were very friendly. I was put off, however, by a loud, poorly supervised Boy Scout troop whose members kept running back and forth along the path without looking where they were going, screaming at the top of their lungs, often profanities. Nor was I pleased by the numerous hikers smoking cigarettes, something you don't see in California. There is nothing more unpleasant on a hike than having the pristine air ruined by a noxious cloud of cigarette smoke.

The Pinnacles Trail was fairly easy for almost 2.5 miles as it made its way steadily up the combined flanks of Mount Emory, Casa Grande Peak, and Toll Mountain. At mile 2.5 the route steepened considerably, swung sharply left, then right, then began a series of rocky switchbacks to Pinnacles Pass. I passed a few scattered trees and rock overhangs, but most of the route was out in the open.

Even though it was only 10:30 A.M., I approached Pinnacles Pass sweating profusely. I'd estimate the temperature at perhaps eighty or eighty-five degrees, which is warm for that high up. The temperature, I knew, would grow much warmer as the day wore on. If it was 85 in the Chisos, that meant it was 100—heading toward 110—in Presidio and Terlingua.

The narrow Pinnacles Pass, with Toll Mountain on one side and Emory Peak on the other, was lovely. I presumed it was called the "Pinnacles Trail," and

"Pinnacles Pass," because of the many rock outcrops, not to mention the high peaks all around. I sat down on the edge of the trail, on the south side of the pass, beneath a large ponderosa pine, with my feet dangling over a drop-off. The trail started back down on the south side, toward the canyon of Boot Creek.

Despite the heat, I'd been trying to avoid drinking from my canteen. My standard tactic on hikes, unless I'm dying of thirst, has always been to save my water until I arrive at my destination, then dole it out on the return trip. But with the steep switchbacks, the intense heat, and the lack of shade, I broke my rule and chugged down maybe a quarter of the contents. I immediately regretted drinking so much because I still had the much steeper Mount Emory hike ahead of me.

When done drinking, I set the canteen down at my side. I did not put the cap back on because I planned to treat myself to one last sip before I started hiking again in a minute or two, after I'd rested a little and my initial huge drink had settled in.

In retrospect, the expenditure of energy required to screw the cap back on, then off, then on again would have been minuscule compared to the ultimate cost of my failure to replace the cap. All I can say is that in every hike since, I've screwed the cap back on immediately after each drink, even if I planned to take another drink in a couple of minutes.

I learned my lesson.

I don't know how I managed it but somehow, as I gathered my camera (I forgot to mention I had a camera with me, a bulky old Nikon) and prepared to get up, I knocked the opened canteen over the edge of the trail, down the rocky incline, and into the canyon. The container tumbled about 50 feet, then came to rest, upside down, in some bramble bushes.

"Crap," I said out loud, quickly assuaging my initial panic by reassuring myself that with all those hordes of fellow hikers, and "only" 5.5 more miles to hike, I could manage without the canteen. Probably. Possibly. The nearest water source, at Boot Spring, lay 1.25 miles beyond Pinnacles Pass. Of course, I'd also read in the park brochure that in September, the driest month of the year, Boot Spring was as dry as a British sense of humor.

The park brochure hadn't quite used those words.

I was able to climb down and retrieve the canteen with little difficulty. But boy, oh boy, was it ever empty.

Forty minutes later I stood atop Mount Emory, surrounded by Boy Scouts and cigarette smokers, still perspiring and anxious to start back down.

The view, spectacular wherever you looked, was better to the west than any other direction. To the east, Toll Mountain and Casa Grande Peak continued to get in the way. To the south, the South Rim blocked the near view somewhat but I could still see all the way to Mexico and eighty miles beyond.

All in all, I was glad I'd come.

I actually managed to scrounge a drink of water from a Boy Scout while on the summit. He was a fat, squeaky-voiced, nervous kid with an untucked shirt and an incipient, never-before-shaved mustache. The young fellow was very nice about it. I figured that since it was downhill all the way home, the offering from the Boy Scout should suffice for the remainder of the trip.

I was wrong.

I started back down at eleven-thirty. Remember that I'd hoped to be back at the trailhead by one o'clock, and it was still two and a half hours away. While the return trip was all downhill, which made the going faster and easier, I now had the midday sun to contend with. And even though the 7,800-foot elevation cooled things considerably, there was little shade and intense solar radiation.

By the time I got back to the pass, my mouth felt as though somebody had stuffed it with ultra-absorbent diapers. I had all the early symptoms of dehydration: fatigue, headache, slight dizziness, nausea, spots in my peripheral vision, extreme dry mouth, and bright yellow urine. I hasten to add that I'd experienced all those symptoms before, some many times. But never when totally without water in a place this hot and arid.

I'm not sure why I didn't just ask a passerby for a drink at Pinnacles Pass, as I'd done with the Boy Scout. It seemed like an imposition. They undoubtedly needed their water as much as I did.

The fact that I continued to perspire on the way down from Mount Emory was both a good sign and a bad sign. According to the *Red Cross First Aid Handbook*, it meant I still had the raw materials in my body with which to manufacture perspiration. It also meant I was depleting those raw materials. If and when my body ran out of water and electrolytes, I would be in big trouble. They call that "heatstroke" and it can be fatal.

Back at Pinnacles Pass, a passing hiker informed me that contrary to the park brochure, there was still a little water at Boot Spring. The news touched off a lengthy internal debate. Should I head back toward the trailhead without water or hike an extra 1.25 miles—2.5 miles round trip—to Boot Spring to obtain the precious fluid? The side trip would delay my arrival back at the trailhead by more than an hour, and I was already an hour late.

I pretty much decided to forget Boot Spring and take my chances. Nevertheless, I inexplicably found myself walking a short ways down the trail in the Boot Spring direction, ostensibly looking for a good photogenic view into the Boot Spring Canyon.

That was when I noticed a faint, unmarked side trail taking off to the left. It appeared to drop down to Boot Creek, meeting the stream in a quarter-mile, at a point, I estimated after examining the map, 1 mile below Boot Spring. The map showed the creek but not the side trail. While kind of steep, the shortcut could possibly get me to water in far less distance than the Boot Spring hike on the main trail. I couldn't tell from my vantage point if there was water in Boot Creek or not.

If I followed this path and did not find water, my situation would be worse than ever. On the other hand, if I did find water, my problem would be solved and I'd have lost only twenty minutes or so.

"Hmmm," I said out loud, unscrewing the cap from my canteen and peering with one eye into its dank, echoing emptiness. I took a dozen or so steps down the side trail, which turned out to be not as steep or as faint as it appeared from the junction. I ended up following it all the way to the creek.

The creek was completely dry. My heart sank as I pondered the prospect of hiking, empty-handed, back up to the pass. Then I noticed that there seemed to be a fair amount of dampness in the creekbed under the top layer of pebbles and cobbles. And a lot of green streamside vegetation. If I hiked upstream a short ways, I wondered, would there be water in the creek, especially if I dug it out a little?

I was not anxious to return to the main trail without achieving my objective. Besides, my spot by the creek felt good, a little cooler than the main trail and much more secluded. The short side trip had transformed my journey from an irritating battle with crowds to pleasant seclusion, the way a hike should be. I walked a little farther upstream, looking for signs of water.

My judgment was not 100 percent just then.

After hiking a hundred feet or so, I scolded myself for taking such a huge risk. What I should have done was ignore my fatigue and thirst, tough it out, and get on home while I had a little energy left. Were something to happen to me—if I passed out from heat exhaustion, say—nobody would ever find me at this spot. I absolutely had to get back on the main trail. And soon. But I was too tired. And my head hurt. And I kept hearing an annoying buzzing noise in my ears. And man, was I ever thirsty.

I debated lying down but I knew that would not quench my thirst. My most prudent course of action was still to get back to the main trail. And I still kept hearing that buzzing noise. In fact, it was growing louder.

I stood pondering for a minute or two, then started walking back toward the side trail with as much resolve as I could muster, which wasn't very much. I'd taken maybe three steps when I felt a stabbing, pinprick pain in my calf, eight inches above my ankle.

That's when I saw the rattlesnake.

That's when I figured out what the buzzing noise had been.

PART 4

ACCORDING TO THE *RED CROSS FIRST AID HANDBOOK,* THE RECOMMENDED treatment for snakebite is to get to a doctor within two hours. It was, however, 12:15 P.M. Even if I had plenty of water, felt 100 percent, and had not just been bitten by a rattlesnake, I was at least two hours from the trailhead. Probably more. The other recommended snakebite treatment is to do everything possible to slow your body's rate of metabolism so your kidneys can detoxify the venom before it does all the damage of which it's capable. Slowing my metabolism was the best excuse I could think of to sit down, which was what I'd wanted to do all along.

I should add that I was terrified. Thoughts of dying whirled around in my brain even though I kept reassuring myself that snakebites usually aren't fatal to adults. Especially 180-pound adults. According to the *Red Cross First Aid Handbook.*

The Red Cross First Aid Handbook didn't say anything about the effect of snakebite on 180-pound adults severely weakened by dehydration.

I'd read somewhere else that the rattlers don't always get their venom out when they bite. This guy, however, had gotten off a pretty good chomp. I would have been very surprised if he'd failed to deliver his package. He'd apparently crawled up under my pant leg, so I couldn't even rationalize that he'd bitten me through denim. The fact that he'd crawled up my pant leg is a testimony to my inattentiveness at the time.

At least the buzzing noise was gone.

I sat down on the ground, in the scant shade provided by the creekside bushes, pulled up my pant leg, and examined my wound. It was a flaming, nasty red and hurt terribly. I squeezed the wound and two very small drops of venom oozed out. I squeezed some more, with all my might, but those first couple of drops were all I was going to get.

The circles of redness kept growing. And my lower leg was becoming numb, which would have made it difficult to walk should I take a notion to try to hike out. I had no such notion. I was becoming more nauseous and dizzy by the minute. And feverish. The fever was a new, ominous development. I lay down in the shadiest spot I could find and prayed that my body would have the strength to fight off whatever was about to happen.

That's when I vomited. If I was dehydrated before, I was really dehydrated now. Vomiting does that. I don't know where all that stuff inside me came from because I'd made no attempt to eat the peanut butter and jelly sandwich I brought for lunch. With no saliva in my mouth or water in my canteen, I'd never have been able to swallow the chewed food. Without water, I could not wash the taste of vomit out of my mouth. I was able to scoot away from the little puddle before I blacked out, using just about my last iota of strength.

Actually, I didn't exactly black out. At least not totally. I guess you could describe my condition as semidelirious. Or that's how I remember it. I kept dozing, then half waking up, then dozing again. I never regained full consciousness because whenever I got too close to being awake, I'd feel the nausea, or the pain in my leg, or the dryness in my mouth, or the fever. Or all of the above. It was just too uncomfortable.

I remember dreaming I'd been bitten by a garter snake, not a rattler, and that I was running desperately up and down the trail, showing everyone the terrible, bleeding, festering wound on my leg and begging for somebody to help. But they all kept laughing at me because, as everyone knows, garter snakes are completely harmless. Unless you happen to be a frog or mouse.

After a while, heaven only know how long (I never thought to check my watch), I returned to full consciousness. Or almost full consciousness. I knew I wasn't dreaming anymore because I was aware of minute details, like the pebbles in the creek, the dust on my pant legs, the awful taste in my mouth, and the smell of vomit a few feet away. Dream pictures are usually painted with much broader brush strokes and much less detail.

In that moment of clarity, it occurred it me that there was a good chance that I was about to die, in which case they probably wouldn't find me for weeks, if ever. While I didn't so much mind becoming buzzard fodder (I did mind, actually, very much), I didn't want Pat to worry. I tried once again to get up, but I still didn't have the strength and my wound hurt too badly. My lower leg throbbed like a jungle tom-tom. And the nausea, dizziness, thirst, and fever had not abated. Not in the slightest.

All in all, I preferred the delirium.

That's when I prayed for help, something I'd done maybe four times before in my life. It had never done much good in the past but I figured, in my delirium, that it couldn't hurt.

In the middle of the prayer, I heard a rustling in the bushes. I looked in that direction and saw nothing at first. Then I noticed an animal hiding in the foliage.

"Come on out, fellow," I said, holding out a bit of sandwich. "I won't hurt you."

Slowly, warily, a strange-looking creature crawled out of the bushes. It was about 3 feet long with a doglike face, very short legs, and long, smooth white fur that dragged on the ground. It had a musky smell that I found kind of pleasant.

The animal reminded me of a cross between Flub-a-Dub from the old Howdy Doody show, and Falcor, the friendly Luck Dragon from the movie *Never-Ending Story*. Flub-a-Dub was a marionette with floppy dog ears, feet like a seal, a duck's bill, a cat's whiskers, a bunny's tail, and a body was that was mostly a plaid dog coat. Falcor was 20 feet long and had a sweet, doglike face and a long, furry, snakelike body with silvery white fur. The animal I saw did not have a duck's bill or a plaid dog coat and was not 20 feet long. But aside from that, the resemblance was striking.

My mysterious animal seemed to have no interest in me as a person. Not at first, at least. It had no interest in my piece of sandwich, either. The thing was mostly interested in my wound, which it walked up to and started licking. I was lying with my pant leg pulled up so the bite was exposed for all to see. My initial instinct was to shoo the animal away and try to protect myself. But the beast seemed so unthreatening, and the tongue felt so soothing, and I was so intrigued, that I just sat there and took my licks. The licking lasted perhaps ten minutes. After two or three minutes, I noticed that the swelling and discoloration had improved and that I felt much, much better.

Eventually, when the animal had satiated itself, it wandered off, back into the bushes. That was when I finally remembered my camera.

When I stood up a few minutes later, after briefly dozing again, my leg felt fine, my stomach felt fine, my head felt fine, and my fever was completely gone. Even my mouth felt better. And the weather didn't feel nearly as hot. Of course, it was now four-thirty.

"Takes a licking and keeps on ticking," I said out loud.

Then I started back up the side path toward Pinnacles Pass, the Pinnacles Trail, and the Chisos Basin Trailhead.

I know what you're thinking. The animal was a dream. Or a hallucination. Or a dog or a bobcat. And I might simply have fought off the snakebite on my own. You're probably right. Besides, as far as anyone I've talked to knows, there are no animals in Texas even remotely like the one I saw.

Then again, you never can tell. There are all sorts of strange animals in Texas.

PART 5

WHEN I ARRIVED BACK AT THE CAMPGROUND, AT SIX FORTY-FIVE, PAT WAS FRANTIC. Who could blame her? All the park rangers were out looking for me when I came sauntering in. Somehow they'd all failed to spot me during my return hike.

An emergency medical person examined the snakebite and said it didn't look very bad. He said my body seemed to have done an excellent job of shaking off the venom. He put some antiseptic on the bite so it wouldn't get infected, then sent me on my way.

I didn't mention to the medical person about the little animal that saved my life. I didn't mention it to Pat, either. Or Jenny. I didn't figure they'd believe me. Besides, it's not up to me to persuade them that such animals actually exist. They'll run across their own Category Two, Three, or Four animals one of these days. Then they'll understand.

I also did not mention to my wife, or the Big Bend rangers, the conversation I had with the strange little animal. It happened just as the creature was leaving. It turned to me and said, in perfect English,

"I'm happy to help out but let's just keep this our little secret."

I figured they really wouldn't believe that.

PART 6

HERE'S A LITTLE FOLLOW-UP STORY THAT I THINK IS KIND OF CUTE: AFTER TOURING Big Bend, we drove past San Antonio and Houston, taking a car ferry from Galveston to the Texas Gulf Coast. From the Gulf, we visited New Orleans, then headed up Mississippi and across Tennessee, Kentucky, and Ohio to Detroit. We pulled into my mother's Detroit driveway at around noon, spent and exhausted but happy. Two days later, amazingly, we found an apartment in Ann Arbor. And a week after that, school started.

Eight months later, degree in hand and several bound copies of my thesis in the trunk of the car, we returned to California. This time we followed a northern route across Indiana, Illinois, Wisconsin, Minnesota, and North Dakota to Glacier National Park in Montana. Then we swung up into Canada, taking in Banff, Jasper, and other spectacular parks of the Canadian Rockies. In Washington State we rode a ferryboat from Whidbey Island to the Olympic Peninsula. Then we headed home.

My daughter Jennifer's conclusion after all that traveling (given her age at the time, she now doesn't remember one single second of the trip) was the observation that to get from California to Michigan and back, you have to take a ferryboat.

THE HIKE: *Pinnacles Trail and Mount Emory Trail, Big Bend National Park, Texas.*

LENGTH *(one way): 4.5 miles.*

DIRECTIONS: *From I-10 at Van Horn, 118 miles east of El Paso, take US 90 south for 136 miles to Marathon. In Marathon, follow US 385 south for 69 miles into Big Bend National Park, and on to the Panther Junction Visitor Center. Head west from Panther Junction for 3 miles, toward Terlingua and Presidio, to the Basin Junction, then go south for 6.5 miles to the developed area in the Chisos Basin. The trailhead for the Pinnacles, South Rim, and Laguna Meadows Trails is located near the Chisos Basin store and ranger station.*

HIKE TEN

THE WEIRDEST HIKE OF ALL

PART 1

MAN, JUNEAU IS A WEIRD CITY," I SAID TO MY WIFE AS I GAZED OUT THE window of our room at the Baranoff Hotel at the two nearly vertical walls of green mountainside only a mile or two away, one on either side of Gold Creek. I found it extremely weird that slopes so steep and massive would be located so close to town. One minute you're in the middle of Juneau, the next you've bumped into a 3,000-foot-high stone barrier. It was raining out, and I could see streams cascading down the slopes, from summit to base. The dense conifer rain forests for which Juneau is known lie mostly in the canyons, not on the mountain slopes visible from my window. The slopes were covered with brush, grass, and bare rock.

In addition to forest, many of the side canyons contained immense valley glaciers, which we had seen from the airplane and during the bus ride from the airport to the hotel. Seeing glaciers was also pretty weird for a non-Alaskan. For an Alaskan, it wasn't weird at all.

The city smelled of dampness, conifer forest, and amazingly fresh air. That, too, was pretty weird for a city. But it was good weird. The weird green wall of mountains, and the weird valley glaciers, were also good weird.

Something else weird was the time, ten o'clock at night on July 1, 1981. Back home in Oregon I would never be looking at mountains out the window and commenting on the scenery at ten o'clock at night. Back home, at 10:00 P.M. you couldn't even come close to seeing the puny little far-off mountains that surrounded the town where we lived, let alone be able to make out cascades running down the side.

"It's pretty weird, all right," Pat agreed as she unpacked our luggage. I wasn't exactly sure why she was unpacking since (1) we were both exhausted and could barely stand up, and (2) we were leaving for Glacier Bay National Park first thing in the morning.

167

"Very weird," I said.

"But good weird," Pat hastened to add.

"Very good weird," I agreed.

We had every reason to be exhausted. A scant thirty-six hours earlier, we'd gone to bed in Grants Pass, Oregon, our hometown, intending to get up bright and early and drive the 400-plus miles to Sea-Tac Airport, near Seattle, where we would put our car in long-term parking and board an Alaska Airlines flight to Juneau. Except we couldn't sleep. Not a wink. Not a snore. Not a REM. Nothing. Neither of us.

I'm not sure how we made it all the way to Seattle on no sleep, but we did. It would have taken a lot more than just fatigue to dissuade us. We each got a little sleep in the car but it wasn't nearly sufficient.

We couldn't sleep on the plane, either. And after landing in Juneau at six in the evening, we were too excited to sleep and ended up walking all around the waterfront, eating dinner in a fancy restaurant, and having a couple of drinks in a bar. Those drinks should have knocked my wife and me on our respective tails. But they didn't, which was also kind of weird.

We returned to the hotel room only to discover that in summer in Juneau, the gently relaxing, sleep-inducing blanket of night simply did not exist. It gets dark at ten-thirty or eleven but even then, it doesn't get all the way dark. By 3:00 A.M it's daytime again. That is definitely not conducive to sleep if you're not used to it.

"How in the hell do they expect you to sleep with all this daylight?" I asked my wife.

"Beats me," she said. "I'm sure the reason it gets dark so late is solely to inconvenience you. There can be no other explanation."

The trip to Juneau was conceived, if you'll pardon the expression, because of the failure of my wife and I to produce a second child after five years of trying. Or a third child, if you count Pat's daughter Jennifer by her first marriage. And Pat and I definitely do count Jennifer. Our first child together, Sara, had taken all of one month to conceive. She made her debut in the Bernstein pantheon in December 1973. Our next effort, which would ultimately prove to be our last, was another matter. It began in 1976, three years after Sara's birth, when we decided that Kid One and Kid Two were so successful, we just had to go for Kid Three.

Unlike Sara, this third and final progeny just didn't want to happen. After four years of diligent attempts at procreation, we ended up seeing a fertility specialist, who among other things, suggested we go on a trip together to relax and take our mind off things. He said we had fallen into the *trying-too-hard* syndrome and that the best cure was to just have fun together and forget about having a baby.

He was right, of course. Partly because of the baby problem, and partly due to numerous minor issues that gradually built up over the course of day-to-day existence, our marriage was becoming strained and we hadn't been getting along very well. With our tenth anniversary coming up and my aunt Blanche in New York offering to foot the bill, we planned the Alaska trip with great excitement. Pat's parents graciously flew out from Michigan to watch Jennifer and Sara during our ten-day odyssey.

I'd always wanted to go to Alaska. For a naturalist and outdoors writer, a trip to Alaska is the closest thing to heaven to be had in this world. It's like Cannes for a film critic. Besides, as of 1981, I'd been to forty-seven states and was anxious to add the last three: Alaska, Hawaii, and Delaware. I finally made it to Delaware in 2000, when I visited my sister in Virginia, then drove to New York to see my aunt. As of 2001 I have still not been to Hawaii.

I will, though. One of these days.

No offense to Delawarians, but I liked Alaska better. Especially Juneau. Even if it was a pretty weird place.

PART 2

PAT AND I SLEPT WELL ENOUGH OUR FIRST NIGHT AT THE BARANOFF. NOT GREAT BUT okay. We had reservations the first thing in the morning to hook up with a tour group in the hotel lobby and fly to Glacier Bay National Park. It's much cheaper if you go with a tour. From the suddenly mobbed lobby, they bused us to the airport, put us on a plane, flew us to the remote village of Gustavus (pronounced *Gus Davis*), and put us on another bus to Glacier Bay Lodge.

We ended the day having dinner in the lodge's beautiful restaurant, which featured an immense picture window overlooking the bay. Pat had king crab and I ordered the grilled salmon. Had it not been overcast out, we could have seen, through the immense window, Mount Fairweather (an oddly inappropriate name for place that receives hundreds of inches of rain a year) rising on the other side of the bay. It would have been the first summit I'd ever seen that was higher than California's Mount Whitney. I've climbed

Whitney, which is the highest peak in the lower forty-eight. Fairweather beats Whitney by about 800 feet. Mount McKinley (now called Denali), also in Alaska, beats Whitney by 6,000 feet. I have never seen Mount McKinley.

While we were eating dinner, a bald eagle flew past outside the window, skimming just above the surface of the bay, with a salmon in its talons. Neither Pat nor I had ever seen a bald eagle before, although we'd seen a golden eagle once, on a dirt road in Nevada. We both just sat there in the restaurant staring in disbelief. We would see many bald eagles before the trip was over. They are my favorite bird.

Pat and I may have arrived at Glacier Bay on schedule, but our luggage ended up in Skagway. It was later flown to us on a special charter flight and we were finally reunited with it just before going to bed. I envied our luggage and its free trip to Skagway.

Glacier Bay was predictably magnificent. Pat and I had a fabulous time. In fact, we had a fabulous time the entire trip. It was the trip of a lifetime, although we never did catch up on our sleep until we got home. More than anything else, we were pleased to be getting along so well. We enjoyed each other's company, never argued, and managed to avoid worrying about having babies.

Just what the doctor ordered.

Despite our perpetual exhaustion and hectic schedule, we engaged in a little bit of baby-making activity during the trip. But per the doctor's suggestion, we did not talk about babies or call each other "baby." We also tried not to think about babies, but that was pretty much a losing battle.

After spending the night in Glacier Bay Lodge, we boarded the little National Park Service boat after breakfast. The craft was small and crowded but great fun. Most of the day was spent sitting at little tables inside, except when we went on deck several times, briefly, for a better look at some wonder pointed out by the ranger on the loudspeaker. The deck was cold, windy, and overcast, which was supposedly weird for July in this part of the world.

Gigantic excursion liners also plied the serene waters of Glacier Bay. I much preferred our little boat. Our tablemates for the trip were a recently retired druggist from Detroit and his wife, finally getting around to the travel they'd always dreamed about and had been putting off for forty years. They'd just returned from Barrow, North America's northernmost town. I could not imagine them in Barrow.

After a couple of hours of salt air, puffins, bald eagles, killer whales, humpback whales, seals, walruses, icebergs, high mountains, and some of the most incredible scenery imaginable, we arrived at the tidewater glacier that was our destination and turnaround spot. The glacier was half a mile wide and 20 miles long. It flowed from the mountain into the ocean, or the bay, where it broke off into small icebergs, exposing the eeriest blue ice I've ever seen. The Glacier Bay icebergs were much smaller than the titanic icebergs that separate from the Greenland ice cap in the North Atlantic.

The color of the glacial ice was weird. Even weirder was the fact that the glacier had been retreating at the rate of half a mile a year. It still is. The last half mile of our boat ride took us through an area that, only one year earlier, had been buried beneath the very glacier we were visiting. In the 1890s, when John Muir, the famous naturalist and writer (and my personal hero), visited Glacier Bay, the entire bay, including the lovely forested setting where the lodge now stands, was beneath a glacier.

The next day, back in Juneau, the overcast had turned to steady rain, which pretty much continued for the remainder of our stay. In ten days we never saw the sun once, except as we were leaving on the ferry, the last day.

Beginning our third night we moved to a smaller, much less expensive, though perfectly nice motel. The best feature of our new accommodation was that the room looked out on an enclosed parking structure. Normally, I would have hated such a restricted view and lobbied vociferously for a something more scenic. But in Juneau in midsummer, it was a godsend, the only reason I got any sleep at all during the trip.

The next few days were spent attempting to keep busy and dry. We were told repeatedly that so much rain in midsummer in Juneau was weird, very weird. Except that the souvenir shops all sold T-shirts that said, JUNEAU RAIN FESTIVAL, JANUARY 1 TO DECEMBER 31. So it couldn't have been that weird.

It absolutely poured during our Mendenhall River raft trip. The river is only 3 miles long, beginning at the little lake at the tip of the Mendenhall Glacier, 5 miles north of town. The tour operators pick you up at the Baranoff, bus you to the glacier, put you in a raft, serve "lunch" halfway down on a sandbar (mariner's crackers, salmon jerky, and some kind of sweet-tasting wine drink called "Mendenhall Madness"), then put you back on the bus where the river crosses under the highway and runs into the Gastineau Channel. It's not exactly a solitary wilderness trip, or a major whitewater river run, but it's Alaska and it's gorgeous.

Two days later, with the weather easing up slightly, Pat and I returned to the Mendenhall Glacier. This time, we hitchhiked because it was the Fourth of July and the buses weren't running. It was a busman's holiday.

From the Mendenhall Glacier vista point and visitor center, we followed a little trail along the edge of the massive ice sheet for about half a mile. We'd have hiked farther but the path disappeared and it started raining out again. The glacier was fascinating, full of deep crevasses. We were content to walk alongside the glacier rather than on the ice itself. The ice did not look very safe.

At the end of our brief and somewhat unsatisfying Mendenhall Glacier hike, Pat and I hitchhiked back to town. We were given a ride by two very friendly, and very intoxicated Native Americans, Tlinkits probably. One of them, a young woman, insisted that I must be Native American (I have dark brown eyes and slightly tannish skin, but I also have curly hair). And she made a pass at me right in front of Pat. Fortunately, the woman was too drunk to be taken seriously, and Pat mostly thought it was funny. The woman was kind of cute, though I never expressed that opinion to my wife.

Making a pass right in front of Pat was weird.

The day after our Mendenhall hike, Pat and I had dinner at something called the "Juneau Salmon Bake," a highly recommended local institution. A bus picked us up at, you guessed it, the Baranoff Hotel. It then hauled us out of town and up a little side creek to an outdoor picnic area with a huge brick barbecue pit. They served salmon fillets, baked potatoes, salad, bread, and lots of beer. The aroma of the sizzling fish was intoxicating. While the method of preparation may not have met the legal definition of *bake*, the food was excellent.

I should point out that fresh salmon, in Alaska, may be the world's greatest delicacy. It tastes nothing like the salmon you buy in supermarkets in the lower forty-eight. Not even in supermarkets in Oregon, where salmon also abounds. Alaskan salmon tastes like the most tender steak you can possibly imagine. I had salmon nearly every night during my stay in Juneau. And the very best salmon was at the Juneau Salmon Bake.

It absolutely poured during our evening at the Salmon Bake. A creek next to the property was near flood stage, and they had tarps and canopies set up over the barbecue pit and tables.

Except for the rain, the Juneau Salmon Bake was not the least bit weird.

After eight days in Juneau, visiting every visitable sight and partaking of every imaginable activity, including baby making, while waiting for the rain to let up, we ended up sitting in the little bar on the waterfront that had become our hangout. That's where I complained to Pat about the one thing caused by the incessant rain that frustrated me more than anything else.

"I can't go to Alaska and not go hiking," I informed my beloved spouse for the millionth time. "Hiking is what I do."

"I understand," said Pat, pat-pat-patting me gently on the hand while taking a sip of her Denali Delight. Pat liked drinks with seventy-five ingredients and lots of sweet stuff. I, on the other hand, tended more toward plain old beer in my boozing.

"I don't care what you say," I announced. "Rain or shine, I'm going hiking tomorrow."

"Did I say you shouldn't?"

"I hope you'll come with me. But if you don't . . ."

"I'd be happy to go with you. Where did you have in mind to hike?"

"I'm not sure. The Mount Roberts Trail, I think. It begins right in town but from the map, it looks kind of steep. It ends up at a cross on top of a mountain after 2.5 miles. You can also hike for 3.5 miles to another mountaintop, or 4.5 miles to a third mountaintop. Mount Roberts is the third summit."

"How about we just go to the cross?" said Pat.

The statement sounded kind of weird: *Just go to the cross.* I'm sure she didn't mean it in a spiritual sense, although you never can tell with Patricia. Mostly I was surprised that she agreed so readily to accompany me, without any persuading whatsoever. She didn't enjoy hiking nearly as much as I did. While she didn't despise hiking, she had nowhere near my passion for the activity.

Pat agreeing to go hiking with me was weird.

PART 3

IT DIDN'T POUR THE DAY WE WENT HIKING IN ALASKA, AS IT HAD THE DAY OF THE Mendenhall River raft trip and the day of the Salmon Bake. It mostly drizzled steadily. The relentless ooze from the perpetually gray sky reminded me of winter in Oregon, where it can rain for days at a time but you can often spend the whole day outdoors in it and barely get wet. It's more of a very heavy mist than actual rain.

Nevertheless, Pat and I stopped by a drugstore before leaving on the hike and purchased a couple of those eighty-nine-cent plastic ponchos that come in a little 3-inch by 4-inch plastic bag. We hadn't brought any rain gear or warm clothing. It was summer after all. We both had on jeans and T-shirts for the hike, with plaid flannel shirts as a jacket. As it turned out, we didn't need the plastic ponchos. But it was comforting to have them just in case.

The trailhead was located ten blocks from the motel, and we did a little sight-seeing in downtown Juneau on the way. Our route took us past the Alaska State Capitol and the Alaska State Office Building (Juneau, in case you didn't know, is the capital of Alaska). The capitol was about the size of the county courthouse in our hometown. The state office building was an interesting architectural structure, built over the side of a cliff. You could enter on either the first floor or the eighth floor.

That was weird.

Even more weird was the Mount Roberts Trailhead, a few blocks away. Following the instructions in the little hiking guide we'd purchased, we walked to the end of Sixth Street, a quiet, paved, steeply uphill residential street. The road abruptly ended at a dense green woods, with the mountainside rising up immediately beyond. The actual trailhead consisted of a little wooden stairway. I'd never seen a trailhead like that before or since, and I've seen a lot of trailheads.

A sign at the trailhead warned of black bears, brown bears, and grizzly bears (but not polar bears). Black bears, we knew, were pretty timid, but brown bears and grizzly bears have been known to cause serious injury or worse. Kodiak bears, the world's biggest, are a variety of brown bear. None is to be trifled with, not even the black bear. Neither Pat nor I, at the time, had ever encountered a bear on a trail before. We hoped our initial ursine meeting, if there had to be one, whenever and wherever it occurred, would be with a small, docile black bear, waaaaaaaaaay off in the distance, which would wander off into the woods long before becoming aware of our presence.

The best way to avoid bear encounters, according to our guidebook, is to make lots of noise as you hike, so you don't catch them by surprise or accidentally corner one. Following this exquisitely simple bit of wisdom, we spent the entire hike singing at the top of our lungs and keeping up a constant chatter. The procedure eliminated any possibility of a quiet wilderness-type experience, but it did keep the bears away. Something kept the bears away, at least. Whether or not it was our singing, I cannot say for sure.

Perhaps the bears were simply much smarter than us and knew not to come out in such weather.

Our melodic repertoire began with "Garryowen," General Custer's Scottish battle march. It's a fabulous hiking song except it has no words as far as I know. I often find myself humming it under my breath when I hike, to the cadence of my steps. Pat and I moved on to another song when it dawned on us that Custer's musicians were probably playing that very tune during the battle of the Little Big Horn, while Native American arrows were penetrating the rib cages of the general and his troops.

From "Garryowen" we moved on to old show tunes: "The Hills Are Alive with the Sound of Music," "Climb Every Mountain," "I'm as Corny as Kansas in August," and "Put on a Happy Face" ("Gray skies are gonna clear up"). Then we moved on to some 1960s stuff, "Summer in the City" and "Sunshine Superman." We ended up with a medley of camp songs and old Girl Scout songs, "The Kookaburra Song," "The Worms Crawl in the Worms Crawl Out," and "The Bear Went Over the Mountain."

We found that last one very appropriate.

The little staircase at the trailhead was not the only weird thing about the Mount Roberts Trail. Ten steps beyond the stairway, we found ourselves in a mysterious world that reminded us of *The Land of the Lost*, a children's TV show from the 1970s where the characters get shrunken down so that a lawn becomes an impenetrable jungle. We fully expected to encounter animals so large, we could barely see over the tops of their paws.

While most of the plant species along the trail were native to Oregon as well as Alaska, they were all much bigger than their Oregon cousins. Much, much, much bigger. I mean, I'd seen devil's-club before (a nasty plant consisting of a tall, upright stalk with a maplelike leaf at the end, with stalk and leaf covered with barbed spines). But I'd never seen devil's-club 15 feet high. Usually it's 2 or 3 feet. The ceaseless summer rain undoubtedly had something to do with the immense, freakish size of the devil's-club and other understory plants. Summer daylight that lasted until ten-thirty at night probably also played a part. Plants do love their daylight.

Suffice it to say, it was all very, very weird.

I wasn't exactly sure how all that old-growth forest and giant foliage fit into the overall picture because we were climbing the very same nearly barren mountainside that I had viewed from my window at the Baranoff

Hotel our first night in town. Apparently there were nooks, crannies, benches, ledges, and foreshortened gaps not noticeable until you got up close. For the first 2 miles, the trail remained largely beneath a rain-sheltering canopy of Sitka spruce and Douglas fir.

The pathway, as the guidebook predicted, was pretty steep. According to the book, it rose 2,500 feet in 2.5 miles. That's a thousand feet per mile, a challenge in anybody's book. Since Pat had no burning ambition to reach the summit, or the cross, or any other landmark on the route, and since she hikes much more slowly than I, she urged me to go on ahead, then rejoin her on the way down. I stayed with her on the sinuous, twisting path as long as I could. But the higher we got, the more the trail steepened, the slower Pat's pace became.

After 1 mile the route started passing occasional rock outcrops with panoramic views of Juneau, the Gastineau Channel, and Douglas Island. Pat and I were very impressed. She seemed to really enjoy those little catch-your-breath breaks. But invariably, the path would return to the woods and become even steeper than it had been.

At mile 2, finally, the route broke out into the open for good, at a tremendous overlook near a large green meadow atop a cliff. Although the trail leveled off briefly as it crossed the meadow, it also grew extremely muddy. Despite the low, ozone-scented cloud ceiling, we could see the 15-foot wooden cross, our destination, atop a little green knob half a mile away. To reach the cross, the route climbed 500 feet in half a mile from where we stood.

Pat concluded that the overlook was a perfectly good spot to sit and wait. That's the main difference between us when we hike. She likes to find a really nice spot and stay there, while I need to keep moving. She also wasn't that anxious to get her Levi's all covered with mud. Reluctantly, I kissed her on the cheek and started up toward the cross by myself. I could see her most of the way, waiting patiently on her rock. If she turned around, she could see me. While I didn't especially like leaving her alone, the fact that we could see each other eased my mind.

"Keep singing," I advised as I slogged off into the mist.

"You too," she replied with a smile and a wave.

Twenty minutes later I arrived at the cross. Far below I could see Juneau, all the surrounding landmarks, and Patricia, still on her rock, still admiring the view. In the opposite direction I mostly saw cloud cover. But it was obvious that an imposing row of jagged, snow-covered, heavily glaciated peaks lay not too far off. One of those peaks was Mount Roberts.

Juneau from Mount Roberts Trail

I'm not kidding when I say *imposing*. That mountain barrier is the reason there are no roads into or out of Juneau. If you want to operate a car in Juneau, you must either rent one or haul one in by ferry. Only then are you free to drive on the 27-mile road system around the city. The nearest road connecting to the Alaskan or Canadian interior is at Haines, a hundred miles or so up the channel. The road from Haines goes over Chilkoot Pass to Whitehorse, Yukon. It's the same pass that the Klondike gold prospectors climbed by the thousands, in the snow on foot, to reach the Yukon gold fields at the turn of the twentieth century.

As I said earlier, I'm not usually one to linger at my hiking destinations. I like to keep moving, and I get bored just sitting there. Once I've achieved my goal, I catch my breath, stay a few minutes, maybe eat something, then start back. But I liked this place. Despite the rain, it felt comfortable and serene. I'd have hiked the additional 2 miles to Mount Roberts in a heartbeat had Pat not been waiting for me.

I waved at my wife from beneath the cross and she waved back. Then, since I wasn't quite ready to start down, I did something uncharacteristic:

I sat down to rest for a few minutes. I didn't intend to stay very long. For one thing, the rain was increasing in intensity and there was a good chance that I might actually get soaked. I debated putting on the eighty-nine-cent poncho but decided against it. The garment was just too silly looking.

As I sat there, an Eskimo walked by, coming from the Mount Roberts direction. He might not really have been an Eskimo, he could have been a Tlinkit, but he sure looked like an Eskimo. The man was stocky, about five-foot-five, and had a round, copper-skinned, slightly Asian-looking face that was unmistakably Native American. I guessed him to be in his midsixties but could have been off by ten years either way. He had on a bulky parka with a fur-lined hood pulled up around his head. It was the coat more than anything that made me think he was an Eskimo. Being July, it wasn't really the season for bulky winter coats.

"Hey, man," I said, with a smile and a nod, as he approached.

"How's it going?" said the Eskimo.

"Pretty good," I said. "Did you climb Mount Roberts?"

"Yeah. I climb it just about every weekend. Keeps me in shape."

"Is there much snow up there?"

"A little."

Then the Eskimo, or Tlinkit, or whatever he was, continued walking, down toward my wife, down toward Juneau. He was the only other hiker Pat and I saw on the trail that day. He probably would have hiked the trail even if it had been snowing out, which was no doubt often the case in winter. The drizzle that Pat, myself, and apparently every other potential hiker in Juneau found so intimidating didn't faze him in the slightest. Not with that coat.

At the time I didn't think meeting an Eskimo at the cross on the Mount Roberts Trail was the least bit weird. It was Alaska, after all, where Eskimos live. Had this incident occurred a year later, though, I would have found it extremely weird. That's because I joined a twelve-step alcohol recovery program a year after my Alaska trip. There's a favorite story in the program that has to do specifically with encountering Eskimos on trails.

It goes like this:

A guy was stranded in the middle of the Alaskan tundra at night, in winter, during a blizzard. He had no food, it was a hundred miles to the nearest settlement, he was completely lost, and his dog team had been devoured by wolves. In desperation, the man prayed to Almighty God to rescue him from this dilemma.

A few minutes later, so the story goes, an Eskimo came by on a dogsled. The Eskimo stopped and offered the man a ride.

"No thanks," said the man. "God is going to rescue me. I don't want to miss it."

Two more Eskimos came by and still the man refused their offers of assistance, preferring to wait for the divine answer to his prayers to extricate him instead of a mundane old dogsled. Hours later, as the man lay in the snow near death from frostbite and exposure, he prayed again.

"Why didn't you rescue me?" the man pleaded. "What kind of a God are you?"

"What are you talking about?" came a booming voice from the heavens. "I sent you three Eskimos. What more do you want?"

I think that's how the story goes. I could be wrong. It was something like that. In recovery, because of that story, clearly beneficial happenings are called "Eskimos."

I had not yet heard the story when I encountered the Eskimo at the cross on Mount Roberts. Shortly after he passed by me, or passed me by, I started back down myself. The rest of the hike was pretty uneventful. It was much like the hike up except in reverse.

The only incident worth repeating on the way down came when Pat and I were almost back at the trailhead. We passed a profusion of blackberries, all deliciously ripe in the extended Alaskan daylight. Since we were kind of hungry, and we both loved blackberries, we began grabbing great handfuls of them and stuffing them in our mouths. The array presented a veritable blackberry smorgasbord: Every species I'd ever heard of was there, in that little patch, plus a couple with which I was totally unfamiliar. I specifically identified blackcap raspberry, common blackberry, Himalaya berry, thimbleberry, salmonberry, and cut-leaf blackberry.

One species in the "unfamiliar" category looked like an oversized salmonberry. Pat and I had a big debate over whether it was a salmonberry or not. Regardless, we concluded, it was definitely a member of the blackberry/raspberry family. Pat plucked one, stuffed it in her mouth, and immediately spit it out.

"That's no salmonberry, " she announced, continuing to spit until all traces of the fruit were banished from her system. "That's the worst-tasting thing I ever ate."

"Probably just not ripe," I suggested, although it certainly looked ripe.

As we climbed down the stairway back onto Sixth Street, I put my arm around my wife. It had been, all in all, a very good day. She'd enjoyed herself and I could now boast to the world that I'd been hiking in Alaska. You couldn't ask for too much more.

"That was a very weird trail," Pat commented as we approached the motel. "I kept expecting something strange to happen. I guess we just lucked out."

"I know what you mean," I said. "I thought it was weird, too. It was probably just our imagination. But it sure seemed weird."

"It sure did," said Pat.

PART 4

THE SUN CAME OUT, FINALLY, AS WE WERE PULLING AWAY FROM THE JUNEAU harbor in the ferryboat at six in the evening of our tenth day. The first few hours out of Juneau were fabulous as the boat passed through Misty Fiords National Monument. Everywhere you looked, there were craggy peaks, deep, spooky inlets, and huge valley glaciers. After it got dark, and for the next two days, we settled into what turned out to be a pretty boring routine. We whiled away the time by pacing around the deck (I probably did a thousand laps), checking out occasional scenic spots on shore, and consuming alcohol in the little bar. That's about all there was to do, except when the captain had everybody run out on deck a couple of times. This happened once when he spotted a killer whale (actually, the animal was already spotted), and once when a pack of dolphins showed up. It was kind of interesting when we passed the Queen Charlotte Islands and hit the open ocean for a few miles instead of the much calmer Inside Passage. The channel between Vancouver Island and the British Columbia mainland was also pretty interesting.

Pat and I were fortunate in that unlike most passengers, we'd rented a sleeping room. I can't bring myself to call it a "stateroom" because there was nothing the least bit stately about it. It contained a bunk bed, a sink, and about four square feet of walking-around space. Most of the passengers slept on deck or in the lounges. Not that Pat and I slept very well. The room set us back all of twenty bucks.

We debarked at 5:00 A.M. in downtown Seattle, 12 blocks from the place where the airport bus picked up its passengers. The only way to get from the ferry dock to the bus stop was to walk, which we did. On the way, we passed a little dress shop that had the same name as the little girl who lived next door to us in Grants Pass, Courtney Branch.

We thought that was weird.

PART 5

IN RETROSPECT, FOR ALL THE SUPPOSEDLY WEIRD THINGS THAT HAPPENED on our trip to Alaska, only two turned out to be truly weird. Both involved the ferry ride home.

They had a little gift shop on the ferry. A very little gift shop. One item for sale was a guide to edible plants of Alaska. I got to browsing through it and came to the section on blackberries and raspberries. What I read made my flesh crawl. I immediately called Pat over and showed it to her.

It seems that of the dozens of species and varieties of blackberry and raspberry in the world, there is a single species that is deadly poisonous. It's called "baneberry" and it looks a lot like salmonberry. Except it's a little larger and very, very bitter.

The blackberry that Pat spit out was a baneberry. Had she not spit it out, she would have gotten very sick. Or worse.

Eating the baneberry sort of ties in to the other truly weird thing that happened on the trip. Pat kept complaining of severe nausea and spent most of the ferry ride home vomiting and unable to eat. I mean, I've heard of violent seasickness before but only on violent seas. Except for the area around the Queen Charlotte Islands, most of the homeward voyage took us through extremely placid waters. Besides, she'd never complained of seasickness before.

I eventually began to suspect that neither the boat ride nor the baneberry was the cause of Pat's problem. Sure enough, the nausea continued after we got off the ferry. And sure enough, when she went to the doctor a couple of weeks later, still complaining of nausea, it was definitely confirmed, she was pregnant.

At the time all I could think to say was, "Thank God you didn't swallow the baneberry."

I know, I know. As much as I love the idea, the baby could not possibly have been conceived in Alaska. But realizing that my wife was pregnant after five years of trying, during a trip we'd taken on the advice of my wife's gynecologist to take the pressure off us in our quest for a third and final child, made the trip much more memorable.

The trip would have been even more weird had the Eskimo turned out to be the Messiah or something, materializing at the cross to save humankind just as I was sitting there. Especially if his appearance changed my life, Pat's life, and the course of human history, forever. But I don't think he was the Messiah. Regardless, our third child, Anna, born February 28, 1982, certainly changed our lives.

PART 6

THERE IS ONE MORE WEIRD THING—BAD WEIRD NOT GOOD WEIRD—ABOUT PAT'S and my trip to Juneau. I did not learn about it until I began researching this story, in the year 2000. Apparently Pat and I were not the only people impressed by the spot on the Mount Roberts Trail where Pat waited for me—where the path levels off at mile 2, with the fabulous overlook, half a mile from the summit with the cross. There is now an aerial tramway from downtown Juneau to that very spot. There are also a gift shop, a visitor center, and a restaurant at that spot. It costs twenty bucks to ride the tramway up and takes six minutes. If you hike up, as Pat and I did, you can ride the tramway down for five bucks.

I don't know this for sure but my guess is that with the tramway, and the increased visitor use that goes along with it, hikers don't have to worry nearly as much about grizzly bears as Pat and I did in back 1981.

Weird.

THE HIKE: *Mount Roberts Trail, Tongass National Forest, Juneau, Alaska.*

LENGTH *(one way): 2.5–4.5 miles.*

DIRECTIONS: *Juneau, Alaska, cannot be reached by road. However you arrive there, find your way to Sixth Street, then walk up Sixth, past the historic old Russian Orthodox church, to the end of the street. It's only a few blocks. The Mount Roberts Trail begins at a wooden stairway at the end of Sixth Street.*

HIKE ELEVEN
THE BARRENS

*The destination is nothing,
the journey is everything.*

PART 1

WHEN I WAS TWENTY-ONE YEARS OLD, I RAN AWAY FROM HOME. I planned my escape for days, down to the finest detail. The details were important because for me, the ritual surrounding my escape was as meaningful as the actual act. My getaway had to be unannounced, it had to be at night, and I had to arrive at my destination at dawn. That way the journey would feel like a clean break, a rebirth, a spiritual transformation.

It was the first of many journeys I would take in my journeyman life. While each transformed me a little, and brought a small measure of increased spiritual awareness, I always ended up disappointed that the effect was not more profound.

Other people experienced major transformational journeys, with many wonderful surprises at every turn. Why couldn't I have one? Jacob, in the Bible, encountered a ladderful of angels on a journey through the desert to Haran. Saul of Tarsus found his personal savior on a journey to Damascus. Moses and the Israelites journeyed for forty years, then finally arrived at the Promised Land. Siddhartha Gautama became the Buddha when he left his life of luxury and set out on a journey of truth. Abraham spent the most spiritually productive part of his life as a nomad, wandering the desert in search of green pastures and good water for his sheep.

And Art Bernstein, also in search of green pastures and good water, ran away to New York City in November 1964. I didn't know it then, but of all the wondrous experiences of my runaway year in New York, the most profound and life altering would occur on a nondescript trail in the New Jersey Pine Barrens. In November 1964 I hadn't even heard of the New Jersey Pine Barrens.

As I write this story, most people still haven't heard of the New Jersey Pine Barrens. Many residents of New Jersey have not heard of the New Jersey Pine Barrens.

At the time of my midnight journey to the biggest apple on the North American tree, I'd recently graduated from college, the University of Michigan, with a major in anthropology. I had little interest in anthropology. I'd picked it only because nobody else I knew was majoring in it. That kind of thing mattered to me in those days. Mostly I was confused about what to do with my life and grasped at anything that seemed to offer even a modicum of direction. Things grasped under such circumstances, however, tend to be let go of pretty quickly.

In retrospect, if you're going to choose a major in which you have little interest, my advice is to select one that pays good money, like accounting or business administration. But I'd been raised to concern myself more with "personal fulfillment" than cash. As my father used to say, in his flawed wisdom, "Find a profession you like, pursue it with everything you have, and the money will take care of itself." I suspect my father's advice was more wishful thinking than anything else. He gave up a promising career as an artist to work in engineering, a field he hated, solely to better support his family. When I was twenty-one, however, I foolishly believed everything my father told me. My father was a fine fellow and otherwise very bright, but like most humans, he was not 100 percent right all the time.

Because of the lessons learned from my tendency to blindly accept my father's dubious advice, I was careful to raise my own children to question everything, including me. All and all, I am pleased with the results. Except I may have gone too far. My kids don't listen to anything I tell them, no matter how wise. No grasping for them.

Anyhow, I realized the stupidity of my choice of majors when, brand-new degree in hand, I started looking for work. No matter how thoroughly I scanned the want ads in the *Detroit News*, I could not find any jobs requiring a B.A. in anthropology. Not one. Ever. And I didn't like the subject well enough to consider graduate school. Besides, my grades weren't that good. Not to mention the University of Michigan Anthropology Department, at the time, flunked out 80 percent of its graduate students in the prelim exams.

My plan was to attend graduate school in the fall at the University of Michigan School of Social Work, which for some reason had accepted me despite my mediocre grades. I wasn't much more interested in social work than I was in anthropology. But at least there was the prospect of gainful employment, and I could tell myself that my work would be "doing good" for humankind. That was important.

I spent the summer of 1964 living at my parents' house and driving around in a 1957 Plymouth willed to me because my parents no longer had any use for it. It was a huge copper-colored monster with a stick shift on the column and tail fins in back. I loved it. My lifestyle, in the summer of 1964, was to use the Plymouth to go bar hopping every night, and to drag myself to work at a day camp every morning.

My worst day at the day camp occurred after a particularly raucous night of drinking that lasted until five in the morning. Somehow I made it to work on time the next day. Our agenda was to take the kids to the beach at Kensington Metropolitan Park, way out in the country. I spent the day chasing children, swimming, playing baseball, and nursing a hangover, all on two hours' sleep. I ended up with a terrible sunburn.

I returned home exhausted, dehydrated, and miserable, with an overwhelming desire to collapse in a heap in my bed. On my way through the living room, I was accosted by my sister Barbara, who also still lived at home.

"Daddy died," she announced, in a soft voice.

"Really?" I replied. "That's terrible. How is he?"

It took a few minutes for my mind to grasp what my sister had just said. The next thing I knew, instead of taking my much-needed nap, I was in a funeral home showroom with a bunch of aunts (my mother was too distraught to go), having been assigned the task of picking out a casket. At one point the aunts began arguing over whether oak or mahogany was more "him."

Attending the Graduate School of Social Work was challenging, interesting, and a terrific thing for me to be doing. But my heart wasn't in it. I'd sit and stare out the window, wishing I was off in the redwoods, or the High Sierra, or the Grand Canyon, or the Swiss Alps. My thoughts kept returning to my father and how he'd always dreamed of traveling but never got the chance because he'd worked himself to death, up to seventy hours a week, at a job he hated.

It occurred to me that I had been doing as I was told, doing what was expected, since the day I was born. The time had come to do what was most meaningful to me. That's when I began plotting my getaway.

I formally withdrew from the social work program on a Wednesday afternoon. I moved all my belongings out of my little furnished room, loaded them into my car, and drove to my mother's house in Detroit. My mother just happened to be visiting her sister in New York, my aunt Blanche. My plan was to drive to New York and stay, temporarily, with a former roommate who was living in Brooklyn, and then call my mother in a couple of days.

The journey of a lifetime, which I fully expected would change me forever, began right after dinner. I started up the Plymouth and slowly backed out of the driveway. While I was anticipating many wonderful surprises, my main hope was that I would not be struck blind, like Saul of Tarsus. Not while I was driving, anyhow.

Given a choice, I'd prefer angels on a ladder to being struck blind.

PART 2

FOR HOUR AFTER HOUR I DROVE THROUGH THE DARKNESS, LISTENING TO STRANGE radio stations from places like Waterloo, Iowa, and Fargo, North Dakota, feeling more transformed with every mile I put between myself, Detroit, and school. I loved the process of "just driving." I still do. Actually arriving somewhere would be anticlimactic because it meant the journey had ended and reality would once again rear its ugly head. From Detroit, Interstate 75 took me to the Ohio Turnpike, which blended into the Pennsylvania Turnpike, which led to the New Jersey Turnpike, which led, unwaveringly, to New York City.

In that part of the country, all roads lead to New York City.

I arrived in New York at seven A.M., emerging from the Holland Tunnel smack in the middle of the Garment District at rush hour. Somehow my big old Plymouth made it through the morning traffic, over the magnificent Brooklyn Bridge, and across Brooklyn to my friend's apartment in Bensonhurst. I phoned my mother the next day. She took the news surprisingly well and, in fact, seemed glad to see me. We spent a memorable couple of days together, visiting the Guggenheim Museum and having lunch in a Chinatown dim sum restaurant with my aunt and a bunch of my mother's old friends. My mother collected old friends the way some people collect gnome figurines, kitten postcards, or Barbie dolls.

Two weeks after moving to New York, I managed to land a job as a social worker in the world's second largest mental hospital, which happened to be located 10 miles from the world's first largest mental hospital. That was before they let all the mental patients out on the street rather than risk violating their civil rights.

The best thing about the job was that it came with accommodations in the residence hall for unmarried medical and professional staff, complete with three meals a day. The work was fascinating, too. The hospital setting, in a quiet village on Long Island Sound, 40 miles from New York City, was serene and beautiful. As an added benefit, there was an endless supply of young, single, socially aware female practicum students who worked temporarily at the hospital while studying things like occupational therapy at various surrounding colleges.

One of the people I dated was a girl name Mikki. A nursing student at Brooklyn Jewish Hospital, Mikki was spending a semester at our establishment to learn the ins and outs of psychiatric nursing. Mikki had a beautiful personality and an even more beautiful figure. We spent many a happy evening discovering the wonders of Greenwich Village, the Canarsie Pier, and Nathan's at Coney Island, the original hot dog stand.

More than anything else, I liked the patients. One patient with whom I became especially close was a good-looking Italian in his late twenties. His name was Al, which was short for Alphonso. It was Al who first made me aware of the New Jersey Pine Barrens. Al had spent his entire life in the Little Italy section of Lower Manhattan, and his family was strongly Mob-connected. Al was in the hospital because of an attempted suicide. He had been diagnosed by the hospital doctors as a "sociopathic personality," which meant he was technically "without mental disorder," which meant he would be quickly released.

Al hated his diagnosis. The label upset him even more than the events leading up to his suicide attempt. It branded him as having an inborn "inability to internalize the morals and values of society." Cold-blooded, unfeeling murderers are considered sociopaths. Al saw this diagnosis as an irreversible life sentence that meant he would continue to get into frequent trouble, always be in and out of jail, never truly feel love for another person, and constantly manipulate to satisfy his immediate needs. Sociopathic personalities are fairly common among Mob types.

There was one truly odd thing about Al that set him apart from every other petty New York gangster. Al wrote some of the most beautiful, sensitive poetry imaginable, about his girlfriend, about what it's like to be in jail, and about how it feels to be unable to control your violent impulses. He also wrote a lot about nature. His poems did not sound as though they'd been written by a criminal sociopath and mobster.

For three weeks Al was a patient in the minimum-security intake ward to which I'd been assigned. Then he was released. A month later I received a message that Al was back in the hospital, this time in the maximum-security ward. He'd been arrested for attempted murder and tried to hang himself while in jail at Riker's Island.

My visit with Al was the one and only time I'd ever been to the maximum-security ward. An oversized skeleton key, carried by all employees including myself, allowed me unescorted access into the building and into the dayroom of Al's ward. This dayroom was one of the most frightening places I've ever been. The huge, barred room was furnished with wooden benches, which accommodated maybe a third of the patients, and a TV behind a protective, Plexiglas shield. That was it. The shield in front of the TV was caked with dried "stuff," as were the walls. The room reeked of fecal material, sweat, and vomit. It was mobbed with shouting, cursing, psychotic-looking men acting out various stages of rage. Thrown objects kept flying past my head. Skirmishes broke out every few seconds. Heironymous Bosch could not have imagined a more terrifying place.

I quickly made my way through the melee to the attendant's station, wondering if this insanity went on all day every day. Along the back wall I passed a row of patients in "double restraints," straitjacketed and shackled to a mattressless bed frame. It made me want to cry.

One of the men in double restraints was Al, looking very sad and tired. After I announced my presence to the head attendant, I talked to Al.

Al talked constantly about suicide, as he had when I first met him. He was in the double restraints, however, not as suicide prevention but because he'd severely beaten another patient. The person back in the city whom he'd attempted to kill, which landed him on Riker's Island, had been sleeping with his girlfriend.

Al asked if I would talk to the head attendant about letting him out of the restraints. I said I would.

"Hey man," Al said, as I was about to leave. "I thought about you one day while I was out. Me and my girlfriend drove out to the Pine Barrens, over in New Jersey. You'd like the Pine Barrens. I know you get a kick out of nature and stuff."

"Thanks," I said. "Maybe I'll check it out."

"The Forked River Mountains," said Al.

"I beg your pardon?"

"I said the Forked River Mountains. That's where we went. Great place. Full of surprises."

That was the only time during the conversation that Al smiled.

The truth was that I had no intention of driving halfway across New Jersey, which had never impressed me as very scenic, just to see some barren place that was covered with pines. I did not tell him that, though. I just smiled politely and acted interested.

The next morning, shortly after I arrived in my office, I received a phone call from my supervisor, a sweet little lady in her sixties. She informed me that Al had died the previous night.

"The staff at maximum security thought you'd like to know," she said.

According to my supervisor, after Al was unshackled from the bed frame and straitjacket, as a result of my intervention, while being interviewed in the attendants' station (maximum-security attendants rarely ventured into the dayroom if they could avoid it), he'd apparently fished the pull-tab from a soda can out of the wastebasket, hidden it his pocket until night, and used it to slice open his wrists.

PART 3

WERE IT NOT FOR AL'S PASSING, I NEVER WOULD HAVE TRIED TO FIND THE FORKED River Mountains. But I figured I owed it to him. Conning me into driving all the way to central New Jersey was Al's last act of sociopathic manipulation, unless you count stealing the pull-tab. Still, Mikki and I liked to take drives out of the city every now and then. The urge grew particularly compelling as spring gathered into full blossom after a long and dreary winter. We'd spent a day in New Haven, we'd driven up the Hudson to Nyack, and we'd visited the tip of Long Island. Why not check out central New Jersey?

Mikki was an excellent traveling companion: game for just about anything, appreciative of good scenery, and easy to get along with. Not to mention damned pretty. If the scenery got boring, there was always Mikki to look at. In addition, she was very well organized and good at following maps. What more could I want in a traveling companion?

Locating the Forked River Mountains, the place Al recommended we go, was not easy. They didn't appear on any map that I could find. I did mange to find, on the New Jersey map, a little town on the Atlantic shore, 45 miles north of Atlantic City, called Forked River. That sounded promising. Actually, Mikki found it by looking through the index of towns on the back of the map. For a tiny state, New Jersey had an awful lot of little towns. And for a densely populated state, it contained an awful lot of blank holes, like the Arabian "Empty Quarter." Most of those "holes," it turned out, were the Pine Barrens.

Technically, the town of Forked River, New Jersey, was not located on the Atlantic shore, although it is a classic coastal fishing village. It was located on Barnegat Bay, part of the Intracoastal Waterway. A long, narrow barrier island on the other side of the bay faced the actual ocean. That is true of most of the Atlantic coast in the United States. And while we're being technical, the town was not exactly on Barnegat Bay, either. It was on an inlet off the bay, the estuary at the mouth of the Forked River. Except for the wide estuary where the Forked River emptied into Barnegat Bay, it wasn't much of a river. True to its name, the stagnant, slow-moving waterway forked 5 miles upstream, into the North Branch of the Forked River, the Middle Branch of the Forked River, and the South Branch of the Forked River.

In New Jersey they call divided rivers "branches," not "forks"— as in the town of Long Branch, 40 miles up the coast from Forked River. It's a good thing, too. Talk of the North Fork of the Forked and the South Fork of the Forked would have gotten very confusing, not to mention difficult to say.

On a warm morning in late April, as apple and cherry blossoms filled the universe with visual and aromatic magic along the East Coast, and in little magical pockets in the city, Mikki and I jumped into my big old finned Plymouth and headed out of town on the New Jersey and Garden State Turnpikes to find Forked River. Our sole objective was to drive around, visit some pretty places, hopefully have a look at the mountains (although I could not imagine there being anything in New Jersey that resembled real mountains), and honor Al's memory.

If the Forked River wasn't much of a river, the town of Forked River wasn't much of a town. It consisted, in 1965, of a gas station, a smoky little cafe, a few stores, and a cluster of houses. The population was perhaps a thousand. Maybe two thousand. The stores catered mostly to commercial and recreational fishermen.

It was fairly early in the day when Mikki and I invaded the town. We stopped by a little convenience store, called a "general store" back then, to purchase a bag of pretzels and inquire about the Forked River Mountains. The store had an ancient, musty smell. The owner, or somebody, collected antique kitchen utensils. Old egg beaters, food whips, and unidentifiable gizmos covered with gears and cranks dangled by the hundreds from the ceiling, suspended by wires.

"Very inventive," said Mikki as we stood in the middle of the store looking upward. "Hanging stuff from the ceiling displays the collection without taking space away from the sales racks."

"I guess. Except it takes your eyes off the merchandise. Not to mention you're liable to bump into a counter and knock something over."

"Which is also a great merchandising ploy," said Mikki with a laugh. "If you break it, you buy it."

After analyzing the store's marketing strategy, we approached the proprietor, who was standing near the cash register, about the Forked River Mountains. The white-haired guy in his late sixties must have weighed four hundred pounds. His apron was the size of a bedsheet.

"You wanna see the mountains, do you, kiddos?" he replied with an effusive grin. "Well I think we can help."

"Great," I said. "How do we get there?"

"It's not quite that easy, kiddos. The mountains are on private property. I need to call the owner and let him know you're coming so he'll have the gate unlocked. It's no problem, though." The man picked up the telephone receiver and started to dial.

"Hold on a second," I said. "Can't you see the mountains from the road?"

"You can see them from County Road 614 but they're way off in the distance and don't look like much. I can get you right up close. To the top even, if you want, although that requires a little hiking. You kiddos like hiking?"

Then the man started dialing again.

Going hiking had never entered my mind. Or Mikki's either, I presume. Hiking just wasn't in our repertoire of things to do, even though we both enjoyed nature and the outdoors.

"How long are the trails?" I quickly interjected, which to my relief caused the man to pause in his dialing. "And are they very hard?"

"Not hard at all. Pretty soft in fact. Very sandy. They're also pretty easy. Not too steep and only a couple of miles long. You might want to buy a compass, though. Not that you're likely to get lost. But there are surprises."

"Let me guess. You just happen to sell compasses."

"Sure do, kiddo."

"What do we need a compass for?" Mikki interjected.

"In case we get lost," I repeated. The store clerk nodded in support. I certainly did not want to get lost.

"I don't see how a compass will help us even if we do get lost," said Mikki. "But if you want a toy to play with . . ."

"We'll take the compass," I said. "What else do we need for a hike?"

"Well, let's see. A map. Sandwiches. Couple cans of soda. That should do her."

"We'll take all of that," I announced, glancing toward Mikki to make sure she agreed with the decision. She smiled and nodded.

As the shopkeeper made the phone call to the landowner, then prepared the sandwiches, I continued asking him questions.

"Do you send a lot of people to this property to go hiking?"

"Two or three a weekend. Tourists are more interested in the coast than the Barrens. Everybody loves water."

When the man was done making the sandwiches, salami and lettuce on rye with mustard, he gave us instructions on how to use the compass and how to find the property entrance. The gated turnoff onto a dirt road, we were told, was located 8 miles from town, on the left. The mailbox read BARNEGAT JONES.

The man also mentioned in passing, just as we were leaving, that the property owner expected us to fork over $1.00 for the privilege of driving and walking on his land. I felt a twinge of annoyance that he hadn't mentioned this earlier. But I was now getting kind of interested in the prospect of scaling the mighty Forked River Mountains. Mikki agreed that going on a hike definitely sounded fun.

It was certainly worth a $1.00 investment, plus another $4.00 investment in sandwiches, soda, and a compass. Everybody made money off us that day.

PART 4

THE SHORT DRIVE UP THE NORTH BRANCH OF THE FORKED RIVER, THEN OVER a low rise past the "mountains," was lovely. Just the sort of outing Mikki and I were looking for. Much of the North Branch was a stagnant, smelly channel, but with lush, brilliant green vegetation choking the shore. Once out of the river valley, we found ourselves on a narrow, paved county road driving through an unbroken forest of pines and oaks, with occasional openings of grass, small farm tracts, and swamp.

Five miles from town the mountains came into view, off to the left. Some mountains. The 4-mile road segment between the North Branch of the Forked River and the Factory Branch of Cedar Creek crested gently, imperceptibly, at about 50 feet above sea level. To the northwest a series of broad hills, maybe 3 miles away, nudged skyward to perhaps 200 feet in elevation.

Those, we guessed, were the famous Forked River Mountains. As nearly as I could tell, there were three of them, in a small cluster.

"Some mountains," I said to Mikki.

"I like them," she replied. "I think they're cute. The toy poodle of mountains. Or the Chihuahua of mountains."

A 200-foot-high mountain is minuscule even by New Jersey standards. By contrast, the highest point in New Jersey (called "High Point"), a ski area in the state's extreme northwest corner, near the Delaware River where New York, New Jersey, and Pennsylvania all come together, soars to a whopping 1,800 feet above sea level.

Although I found the Forked River Mountains kind of silly looking, I liked the Pine Barrens. I especially liked that they were in New Jersey. When you think of *remote*, the last place that comes to mind is New Jersey, with its small area, heavy industry, and teeming population, not to mention New York City pressing on one border and Philadelphia crowding the other.

The Pine Barrens, Mikki read as we drove, from a brochure she'd picked up in the general store, cover a million acres and are "a land of lakes, swamps, floating bogs, many rivers, and a hundred miles of coast protected by offshore bars." The soil in the Pine Barrens is acidic and very sandy, with a hardpan layer in some places that stunts the trees. In most places the Barrens are densely forested with small pines and even smaller oaks. They are anything but barren.

More than anything else I liked the smells, especially after we got off the paved road and onto the private property. The sweet scent of pitch pine was the most obvious, and the dank smell of decaying organic matter in the creeks, stagnant ponds, and swamps. Then there were the blossoms. And the wildflowers. And the warm spring breezes. Each lent its own special perfume to the intoxicating mix.

We located the Barnegat Jones gate easily enough, on the left, just as the county road drew even with the mountains. The dirt driveway was straight as yardstick for 2 miles, until it crossed a railroad track. Immediately over the tracks we turned left onto another dirt road, following the instructions from the guy in the general store. Half a mile later we arrived at a little clapboard farmhouse with a lawn, a fenced pasture, a small, newly plowed field, a big red barn, and a friendly collie, beside himself with excitement, who barked out a welcome. From the look of things, I guessed that the farmer mostly cut down trees for a living, and milled them into lumber in his barn. There were stacks of rough-cut lumber all around the property.

The land did not look badly abused, however. I saw no clearcuts, skid trails, or even very many tree stumps. That might have been because the land was not very productive. Anything anybody did to make a living off this land would have to be pretty marginal.

A slender young man in overalls, with short, platinum-blond hair and an almost albino complexion, came out of the house to greet us and collect our dollar. I could see his wife inside and a cute little toddler girl in a diaper playing on the front porch. The man looked maybe twenty-eight years old. Thirty at the oldest.

"Howdy," he said, extending a hand for me to shake. "I'm Barney Jones. Hope you have a good time today. If there's anything I can do for you, let me know."

Wow, I thought, farmers really do say *howdy* when they greet people. And they really do wear overalls. I doubt if I'd talked to more than three or four farmers in my life up to then. Maybe none.

Barney Jones had set up a couple of picnic tables under a large oak tree at the edge of the woods, in a little grassy enclosure 200 feet from the house. He'd also built an outhouse nearby. Two trails took off near the picnic tables, one to the right and one to the left. Immediately beyond the twin trailheads, Mikki and I could see the gentle, tree-covered rise of the mountains. The peaks did not look very far away and the hike did not appear very difficult.

"You folks got a map?" said Barney, cleaning his ear with a finger. "If not, I can sell you one for a dime." Mr. Jones pulled a map out of the pocket of his overalls. It was identical to the map for which I'd just paid a quarter at the general store.

"Sure do," I said.

"Good," said the young man, looking slightly disappointed. "Best way to get to the mountain is go in on the left-hand trail and come out on the right-hand trail. Or you can go in on the right-hand trail and come out on the left-hand trail. Either way. There are a few side paths and some cut-acrosses. It can get a little confusing. But if you follow the map, you shouldn't have any problems. If you get lost, or run into any surprises, just head south to reach the mountain and north to come back." Barney could see that I was holding a compass.

"What kind of surprises?" I asked.

"Never can tell," said Barney. "Nothing serious."

"There aren't any bears or anything, are there?"

"I never seen one."

I commented to Mikki afterward that the guy's directions sounded like the Scarecrow's instructions to Dorothy in *The Wizard of Oz:* "That way is nice. Of course that way is nice, too."

After lunching on salami sandwiches at the picnic table, Mikki and I set off on our little trek, taking the path from the left-hand trailhead. How lost could we get armed with a map and compass on a self-contained trail system on only about 4 square miles of ground? Mikki insisted that we take a compass reading at every intersection. I'm not sure she had any real reason for this, except to get our money's worth out of what was probably a pointless purchase. Or maybe to underscore the pointlessness of my purchase. I didn't disagree with her. According to the compass and map, the path from the left-hand trailhead headed south-southeast.

It was not a particularly pleasant trail. Too much dense brush encroached from the sides and clawed at our legs as we passed. Also, there were too many bugs, the soft sand created an extra strain as we walked, and there wasn't much scenery. At least not near the bottom. The pine smell was kind of pleasant, though, and I liked the gnarled little pine trees for which the Barrens were named.

Half a mile along the gently upward sloping path, we arrived at a three-way junction by a picturesque old barn in a field of wildflowers. By *picturesque* I mean the barn was dilapidated and falling apart. The scene didn't strike me as very pretty even though you are supposed to be thoroughly enchanted by sun-bleached barn ruins surrounded by wildflowers. For one thing, there were more weeds than wildflowers. For another, the spot smelled, for some reason, faintly of burning rubber rather than flowers. Neither Mikki nor I felt beckoned to linger.

If you count the path we came in on, there was actually a four-way junction at the old barn, not a three-way junction. But the fork in the route ahead of us was shaped like a trident pitchfork, presenting us with three options. According to the map, the right-hand prong headed south and led, after a mile, to the vista point at the top the main peak. The other two prongs, according to the map, just sort of drifted off into the woods. A check of the compass confirmed that the right-hand prong indeed headed due south. Beyond the vista point, the map showed the path looping back and emerging as the right-hand fork back at the farmhouse.

"Are you satisfied?" I said to Mikki after taking the compass reading, then shoving the instrument back into my pocket.

"Exceedingly," she grinned.

Five minutes up the new path, which was considerably steeper than the initial trail segment, although still not very steep, I began feeling slightly dizzy. The dizziness was accompanied by a cold sweat and a wave of mild nausea. It felt like what I would later recognize as hypoglycemia, except not as severe. I only get hypoglycemia attacks when I haven't eaten in a several hours, however, or when I've eaten too much sugar and not enough protein. In this instance I'd just devoured a high-protein salami sandwich.

"I don't feel so good," I whined, pausing to let my stomach settle and regain my equilibrium.

"Neither do I," said Mikki, also pausing.

"Must be the sandwiches," I conjectured. "Although they tasted okay to me. Maybe we can get rich suing the store owner."

We both stood and rested for a couple of minutes. Then whatever had been afflicting us went away.

"I wonder what that was?" I said. I didn't really believe that our sudden malady had been caused by the sandwiches. The symptoms of food poisoning usually do not include dizziness. Also, the discomfort seemed to descend too quickly and simultaneously, which was kind of unnatural. Then it went away just as quickly and simultaneously.

"Could have been anything," said Mikki, the nursing student and medical expert, after we both felt better. "It was probably just the sandwiches. Plus fatigue from the steep hill and loose sand. Or there might be power lines nearby. That could do it. Or perhaps we ran into a magnetic anomaly. Or gamma rays from a flying saucer."

"I don't see any power lines or flying saucers."

"Well, then, I guess we'll just never know," said Mikki with a shrug. We continued hiking.

Half a mile later the path emerged at a little clearing at the hilltop vista point that was our destination. It was very scenic. We could see all the way back to the farmhouse.

"Nice view," I said, "for New Jersey."

"Very nice indeed," Mikki agreed, "except that the Empire State Building is 5 times as high and Mount Everest is 145 times as high."

We lingered for a few minutes but quickly ran out of ways to occupy our time. So we prepared to head back.

"Don't forget the compass reading," said Mikki, wagging a finger.

"Yezzum," I dutifully replied.

According to the compass, the path we intended to take went north, not south as indicated on the map. That was impossible because we'd just come from the north and had been heading south. We had not passed, nor did the map indicate, any major curves in our route up to that point.

"Let me see," said Mikki.

I showed her my reading. She agreed that the compass showed the continuing path as heading north instead of south. According to the map, if we continued on the trail instead of doubling back the way we came, we should go south for another quarter mile before making the loop back north. To compete the loop back to the farmhouse, we needed to hike straight ahead, which should have been southward.

"So what should we do?" Mikki asked. "Assume the compass is wrong and hike forward, or go the way we came to make sure we don't get lost?"

"Beats me," I said.

I did not mention to Mikki that I was becoming frightened. That I was having fantasies of getting irrevocably lost, of she and I spending the rest of our lives wandering aimlessly through the Pine Barrens, surviving by trapping squirrels and boiling swamp water.

As an experiment, I made a 180-degree about-face. The compass still showed me facing north. And no, the needle was not stuck. When I rotated the casing, the needle held fast to its direction. In case the needle had somehow become attracted to my magnetic personality, I handed the compass to Mikki. Both trail directions registered as north for her, too. East and west registered correctly.

Because of the problem with the compass, we decided to stick to the tried-and-true for the return trek, going back the way we came instead of completing the loop. It was an agonizing decision preceded by much debate. Mikki wanted to forge ahead regardless while I opted for not getting lost. Half a mile later, we arrived back at the old barn. Except we emerged on the middle prong. We should have emerged on the right-hand prong, which we'd taken to reach the vista point. And the compass still showed us heading north, and it still showed the opposite direction as north.

That was when we decided to quit taking compass readings. It was just too exasperating.

From the barn we retraced the trail to the farmhouse, the same trail we'd come in on, passing the same now familiar landmarks. We emerged, however, on the right-hand trail rather than the left-hand. Having entered on the left-hand trail and come out on the right-hand trail, there was only one possible conclusion: Whether we chose to admit it or not, we had completed the loop. We had no idea how we completed the loop but we had. Regardless, Mikki and I were both exceedingly relieved to be back at the farmhouse.

Barney Jones was sitting at the picnic table when we arrived, drinking a beer and playing with his little girl.

"Everything go okay?" he inquired, again cleaning his ear with his index finger.

"Just fine," I lied.

"That's good. Some people seem to have trouble finding the far end of the loop and end up coming back the way they went in."

"Not us. We just followed the map. We did run into some surprises, though."

The man smiled knowingly. "It happens a lot," he said. "Especially to people who insist on bringing a compass along because they don't trust their instincts to tell them which way to go."

PART 5

OF ALL MY EXPERIENCES IN NEW YORK, THE HIKE THROUGH THE PINE BARRENS WAS the one most reminiscent of the life-altering journeys of Jacob, Moses, Saul of Tarsus, and the Buddha. Of course, I didn't see any angels, have visions of the savior, have the Red Sea parted for me, or become an enlightened spiritual master. On the other hand, neither Jacob, Moses, Saul of Tarsus, nor the Buddha ever headed up one life path, doubled back and returned on the same path, only to discover they were on a different path.

Or maybe they did.

I learned from the experience that you can never be 100 percent certain that you're really on the path you think you're on, and that any path you take should be considered a potential life-altering journey. The important thing is to find a path and start walking.

I also learned that the path of my life is mine alone and that of all the billions of people who ever lived or ever will live, nobody else has ever followed the exact same path.

Well, I didn't exactly learn that last thing from the Forked River Mountain Trail. But you gotta admit, it's awfully profound.

THE HIKE: *Unknown trail in the Forked River Mountains, in what is now Pinelands National Preserve, near Forked River, New Jersey.*

LENGTH: *3-mile loop.*

DIRECTIONS: *Take I-95, the New Jersey Turnpike, south from New York City. Where it crosses the Garden State Parkway, near Perth Amboy, go left (south) on the parkway, toward Atlantic City. Proceed to exit 74 and follow County Road 614 North, away from the town of Forked River, for about 5 miles. In 1965 I was given instructions in the general store in Forked River to look for a gated road on private land, with a 3-mile hiking loop. In 2001, if you wish to hike in the Forked River Mountains, you must arrange an escorted tour with the Ocean County Parks Department or the Forked River Mountains Coalition.*

HIKE TWELVE
THE BLACK BUTTE MIRACLE

PART 1

T'S A RECURRENT THEME IN MY LIFE: WHATEVER I LIKE, MY CHILDREN, BLESS their evil little hearts, instinctively hate. And whatever I fanatically love, my children despise. It's the way of the world, a fundamental law of the universe. The template for creation.

It ticks me off.

This elemental rule of nature has been nowhere truer than in my abortive efforts, over the years, to take my children hiking and force them to like it. I hike a lot and frequently observe other parents hiking with young children. The families always look so idyllic and the children so happy, marching along with their little backpacks and water bottles. Hiking would appear to be the perfect family activity, with bonding coming out your ears. As a parent, it's a perfect opportunity to instill all sorts of wonderful values about nature and conservation. As an added bonus, you get your kids away, however briefly, from the city and TV and automobiles and electronics and all those terrible influences. It's just you and the fruit of your reproductive organs, alone in the wilderness, their adoring little eyes looking to you, their beloved parent, for leadership and instruction.

At least that's how it seemed to be with everyone else's children.

My children, alas, were whiners. Had they whined, during a hike, because they were tired, or hungry, I could have understood it. But they didn't. Had they whined because they'd stoically worked their sweet little buns off and deserved a rest, I'd have been delighted to accommodate them. But they didn't. They whined because they could. Because they knew it irritated me. They started whining with the very first step and continued until the blessed relief of our parked car finally came into view.

"Daddy, I'm tired." (Never, "Mommy, I'm tired.")

"Daddy, this is too hard."

"Are we almost there, Daddy?"

"Can we go home now, Daddy?"

"Daddy, my feet hurt."

"Daddy, I'm thirsty."

"Daddy, I have to go to the bathroom."

"Carry me, Daddy."

In fairness, the above was only true when my children, my three beautiful, angelic daughters, were little. Things improved considerably when they reached their teens and adulthood. Adult to adult, they love hitting the pedal pathway with their doddering dad. Or at least they now have the good sense to say they do, whether it's true or not. But in their preteen years, they were miserable company best left at home.

In retrospect, if I'd had any brains, at home is exactly where I should have left them. But I kept passing all those families on the trail, the ones straight out of the family-togetherness commercials you see on TV, and I rationalized that if those people could somehow manipulate their children into being enthusiastic and cooperative, there was no reason why I couldn't. I was a patient, loving parent and, for the most part, my children did not hate my company. Inspired by the passing families, I'd bravely try again. Only to be disappointed yet again.

I never expected their gratitude or anything. I just hoped that after one of the outings, I'd get the feeling when we'd arrive home that they just might possibly have had a good time. Or at least that they didn't have an awful time. Alas, even on the rare occasions when they didn't whine every second of the hike, I never sensed that they'd had much fun.

A case in point is the time I climbed Mount McLoughlin with my oldest daughter, Jennifer, who was eight at the time. McLoughlin is the highest mountain in southern Oregon, a 9,500-foot volcanic cone visible for 100 miles in every direction. It's not a technical climb in that ropes, pitons, and carabiners are not required. You can get to the top via a well-worn trail, with both feet firmly on the ground. But it's a steep and grueling journey and, as you approach the summit, altitude becomes a problem.

On that day Jenny was brave, stoic, and unwavering, as she often is. She did not have an easy time of it but she was determined not to complain. The truth is that the Bernstein tradition of relentless whining began with my second daughter, Sara, not with Jennifer. It continued through my third and final daughter, Anna. My grandchildren, Jenny's offspring, have lately inherited this hallowed tradition.

I realized almost from the outset that McLoughlin was too difficult for Jennifer. As hard as she tried, and as much as I encouraged her, I kept getting ahead of her and having to wait for her to catch up. When the time of day arrived at which I intended to turn back whether or not we'd reached the top, we were still a mile from our goal. I knew from previous hikes up the mountain that the final steep mile, at high elevation over loose rock, took as long as the first 4 miles combined.

When I made the decision to turn back, Jenny and I were well above tree line, at a magnificent rocky overlook where the mountain's flank tumbled dizzyingly down a glacial valley to Fourmile Lake, 3,500 feet below. In my mind no person should ever be ashamed of having made it to this spot. Least of all my resolute little daughter.

I solved the problem by simply announcing that we were at the top, that we'd made it. I gave Jenny a hug and congratulated her on her accomplishment. She never bothered to ask why there was more mountain above where we were standing. If she noticed that at all, she didn't mention it. The spot where we turned around registered in Jennifer's brain as the summit.

Drained, spent, and looking miserable, Jennifer dragged herself back to the bottom of the mountain. We arrived at the car with Jenny acting unsmiling, grouchy, and mostly silent. She slept most of the way home. Even though she later boasted to all her friends about how she'd "climbed Mount McLoughlin," I never sensed much joy during the actual climb, just determination and fatigue.

Jennifer still occasionally brings up the time she and I climbed Mount McLoughlin back when she was eight years old. She's still proud of the accomplishment.

I hope she doesn't read this.

Jenny is now in her thirties, and I doubt if she's been on a hike a since that ascent of McLoughlin at age eight. She's more of a workout-in-a-gym-on-a-treadmill type. Or an elliptical exerciser or StairMaster type.

Sara, my middle daughter, was an entirely different breed than Jennifer. She invented complaining and honed it to a fine art. Admonitions about "stiff upper lips" and being a "brave soldier" bounced off her psyche like water off car wax. I once took Sara on a half-mile hike to a beautiful little lake in the Siskiyou Wilderness. The trail was perfectly level from beginning to end. Sara complained every step of the way, there and back.

I knew she was doing it just to be ornery. Or out of habit. No human being could possibly tire herself out in that short a time or have so many things to complain about. Besides, we later went on a second hike that day, to a place called the "Shrine of the Redwoods." That trail was three-quarters of a mile long but had exhibits all along the way, geared toward children, with carved statues of elves and fairy-tale characters. Sara didn't complain once on that trail.

There's a lesson in that, somewhere.

Over the years I've developed several techniques, some rather pathetic, to counter the whining. When the kids were little, I would agree to carry them for a specified number of minutes if they would walk for a specified number of minutes without griping. As they got bigger, the carrying time diminished and the time required to earn the reward grew longer. After age seven or so, when they got up into the fifty- to sixty-pound weight range, carrying them even a short distance became out of the question.

Carrying was a last resort even when they were little. Although they invariably seemed to end up on my shoulders, all sorts of ploys preceded it. Least effective was singing "The Happy Wanderer" at the top of my lungs and exhorting the kids to join in the choral merriment. The more successful gambits seemed to involve money, or bribery, if you will. I'd pay them for not whining, usually so much per minute. Their earnings would drop to zero the instant they said anything negative.

They almost never ended up with any money.

I'm happy to report that somewhere along the line, for reasons I can't explain, some of my love of the outdoors managed to sink in with Sara. These days she and I try to go hiking whenever she's in town. Our most recent outing was to a lake in the Trinity Alps Wilderness. A talented writer, Sara wrote a chapter in one of my hiking guidebooks, about a trail near her college in Portland that she'd been on and I hadn't. It was a very good chapter, written from a completely different perspective than anything I ever wrote.

All of which leads us to Anna, my youngest child, born when I was almost forty. Early on I was determined that Anna, of all my children, would be the heir to the Bernstein hiking legacy. I'd failed with Jenny and Sara but by golly, I would not fail with Anna. We'd be the archetypical idyllic family if I had to break Anna's arm. Both her arms.

The dream started to fall apart the very first time I took Anna hiking, when she was six months old. My wife and I hiked to the top of Mount Baldy, a small peak just outside the town where we lived. I carried Anna in a back-pack seat for infants. I won't even bring up that it was my first hike of the season or that I was badly out of shape and overweight. Anna's contribution, in addition to constant fussing and squirming, was to spend every instant of the trip either pulling my hair, gouging her fingers into my ears or poking my eyes out.

As it turned out, that was a good day in the saga of Anna the Hiker. I took her hiking a few more times but she proved even more exasperating than Sara, if possible.

That's why I was shocked when, during a drive through northern California to visit our oldest daughter, Anna actually asked me to take her hiking. She was ten at the time and had never asked to be taken hiking before. Most of the time she went to great lengths to avoid being taken hiking. In fact, none of my children had ever asked to be taken hiking.

Heaven forbid.

At the time of Anna's request, we were in the car heading south on Interstate 5, near Mount Shasta. Shasta is an immense, solitary volcano, the major landmark of the California Far North and one of the world's most beautiful mountains.

Where the interstate crests atop a small pass, a large, barren, steep-sided cinder cone rises almost straight up from the side of the road. The formation is called Black Butte and it's 6,200 feet high, which is 2,500 feet higher than the freeway but nearly 8,000 feet lower than Mount Shasta, 5 miles away. On overcast days when Shasta is hidden in fog and clouds, it's not unusual to see tourists pulled off on the side of the freeway, photographing Black Butte, thinking it to be Shasta.

Something in Black Butte apparently sparked Anna's imagination. Maybe it reminded her of a movie she'd seen on the Disney Channel. Maybe it was that she could see not only the entire mountain but also the entire trail, from the freeway. Maybe it was because from the backseat of the car, the path didn't appear that difficult. Whatever her motivation, whatever momentary spell came over her, I quickly agreed to take her.

Besides, I'd never been on the Black Butte Trail myself and always thought it looked pretty interesting. On that, Anna and I agreed. With its barren volcanic starkness, Black Butte, to me, evoked images of the terrible wastelands in the realm of the Mordor, in the last chapters of the *Lord of the Rings* trilogy.

"Please Daddy," Anna said. "Pleeeease take me up Black Butte."

How could I refuse? Anna and I shook hands and agreed to return in a couple of weeks. It was mid-June at the time and Black Butte, unlike most other high-mountain trails in the region, was just about snow-free. So there was nothing to stop us.

At least nothing I could have anticipated.

PART 2

GOOD HIKING SHOES FOR CHILDREN ARE HARD TO FIND. LOTS OF KID'S SHOES ARE manufactured that look like hiking shoes, but they're too often all show and no substance, designed to make youngsters and adults think they've purchased the real thing. Not that there aren't excellent children's hiking shoes to be had. There are lots of them. Parents often have no problem spending hundreds of dollars on hiking shoes for themselves. But when it comes to their children, they are reluctant to spend money on footwear that will be outgrown in a few months. So they too often end up purchasing cheapies that look like real hiking shoes but may not be.

If I've learned anything about hiking with children, however, it is that shelling out a little extra money on shoes is an excellent investment. You needn't purchase a fancy boot, either. A good, well-made, well-fitting gym shoe, walking shoe, or cross-trainer will do nicely, although athletic shoes can be as spendy as hiking boots.

When Anna and I left for our eagerly anticipated ascent of Black Butte, on a sunny October day with the temperature in the sixties, the last thing I worried about was her shoes. She had on a pair of simple, well-broken-in kids' cloth-top sneakers. The kind she always wore. I had on the usual leather-top sneakers that I always wore. My shoes cost eighty bucks. Hers cost eight.

I never dreamed that her shoes would become a problem.

I had attempted to locate the Black Butte Trailhead once before, twenty years earlier, before they built the nice little parking area. I'd started in the town of Weed and just kept circling the mountain in my car, taking every side road that seemed to get close. That was how you often located trailheads in the early 1970s. I never did find the trailhead but I managed to drive a quarter of the way up the peak.

While preparing for my hike with Anna, I obtained the official "Shasta-Trinity National Forest Recreational Opportunity Guide" for the Black Butte Trail. The flyer gave detailed trailhead instructions that bore no resemblance to the route of my adventure of twenty years earlier. With the help of the flyer, I easily located the little trailhead parking area and Anna and I started walking. After a brief, level jaunt through the woods, we emerged on the flank on the volcanic cone, on the section of trail most obvious from the freeway. The segment was very steep, very rocky, very exposed, and above all, very, very long.

Actually, it wasn't quite as barren or exposed as I thought it would be. As seen from a car on the freeway, the impression of Black Butte is of a giant gravel pile devoid of vegetation and hostile to all life. Up close you can see that the steep gravel slopes support a fair quantity of pine trees, sun-loving shrubs, and wildflowers. There are almost enough trees to land you into the shade every now and then, if you play your cards right.

Anna, bless her heart, didn't start complaining until we were almost 1.5 miles into the 2.5-mile hike to the summit, three-quarters of the way up the long, steep traverse of the mountain's main flank. I'd purposely gone very slowly up to that point, so Anna wouldn't tire herself too quickly (or "peak too soon," if you will). I figured if I beat her to the punch by suggesting rest breaks, she'd have less to gripe about. We'd stopped and rested at least twice when the complaining began. That's not counting short breaks.

The first time we rested, I gave her a lesson in compass reading, as part of my master plan to keep her occupied and distracted. With Mount Shasta a couple of miles away and other noteworthy summits dotting the horizon, it was the perfect location for such a lesson. In case you're interested, Mount Shasta lies at a bearing north 52 degrees east of Black Butte. And Mount McLoughlin is N 12 E of Black Butte.

Anna seemed to enjoy the lesson. So did I.

And by the way, I almost never bring a compass on my hikes. In twenty-five years I'd never needed one. I brought it that time for the sole purpose of entertaining Anna.

Our second major rest stop was a long, leisurely lunch under a large, windswept pine tree. My wife had packed tuna salad sandwiches for us, along with trail mix and a Baggie full of Oreo cookies. I love Oreo cookies, although I don't eat them very often because they're too fattening. I also love tuna salad sandwiches but find that they can be a little hard to digest when you're exhausted and have been hiking for miles. Tuna salad produces a fair amount of stomach acid.

Anyhow, just as we were nearing the end of the long initial pitch, just when I thought I just might be home free, Anna started in. As it turned out, her complaint was very legitimate.

"Daddy," my beautiful young offspring announced in an angelic voice, "my shoes hurt."

"You mean your feet hurt," I corrected. "Shoes are inanimate objects that have no feeling."

"Don't be stupid, Daddy. You know what I mean."

After a few more steps and several dozen more complaints, I stopped to have a look. None of my usual "brave-soldier-stiff-upperlip" exhortations had worked (they never do), and she seemed genuinely uncomfortable.

She explained that the seam on the back of her tennis shoes was rubbing on her heels. On inspection, I observed that there were no blisters yet but that the area in question, on her cute little feet, was indeed an angry red. If I'd brought my trusty buck knife (it had been mysteriously lost or stolen five years earlier), I'd have simply sliced off the offending shoe part. But I didn't have a buck knife.

It was actually kind of a grim situation. We were considerably more than halfway up the trail so even if we turned back, Anna was facing a lengthy trek and a situation that could only get worse.

I stood there stalling, trying to act reassuring and in control, trying to figure out what to do. I couldn't think of a thing. Finally I decided to check my pockets to see if anything therein inspired an idea. It was a long shot because I don't usually carry much in my pockets. A little bit of cash, a wallet, and a watch. That's about it.

My hand landed on my checkbook, in the back pocket of my jeans. I wasn't sure why I'd brought the checkbook. Normally I leave it in the car because of the extra weight. I've never once written a check while on a hike.

The checkbook proved to be a lifesaver. Grinning triumphantly and basking in the blinding aura of my brilliance, I deftly removed the check pad and register from the plastic cover. Then I ripped the cover in half, lengthwise along the fold. I had to bite it to get a tear going but it eventually came apart pretty evenly.

I inserted one half of the check book cover in each of Anna's shoes, lining the inserts up so they reached from under the back of her foot, up the rear of her shoe, perfectly and comfortably covering the part of the shoe that was rubbing against her heel.

There were no further complaints from Anna, about either hurting shoes or hurting feet. The only problem was that I had to adjust the inserts every five or ten minutes because they kept trying to either work their way out of the shoe or slide off center.

A small price to pay.

Not long after my ingenious solving of Anna's shoe problem, we arrived at the part of the mountain not visible from a passing car on the interstate. Having just surmounted the peak's conical flank, the path made a sharp switchback, then leveled off and entered a narrow canyon between the main summit and two small subpeaks. Unlike the main flank, there was almost no vegetation whatsoever in the canyon, except for a few brave saxifrages (rock-breaking wildflowers). Mostly the canyon contained giant heaps of ash, pumice, and lava rock in a brilliant color display ranging from pink to purple to gray to white. It was a terrific place, if you like multicolored rocks and don't like plants.

The little canyon was relatively level and posed no impediment to my rapidly tiring child. On the canyon's far end, the path made a second switchback and began climbing the mountain's ultimate summit. This final section was much steeper than any segment heretofore but I could tell from the map that we were less than half a mile from the top.

Anna and I had a long rest and a long debate at the second switchback. It was the same old thing: She wanted to turn back, and I wanted to continue to the summit. After much persuasion, to my great relief, my wonderful child agreed to give it one more shot. So we plodded on, Anna dragging herself painfully with every step. To tell the truth, I was beginning to poop out myself.

I didn't tell Anna that.

The last part of the trail, approaching the summit, passed through some sheltered areas containing lots of pine trees and therefore lots of shade. Then, finally . . . grimy, sweaty, out of breath, and exhausted . . . we arrived on top.

To our surprise, the summit teemed with hiking humanity, even though we hadn't seen a single other person during the rest of the trek. There had been a bunch of cars parked at the trailhead, though. Since there was only room for one person at a time on the summit, we had to wait our turn.

The actual peak was a small, steep-sided rock outcrop about 3 feet square. Getting up it involved a little scrambling. The view was tremendous, though. You could see not only Mount Shasta and Mt. McLoughlin, but also

Mount Eddy, the Marble Mountains, the Trinity Alp, and Castle Crags. Not to mention the entire length of Interstate 5, from Siskiyou Summit in Oregon to somewhere south of the town of Dunsmuir.

I took a picture of Anna at the summit and she took one of me. She looked adorable in her long brown pigtails, T-shirt, shorts, $8.00 tennis shoes, and little day pack (I looked adorable, too, but not nearly as adorable as Anna). I made a point to elaborately congratulate Anna on her accomplishment. I told her to smile and look triumphant for the photo. She tried valiantly but she just didn't have a smile in her.

I understood.

"Do we have to hike all the way back down, Daddy?" she asked.

"I'm afraid so," I replied.

"I'm not sure I can make it."

"You'll make it. It's much easier than the hike up. Besides, what choice do you have?"

PART 3

"COULDN'T YOU CALL A HELICOPTER OR SOMETHING?" ANNA SUGGESTED AS WE started on the return journey, back to the car.

"Wouldn't you know it?" I replied. "I plum forgot my two-way radio."

That was in the days before people started carrying cell phones on hikes, back in the dawn of time, in the distant pioneer era of the early 1990s.

I explained to my daughter that even if we called a helicopter, there would be no place for it to land. And even if it could land, they'd charge us thousands of dollars. So our best plan was to face the music and get it over with.

As I explained all this, I tried to cover as much ground as possible. Anna seemed to do better when I engaged her in conversation than when I left her to her private thoughts. Her private thoughts all seemed to center on how much her legs hurt.

My *engage-her-in-conversation* gambit didn't last long. I could tell that her complaints weren't idle; she was genuinely exhausted. I was well aware, even before we left home, that my daughter was not an active type or very athletic. That's why I'd been trying to go slowly and take it easy. I tried carrying her, briefly, but she weighed eighty pounds and if I did that for very

Anna, refusing to budge on Black Butte

long, I would be the one in need of a helicopter rescue. Suffice it to say, no amount of rest short of several hours in bed would resuscitate poor little Anna or restore her spirits. Unfortunately, it was starting to get late and we didn't have time for too many more lengthy respites.

Despite her complaints, Anna managed to plod on, somehow, until we arrived at the exact same spot where I'd put the inserts into her shoes. They were still doing their job, by the way. Rather well, considering. I'd gotten so adept at shoving them back into her shoes every few minutes that I could do it without either of us breaking stride. Anna hadn't complained about her feet since I'd constructed the inserts.

Thank heaven for small miracles.

At the windswept pine where I'd worked the miracle of the checkbook inserts, Anna stopped, sat down, and announced that she wasn't going any farther; this was the end of the line, she'd had it. She informed me that she was fully prepared to spend the rest of her life at this spot regardless of the consequences. She made it clear that she wasn't just talking about a long rest, either. She was not taking another step no matter what I did or said.

"So there," she concluded, with her arms folded in front of her and the most singularly determined look I'd ever seen on her face. She was not kidding.

I had no idea what to do. I wanted to trip to be fun, memorable. If I yelled, argued, or forced her, it would ruin the experience. And yet we couldn't just stay there. Spending the night was out of the question because even though it was a warm, late-spring day, nights can get pretty chilly that time of year at that elevation. Besides, we had no food left. Not to mention my wife would get frantic if we failed to return home.

I decided just to wait, hoping that once Anna got a little rest, she'd realize how foolish she was being and start walking again. Twenty minutes later, though, she was as resolute as ever. And I was getting angry but trying not to show it.

That's when the second miracle occurred (the first one being the miracle of the shoe inserts). It was a real miracle this time. In all my years of hiking, over hundreds of pathways, I'd never seen anything like it from a hiking trail.

I first observed the miracle out of the corner of my eye and didn't think much about it. I hadn't noticed it at all on the way up. As it was, it took a few minutes for the vision to sink in, to penetrate my awareness. Yet there it was, an aura of light, a shimmering yellow rainbow far in the distance, at the base of the mountain. It beckoned to us like the star in the east had beckoned the Magi to follow, two thousand years earlier.

The Golden Arches.

The McDonald's in Weed.

"I'll be darned," I said, trying to sound nonchalant even though I was in awe. "You can see McDonald's from here. I've never seen a McDonald's from a trail before. It must be a sign."

"Of course it's a sign. It's a McDonald's sign. I want to go to McDonald's. Can we, Daddy, when we're done hiking?"

"Of course. It's only a ten-minute drive from the trailhead."

"Goody. Thank you, Daddy."

With a perfect child's grin, Anna bolted ahead of me, down the trail, like a jackrabbit in a headlight.

We quickly made it to the car, with me praising the Almighty Creator of the Universe, and the Golden Arches, with every step. Soon after, we were feasting on a Happy Meals in air-conditioned, tile-floored comfort. Or Anna was feasting on a Happy Meal. I was feasting on a Filet-O-Fish and a strawberry shake.

Oddly enough, Anna became a vegetarian soon after the McDonald's episode and remains one to this day. I doubt if the Weed McDonald's had anything to do with it. Still, whenever I tell the story of our ascent of Black Butte in Anna's presence, she always closes with the comment,

"I can't believe we ended up at McDonald's."

The caveat came three days later. Back then, I used to write up some of my hikes for the little Grant Pass newspaper. They used a photo of Anna with my story, the one where she was sitting on the Black Butte summit, with Interstate 5 far below in the distance. If you had a magnifying glass, you could barely make out the Weed McDonald's just over her right shoulder.

Everyone in Anna's class at school, including her teacher, made a big deal out of the article and photo. A lot of people did comment, though, that while it was an adorable picture, Anna didn't look very happy.

"She wasn't very happy at the time," I explained. "But she cheered up later on."

THE HIKE: *Black Butte Trail, Shasta-Trinity National Forest, Mount Shasta City, California*

LENGTH *(one way): 2.5 miles.*

DIRECTIONS: *Take I-5 in northern California to the central Mount Shasta City exit. Proceed through town to Alma Street, following signs to the Everitt Memorial Highway. One mile up the Everitt Highway, a dirt road (Penny Pines) takes off left. Penny Pines makes a hard left just off the pavement and a 90-degree right 1 mile later. It's then 1 mile down the power-line road to the short trailhead spur. Turn left for the small trailhead parking area.*

HIKE THIRTEEN
THE LOST MOUNTAIN

PART 1

WELL, THEN," SAID MY WIFE, PATRICIA, WITH ONLY A SLIGHT HINT OF regret, "I guess it's over."

We were sitting opposite each other on oak chairs in the office of J. Wendell Thayer, family therapist. The room smelled of lemon furniture polish, which I presumed was regularly and liberally applied to the oak table, chairs, and desk. No amount of polish would wipe away the years of accumulated tarnish on Pat's and my relationship.

With Pat's proclamation in Dr. Thayer's office, twenty-nine years of marriage, half a lifetime of shared joy, heartaches, and life-cycle landmarks, went down the tubes. They were in the sewer, gone, finished. The year 2000 had been a bad year all the way around and I remember sitting in that office, with a knot in the pit of my stomach, hoping that the Third Millennium, A.D. would eventually get better. It couldn't get any worse.

In 2000 my youngest daughter graduated high school and moved away. As much as I wanted her to stick around, I was at least prepared for it. Then my wife also moved away. That I was not prepared for. She was the same person I'd literally dreamed about since childhood, the same person with whom I'd experienced more miracles than I could count, not the least of which were our three magnificent daughters and three equally magnificent grandchildren. I fully realized, of course, that despite the length of our time together, and despite my profound respect for Patricia as a mother (not to mention as a contributor to the betterment of the planet), our marriage had been shaky from the start. Over the years the situation had grown steadily worse, not better.

Now, finally, there was no other reasonable conclusion. The time had come for us both to move on.

I reacted by doing what I often do. I selected a beautiful, remote place I'd always wanted to visit, drove by myself for two or three days, and went hiking there. On this occasion I picked Great Basin National Park, in eastern Nevada.

I never dreamed I would end up losing a 12,000-foot mountain, or an 11,000-foot mountain, depending on how you round it off, during my hike. Losing the mountain, of course, was no a great tragedy. It was actually lost only to me. To the rest of the universe, it remained right where it was supposed to be. But the experience underscored the irony of my situation. First I'd lost my wife, then I lost an entire mountain. How inept can a person get?

I never did find the mountain, although I eventually figured out what happened to it.

I still haven't figured out what happened to my marriage.

Losing the mountain reminded me of something Pat used to say, that always irritated me: "You'd lose your head if it wasn't nailed on."

It annoyed me when she said that because I knew she was right. She was always right. I lose things all the time. I'm the typical absentminded professor, except I'm not a professor. I'll be working at my desk, set my pen down for two seconds, and when I go to pick it up, it's gone. And instead of writing, and accomplishing something, I spend the next twenty minutes frantically looking for it, shoving piles of papers around my desk while mumbling obscenities.

Realistically, I assume this happens to everyone. It's the way of the world. Part of the human condition. There is no way around it.

As a hiker, on the other hand, I pride myself on my directional sense, my ability to find my way. I've been forgetful, to be sure. Over the years I've left my lunch on the kitchen counter fifty times. And my camera. And my map. And my canteen. But that's not the same as getting lost. I never get lost.

Absolutely never.

Well, almost never.

Coincidentally, the question I'm most frequently asked by readers of my hiking trail guides is, "Do you ever get lost?"

The short answer to that is, "No, of course not, don't be ridiculous."

The long answer is a little more complicated. "That depends on what you mean by lost."

To me, *lost* does not include the thousand or so occasions when the trail mysteriously petered out and it took me a few minutes to find it again. Or the times when the trail petered out and I didn't find it again so I turned around and went home. Or the times when I inadvertently took the wrong path, ended up where I shouldn't have been, and had to retrace my steps.

By my definition, none of those circumstances constituted getting lost because I always knew pretty much where I was and how to get home.

On four occasions, in five hundred hikes, I managed to lose all trace of the trail in both directions. I could not find my way forward and I could not find my way back. All four times I ended up bushwhacking cross-country, on dead reckoning, without map or compass. Each time, miraculously, I emerged precisely at the trailhead, within a few feet of my car, although on one occasion I was forced to spend the night in the forest, high up on a mountain, in the middle of nowhere, without jacket, food, or water.

But only once did I misplace an entire mountain.

My first getting lost experience happened in 1975, a few years after I moved to Oregon. I was hired to teach a summer outdoor recreation class at Rogue Community College, in Grants Pass, where I had moved only three years earlier. One of our outings involved scaling Mount McLoughlin, the 9,495-foot volcanic cone, that happens to be the highest peak in the southern half of our state. It's a difficult 5-mile hike in which the last mile rises 1,700 feet over boulders and loose gravel in rapidly thinning air.

Following the hike, the class planned to spend the night at a nearby campground and do some more exploring of the region the next day.

We had twenty students in the class, and two teachers. The hike to the summit went reasonably well. Amazingly, despite the difficulty, everybody made it, including a sixty-eight-year-old lady. Some made it much more quickly and easily than others. Some made it much more quickly and easily than I did.

On the way back the group became extremely spread out along the trail. As teacher, I brought up the rear to make sure everyone got off the summit and was headed in the right direction. I'd walked with several different students on the way up. On the way down I mostly hiked with the young man who happened to be with me when I hit the top. He was a friendly, nondescript fellow maybe nineteen or twenty years old.

I don't know how it happened but halfway down, we inadvertently started following a false trail. We'd been engrossed in a conversation about how to tell white fir from grand fir, and just weren't paying attention. It was actually the second time we'd gotten onto a false trail and we should have learned our lesson. The first time we'd followed the errant path for only a few feet. Then we noticed our mistake and backtracked to the real trail. The second time we followed the false trail for more than a hundred feet. False trails don't usually last that long.

When we discovered our error, we thought we could see the real trail below us to the left. At least the fellow with me thought he could see the trail. So instead of backtracking, we decided to climb down to it, which was a colossal mistake. It was not the real trail. It was not any trail. It was not anything at all. And we couldn't find the false trail again, either.

We ended up hiking cross-country all the way down the mountain, with no map, no compass, no jackets, and no food. When it got dark, we slept on the ground in the woods, or tried to sleep, with no sleeping bags. Luckily, it was the warmest night of the year. We later found out that the low that night at Lake of the Woods Resort, not far from the trailhead, had been fifty-eight degrees. The low the night before was thirty-six.

The kid and I stopped hiking when it got dark. After lying awake all night, trying not to stare at the shadows, we started hiking again the instant it became light enough to see. Within minutes after we began hiking in the morning, we arrived at a large creek. It was the first water we'd passed. We followed the creek upstream a quarter mile to the trailhead parking lot. From there, we hitchhiked to where we knew the remainder of the class was camping for the night, 3 miles away. We arrived at seven o'clock.

We quickly learned that we were not the only people in the class who'd failed to show up. A nineteen-year-old young lady was also missing. When she still had not arrived by 9:00 A.M., we called the authorities. Within an hour the Klamath County Search and Rescue Team had launched an all-out search, complete with aerial reconnaissance.

They found her at eleven-thirty, walking down the path 2 miles from the trailhead. She'd gotten lost on the exact same false trail as the kid and I had. Except when she discovered she was lost, she correctly reasoned that her best bet for finding the true path was to hike back up, not down. If worse came to worst, she figured, she would pick up the trail at the summit.

That was almost how long it took her to find the trail. She spent the night in the woods in the middle of nowhere, much higher up than the kid and I, so it was much colder. Also, I had the advantage of being familiar with the surrounding landmarks so I always knew which side of the mountain I was on and pretty much in which direction we were headed. The young woman had no such knowledge.

She said that at one point, she saw the search and rescue plane overhead. She knew it was a search and rescue plane because it was flying low and circling. She said that when she saw the plane, she climbed out onto a rock outcrop, took off her bright red T-shirt, and waved it over her head. But the people in the plane did not see her.

I might add that she was a very well-endowed brunette. I couldn't imagine flying that plane and not seeing her.

I've since climbed Mount McLoughlin half a dozen times, the most recent being in August 2000, not long after I lost the 12,000-foot mountain in Nevada. Although the McLoughlin Trail no longer has any false trails, I'm still very careful to watch where I go, and to follow the blazes on the trees as well as the path.

That's the best way to avoid getting lost.

The second time I got lost was in the Yolla Bolly–Middle Eel Wilderness in northern California, in 1990. The Yolla Bolly ranks high among my favorite hiking places, and not just because it has the longest name of any California wilderness. The Yolla Bolly–Middle Eel Wilderness is very different from the nearby, much larger Trinity Alps Wilderness, with a charm all its own.

I'd been hiking many times in the North and South Yolla Bolly Mountains but had never seen the Middle Eel part of the wilderness until the hike on which I got lost. Most of that portion lay to the west and north of a road embarrassingly called "Indian Dick," a 27-mile gravel route that branched off from another mostly gravel route between Mendocino Pass and the Round Valley Indian Reservation. The entire length of Indian Dick Road paralleled the Upper Middle Eel River. The main Eel River eventually emptied into Humboldt Bay, near Eureka.

Not far from the road's end, Indian Dick Road crossed a rocky little side canyon, then climbed up onto a grassy knob topped by a split-rail drift fence, a large rock outcrop, and a small grove of valley oaks. The drift fence marked the trailhead I was looking for that day, one of the best-landscaped trailheads I'd ever seen. I parked the car and started hiking along the Foster Glades Trail, which was supposed to connect with the Asa Bean Trail after a mile, then lead down to the river after another mile.

I'd hiked about 500 feet, around the back of the rock outcrop and a little beyond, when the trail vanished. I did not notice a large wooden post, 300 feet to my left, on the other side of a grassy expanse at the edge of some woods. Had I noticed the post, and had I figured out that it was a trail marker, I would not have gotten lost. But I did none of those things. I kept looking for the trail on the ground, directly in front of me.

With all that available grass, much of the land thereabouts was leased to cattle grazing. The place was therefore riddled with cow paths. The cow paths wove in and out, started and stopped without warning, and were pretty much useless to anyone but cows. I did not realize I was following cow paths at first. I thought I'd found the continuation of the trail. When I finally figured it out, I was too committed to turn back. I doubt if I could have retraced my steps by then in any case.

Somehow I ended up at the river. Or at least I ended up atop a 20-foot bluff above the river. It was very pretty. Well worth the hike. And I'd only walked a mile to get there. My intended route had been 2 miles. Now all I had to do was find my way back.

Actually, returning to my car wasn't that difficult. I just headed uphill, away from the river, making no effort to follow any of the cow paths. Pretty soon the big rock outcrop came into view, and the trailhead, and my car. And once again, the Bernstein homing instinct proved true and accurate.

Unlike the McLoughlin and Middle Eel experiences, the third time I got lost, in Oregon's Sky Lakes Wilderness, I hadn't a clue how to find the trailhead. Had I not eventually located the correct path, I might have wandered aimlessly for days.

The Sky Lakes Wilderness, just south of Crater Lake National Park, contains a wonderfully named path called the Nannie Creek Trail. The trail leads to a place called Puck Lake, also wonderfully named. I hiked the Nannie Creek Trail in June 1998, after an exceptionally snowy winter. A mile into the trek, I began encountering snow patches, some of which were pretty extensive. At one point I lost the trail in a snow-filled ravine. So I climbed a nearby paralleling ridge, which was maybe 50 feet higher than the ravine and out of the snow. I was hoping I could see the lake from the ridge, then reach it by hiking cross-country. I could not. I followed the ridgetop for an eighth of a mile when, to my surprise, I picked up the trail again.

Half a mile later, in the middle of another long snow patch, I lost the trail for good. That time I couldn't see any way to sleuth out the ongoing pathway or continue the trek. There appeared to be continuous snow ahead of me. I saw no tree blazes and no clearly defined ridges or valley bottoms that the path followed. Nothing. So I gave it up, turned around and started back toward the trailhead.

Except I couldn't find the trail out, either. That was not good. The path in had taken me through a maze of steep hillsides and dense woods with no obvious landmarks. I could never have found my way back on dead reckoning, cross-country hiking, or climbing a low ridge for a better view. The low-ridge gambit worked that one time but usually doesn't.

The culprit was the heavy snowfall of the previous winter. What was 2 or 3 feet of snow when I visited had once been 30 or 40 feet, with an exceptionally high water content. So I was essentially walking on ice, not snow, and therefore left no footprints. Had I noticed that, I would have scuffed my feet as I walked, or something, to make sure I left tracks. I do that frequently on faint trails.

On discovering I was lost, I panicked for a second, spent several minutes looking for the trail, then backtracked to where I'd first realized my situation. From there I started fanning out in wider and wider circles, always returning to the point where I'd gotten lost. On the third circle, the reluctant path turned up.

Boy was I relieved.

PART 2

THE 12,000-FOOT-HIGH MOUNTAIN IN NEVADA THAT I MISPLACED WAS CALLED Pyramid Peak. And it was actually only 11,922 feet high, the fourth highest peak in Nevada's Great Basin National Park. Wheeler Peak, 3 miles north of Pyramid Peak, is the park's highest summit at 13,063 feet. Wheeler Peak is also Nevada's highest mountain entirely inside the state. The state's actual high point is in a range called the White Mountains, which lie partly in Nevada and partly in California. The range culminates at White Mountain, which rises to 14,250 feet just over the California line. Nevada's highest elevation is the spot where White Mountain's eastern flank crosses the state line.

Whether or not Wheeler Peak is Nevada's highest, the mountain ranks high among America's most beautiful. You could never lose Wheeler Peak on a hike. Not in a million years. Of course it's pretty hard to lose Pyramid Peak, too. For most people.

I climbed Wheeler Peak in 1982, before it became part of Great Basin National Park. At the time, what is now the park consisted of Lehmann Cave National Monument and the Wheeler Peak Scenic Area of Toiyabe National Forest. The climb was one of those experiences to which your mind returns again and again, especially when things aren't going well in your life. Even though the Wheeler Peak Trail gains 3,100 feet in 4 miles, I didn't find it that difficult. The scenery, the isolation, and the contrast with the stark surrounding desert were so overwhelming that I tended not to think about the difficulty.

Even though I'm a forester by trade and live in one of the nation's most lushly forested regions—or maybe because of those facts—I have a particular fondness for barren mountains that jut starkly up out of the middle of the desert. By those standards Wheeler Peak had it all, great height, great beauty, great juttiness, lots of surrounding desert, barren slopes, active glaciers, beautiful alpine lakes, brilliant aspen groves, piñon and juniper stands at lower elevations, Engelmann spruce and subalpine fir in the more sheltered pockets, and limber pines at tree line. And above all, on the highest, most exposed slopes, there was a significant population of bristlecone pine, earth's longest-living species.

Bristlecone pines are amazing. They live in the harshest places you can imagine, gnarled relics that at any given moment are 98 percent dead, except for two or three barely noticeable living branches. They can survive that way for up to six thousand years. They are not all old and gnarled, either. For their first few hundred years, they stand straight and proud, until the harshness of the environment starts to wear at them.

My day on Wheeler Peak in 1982 went surprisingly smoothly. I spent the night at the Wheeler Peak Campground, located just past the summit trailhead at the end of Wheeler Peak Road. By six in the morning, I was on the trail. For the first mile the popular route ascended steeply to the ridgetop. It then leveled off somewhat, following a dome-shaped contour to the summit, with plummeting cliffs to the east, not unlike Half Dome at Yosemite. Apart from the areas that had been deeply gouged out by glaciers, such as the northwest face of Wheeler Peak, the summits in the South Snake Range—of which Wheeler was the highest—were all rather gently rounded.

By 9:00 A.M. I was standing atop Wheeler Peak looking out across the desert, beautiful Lake Stella and the campground, and the chain of high peaks to the south.

The most interesting Wheeler Peak feature was the heliograph station. During the 1880s the U.S. military used it for experiments in sending mirror messages across the desert from mountaintop to mountaintop. These days it looks like a rock pile, which is exactly what it is these days.

I'd been hiking in Nevada a few times aside from the Wheeler Peak trek. The first time was in the Toiyabe Range, south of Austin, in 1978. I'd also hiked on Mount Charleston, the ski area north of Las Vegas. And I'd hiked in the aforementioned White Mountains, but not the Nevada portion.

I'd been to the Wheeler Peak area several times prior to climbing it in 1982. On my first visit, in 1968, I was by myself and stopped off briefly to take a tour of Lehmann Cave. It was spectacular. So spectacular, I took my wife (now my ex-wife) and oldest daughter, Jennifer, there in 1972.

In 1980 I stopped by with my middle daughter, Sara, on the way to visit my sister in Texas. It was May when Sara and I visited. I tried to drive up Wheeler Peak Campground Road, a paved, 12-mile route leading to a glacial cirque, a huge aspen grove, and trailheads to several small lakes, the bristlecone pine forest, and the main summit. But the road was snowed over for the last mile. Still, the scenery was unbelievably beautiful and very enticing.

In 2000 my attraction to the Wheeler Peak area had not abated. It had been eighteen years, after all, since my last visit. I decided that I wanted to see Wheeler Peak again. If I went hiking, it would likely be on another trail in Great Basin National Park, probably the path to Baker Lake, which I'd read occupied a spectacular, steep walled basin. And if I took the Baker Lake Trail, I might as well climb Pyramid Peak, the highest mountain in Great Basin National Park outside the three-summit Wheeler Peak cluster. Pyramid Peak rises directly above Baker Lake to the southeast.

On a Saturday morning in July, I got into my car and headed east. Well, south, actually, then east. I followed Interstate 5 south to Mount Shasta, California, then traveled through Susanville to Reno. From Reno I found my way via to Fallon, Nevada. Then I lit out across the fabled US 50.

US 50 across Nevada fit my mood perfectly. Especially the 250 miles from Fallon to Ely, near the Utah line. The state of Nevada has posted signs along the route that say US 50 THE LONELIEST ROAD IN AMERICA. Only two towns disrupt the loneliness, Austin and Eureka, both mining towns from the nineteenth century built on mountainsides, mostly because that's where the mines were but also to avoid the intense heat of the valley bottom. Austin looks down on the Reese River Valley, which Mark Twain wrote about in the book *Roughing It*.

The highway crosses the true Great Basin, with long, narrow, north–south trending mountain ranges rising to 10,000 or 12,000 feet and vast stretches of low, sagebrush-covered desert in between. Often, when you come down out of the mountains, you can see the road straight ahead, across the desert, for as much as 20 miles before it climbs the next range and disappears from view. In the expanses of desert valley, there is often not a house, not a person, not a sign of human habitation except for the lonely, endless road.

At one point I was stopped by a flagger due to road construction. I could see cars coming in the opposite direction, cars that needed to get where I was before I could proceed, but they were 10 miles away. I watched and watched but they never seemed to get any closer or move very much until the last mile or so.

Sometimes, when I hit one of those stretches where you can see 20 miles of road, I found myself thinking about Manhattan Island, in New York City. Manhattan is 12 miles long (maybe 12.5) and 2 miles wide, with nearly two million people living on it. You could fit a hundred Manhattan Islands in just one of those barren Nevada expanses. That's two hundred million people. The population of Nevada was 1.8 million as of 2000.

I did not think much about Patricia or the divorce as I drove, although I worried I might, what with all that time alone. As always, the trip proved renewing and uplifting. Any troubles I had been experiencing in my life were quickly left far, far behind as I sped ever-forward in my fragile little world of protected unreality.

After eating dinner in the gambling casino in Ely, I rented a motel room for the night. I planned to backpack to Baker Lake and camp out the following night.

I slept amazingly well, much better than I usually sleep in a motel. I did not have good dreams, though. I dreamed I was twenty-one years old and my father had just died. The scene was as it actually occurred in 1964. Following the Jewish ritual of shiva, the mirrors and pictures in our house were all covered and a steady stream, almost an onslaught, of relative and friends, many of whom I didn't know from Adam, or Eve, came a-calling with food and condolences.

"I'm so sorry," they all said to my mother. "He was a wonderful man."

"Poor dears," they said to my sister and brother, "what a tragic loss."

And to me, everyone kept saying, "Well then, I guess it's over."

I fell asleep at 8:30 P.M. and woke up at 5:00 A.M. I wasn't exactly raring to go but I was reasonably rested and looking forward to two days in the Nevada mountains. Which meant two days away from Grants Pass and my "situation." Until the dream, I thought I'd been suppressing the divorce pretty well. I'd been doing a lot of denying and suppressing. But I never could fool my unconscious.

In the morning, after a fabulously greasy breakfast at the casino, I drove to the park. Wheeler Peak came into view a few miles past Ely, looking higher, steeper, and more lovely than any mountain I'd passed thus far but still just a jutting island in the immense desert. I pulled into the Baker Creek Campground at eight o'clock, to use the facilities and fill my water bottles. The Baker Creek Campground proved to be much smaller than the Wheeler Peak Campground. Situated at 7,500 feet rather than 10,000 feet, it doesn't get quite as cold at night as the Wheeler Campground but is still much more pleasant than the desert. The Baker Creek Campground is located in a stand of piñon pines, one of my favorite trees and the source of the pine nuts they sell in stores. Piñon pines grow at middle elevations in the desert mountains. They are handsome little trees that always looked to me as though they were placed there by a professional landscape architect.

The Baker Creek Trailhead, where I planned to hike, is located 1 mile past the campground. After some last-minute preparations, double-checking that I hadn't forgotten anything, I hit the pathway at 9:00 A.M. My backpack contained a day's worth of food, a tent, a sleeping bag, a camera, and sundry other goodies necessary for an overnight campout.

My intended route, my itinerary, included the 6-mile hike up Baker Creek to Baker Lake, where I would spend the night. At daybreak the next morning, I planned to leave my backpack at the lake and make the difficult 2-mile journey up to Johnson Pass. From the pass I would walk off trail for a final mile, along the supposedly smooth and treeless ridge, to the top of Pyramid Peak. Then I would return to Baker Lake, gather my belongings, hike back down to the car, and spend the night at Baker Creek Campground.

The Baker Creek segment of the trip proved relaxing and scenic, even though it climbed 2,600 feet in 6 miles. I marveled as I hiked how "user friendly" this particular mountain range was, how even the most difficult trails seemed to welcome and offer comfort. Other mountain ranges where

I'd hiked often felt foreboding, as though the mountains were letting you visit as an indulgence and you really were not welcome. This range—higher, prettier, more densely vegetated, and more botanically diverse than other Nevada ranges—offered an oasis of otherworldly tranquility amid the surrounding bleak desert. It was precisely the spiritual and psychological oasis that my heart and mind craved.

The wonderful desert smells, juxtaposed against cooling breezes off the high peaks, kept me cool, comfortable, and happy as I hiked. The path began in a series of broad, open slopes covered with sagebrush, scattered mountain mahogany bushes, and piñon pines. After a mile the path made its way to Baker Creek, which it followed for the next 2 miles, passing some enchanted little spots. Many welcome level pitches greeted me in this section.

At mile 3 the path began climbing a series of steep talus slopes and glacial moraines, with occasional breathtaking vistas into the cirque basins above that encouraged me to keep going despite the steepening path. After 4 miles the path passed the remains of an old cabin. It then swung away from the creek as it continued its ascent of the rocky moraines for 2 more miles. Beginning the second mile, most of the path was in the shade, with quaking aspen in the upland areas and mixed conifers closer to the creek.

The aspen, I should point out, is a fascinating tree. Because of the way the leaves are built, they flutter wildly at the slightest breeze so they appear in almost constant motion. You'd think that with all that fluttering, the presence of aspen would make a person nervous. Quite the contrary; they are very calming. Aspens have a proclivity for seeking out the most beautiful places in the mountains in which to grow and their presence makes those places even prettier. It's a clonal species, which means that when you walk through a forest of the beautiful, light-barked trees, they are actually all the same tree, with interconnected roots.

Just before the trail arrived at the lake, it offered a view into the yellow rock cirque basin adjacent to the Baker Lake Basin. The adjacent basin was a little lower than the Baker Lake Basin and had no lake at the bottom, just a green meadow and an aspen grove. To climb Pyramid Peak, I had to follow a trail from the lake into this adjacent basin. Above the adjacent basin, I could see Johnson Pass and Pyramid Peak. The route from the basin to the pass looked extremely difficult, rising 1,500 feet in one mile. But the route from the pass to the summit appeared to be an easy stroll in the park.

After four hours I arrived at Baker Lake, a ten-acre gem at the base of some absolutely vertical yellow cliffs that rose up from a third of the lakeshore. The rest of the shore was forested with small conifers. The lake's water level obviously fluctuated greatly so only about half the rocky lakebed, the portion closest to the cliffs, contained water.

I didn't want to leave Baker Lake. There was nobody else there, and I found the beauty and serenity overwhelming. It nearly made me cry. I set up my tent, relaxed, cooked a meal, and generally puttered around until dark.

One thing I never could do during my puttering, although I tried, was locate the trail from Baker Lake to Johnson Pass, the one I needed to follow to climb Pyramid Peak. I'd been warned in a chat with a park ranger that the path might be hard to find. I was told to look for rock cairns at the lake's southeast end, but I saw none. Nevertheless, the route was obvious. If I climbed over a small talus slope, I discovered, I could see the adjacent basin and most of the remaining route.

I briefly debated doing all that right away instead of waiting for the next day. But my plan was to complete the hike in the morning after a night's sleep, leaving my backpack at Baker Lake. After climbing the peak, I would return to the lake, retrieve my gear, and hike back down to my car.

The next morning, at seven-thirty, I hit the dirt pathway once again, carrying a canteen of water and a little day pack. I never did find the spot where the trail to Johnson Pass left Baker Lake, but, as I said, the route was obvious. One mile and thirty-five minutes later, in the green meadow in the basin below the pass and adjacent to the Baker Lake, I finally picked up the path, which I followed for a second mile to the ridgetop. That second mile, as expected, bordered on horrible. Not only was it extremely steep, but there wasn't a single tree or square inch of shade. A section in the middle wound through a series of rock outcrops that I found somewhat terrifying. I couldn't see Baker Lake from the trail to Johnson Pass, but I kept expecting it to pop into view at any minute as I gained altitude.

Halfway up the slope, amid the smell of dust and grit, with my forehead, T-shirt, and jacket drenched in perspiration, in the middle of the steepest, rockiest section, it occurred to me that I'd left my camera in my backpack, back at the lake. So my intrepid scaling of Pyramid Peak would be recorded only in memory, not on film. Going back and retrieving the camera was out of the question.

Oh well.

I was perspiring because of the intense sun and laborious task, not because of the heat. It was actually rather cool out, and very windy. Taking off my jacket to alleviate the sweating would have been foolish. The steady, howling breeze against the dampness would have made me extremely cold and possibly exposed me to hypothermia.

At nine that morning I stood atop the barren, featureless Johnson Pass, 11,260 feet, where the trail crossed over the ridge. I was pretty hungry when I hit the pass, and more than a little tired, so when I noticed a gnarled old limber pine all by itself beside the trail, offering a postage-stamp patch of shade, the only shade for miles, I sat down under it and gobbled a few handfuls of trail mix and a few large gulps of water. Then I leaned back and closed my eyes, intending to resume the hike in two or three minutes.

I must have fallen asleep. That's what I thought when I woke up. Brilliant deduction. I had definitely fallen asleep, which had never happened to me before while resting on a hike. When I woke up, groggy and feeling like Rip Van Winkle, I noted from my watch that an hour had passed. No big deal. I still had all day.

I stood up, gathered my gear, and looked around to orient myself. Below me, I was pleased that I could finally see Baker Lake. It was the first time I'd been able to see it since leaving the Baker Lake basin. Baker Lake is on the left, or north, when you stand on the ridgetop and face Pyramid Peak, so I immediately oriented myself in that direction. And there was the summit, the object of my endeavor, a mile away, looking very large and very pyramidal.

The peak was a smooth, treeless dome composed entirely of gravel and scree slops. Half a dozen other peaks in the vicinity had just about the same look and were nearly as high, but I'd studied the map pretty carefully so there wasn't any question in my mind which of the summits was Pyramid Peak. It was the one rising directly up from the pass with Baker Lake on the left.

Climbing Pyramid Peak took about half an hour. Maybe less. The view from the 11,922-foot summit was not quite as impressive as the view from Wheeler Peak had been, but it was stunning nevertheless. And a lot less crowded. I could see Wheeler Peak, the rest of the Snake Range, and the surrounding desert.

All in all I was glad I'd come. There is something about standing on a mountaintop that you poured out your personal sweat to reach that is more satisfying than just about anything else in the world. No wonder some people get addicted to it.

Pyramid Peak

Half an hour later I was back at Baker Lake. It sort of occurred to me as I hiked, in the dark periphery of my awareness, that the trip from the summit to the lake seemed a lot shorter than the trip from the lake to the summit had been. Part of the reason, I assumed, was that I was now going downhill, not uphill. Still, I had no explanation as to why the path now led directly to the lake instead of first going through the adjacent basin. At any rate, I was too tired to allow such trivia to penetrate too far into my consciousness. Mostly I just wanted to get back to my campsite.

When I arrived back at Baker Lake, it seemed somehow different than it had a few hours earlier. At first I attributed it to the changed lighting. But the differences really didn't begin to click in my brain until I discovered that all my gear was missing. I panicked and began searching for my campsite but couldn't find any spot that looked even remotely like it.

I combed the lakeshore in rapid, frantic circles, muttering under my breath and praying that I would find some sort of clue to magically set things right. The idea of my camera and all my camping gear being stolen was unacceptable.

It was only after I sat down on a boulder to collect my thoughts and composure that it dawned on me that during my ascent of Pyramid Peak, I'd seen no evidence of Johnson Lake. In fact, I'd forgotten all about Johnson Lake, although it was very prominent on the map, in a cirque basin immediately south of Johnson Pass. When I faced Pyramid Peak, up on the pass, Johnson Lake should have been visible to my right, with Johnson Peak, only 30 feet lower than Pyramid Peak, rising immediately behind me. On reaching the Pyramid Peak summit, I should have been able to see Johnson Peak behind me and several more 11,000-foot-plus summits in front of me.

As I sat on the boulder, studied the map (which I had not looked at during the hike), and reflected on my hike, I remembered seeing what I'd assumed was Johnson Peak behind me from the summit, to what I'd assumed was the west. According to the map, however, there should also have been an 11,700-foot summit less than 2 miles east of Pyramid Peak. When I'd peered east from the summit, in the direction opposite Johnson Peak, the mountain range plummeted abruptly down to the desert. It was as though the 11,700-foot mountain had vanished without a trace.

Slowly I figured out what happened. What cinched it was the sudden realization that when you climb Pyramid Peak, Wheeler Peak should be easily visible on your left. In fact, it had been on my right. Why I failed to notice this, and dozens of other clues that I was turned around 180 degrees and climbing the wrong mountain, is something I will never be able to fully understand or explain.

Apparently when I awoke from my nap, I'd started walking in the wrong direction, toward Johnson Peak instead of Pyramid Peak. I should have been tipped off by the presence of Johnson Lake, easily visible on my right. Except I mistakenly took it for Baker Lake, which was not visible on my left but which I thought should have been. Once the initial mistake was made, my subconscious apparently suppressed any information that didn't fit.

Thinking Johnson Lake was Baker Lake, I'd climbed Johnson Peak, not Pyramid Peak. As I said, the two summits are nearly identical. Not only had I climbed the wrong mountain, but I was now at Johnson Lake, not Baker Lake. And that was why I could not find my gear.

Chuckling to myself at my stupidity, I hiked back up to the pass and back down to Baker Lake, the real Baker Lake, where my stuff was waiting exactly where I'd left it. I debated climbing Pyramid Peak as I passed it on the pass, the real Pyramid Peak, but decided that one mountain a day was enough.

What a silly guy, I kept thinking.

The other thing I kept thinking was a little more bothersome:

You'd lose your head if it wasn't nailed on.

I maintain, however, that losing the mountain in front of Pyramid Peak was an honest mistake. It could have happened to anybody. Therefore it wasn't really my fault. Not really.

The same might be said about losing my wife.

THE HIKE: *Baker Creek Trail to Baker Lake and Pyramid Peak, Great Basin National Park, Nevada.*

LENGTH *(one way): 9 miles.*

DIRECTIONS: *Take US 50 from Carson City or Sacramento; or US 50A from Fallon, east of Reno, and then US 50, to Ely. It's 325 miles from Reno to Ely. Fifty-seven miles past Ely, still on US 50, turn right (south) onto NV 487 toward Baker, 5 miles away. At Baker, NV 488 heads west, arriving at the Great Basin National Park Visitor Center and Lehman Cave entrance after 6 miles. Just before the visitor center, take the gravel road left for 3 miles to Baker Creek Campground, and for 1 more mile to the Baker Lake Trailhead.*

HIKE FOURTEEN
A VOICE CRYING "IN THE WILDERNESS..."

PART 1

O NE THING I CAN STATE WITH ABSOLUTE ASSURANCE IS THAT GOD TALKS to me. And I know what you're about to say so keep it to yourself. Before you have me shipped off to the psycho ward, I hasten to add that no, I do not hear voices, although I suspect that the only reason for that is God's tolerance for my prejudiced view that hearing voices is not normal. God is certainly powerful enough to speak aloud, if he wanted to. Or if she wanted to. With me, however, God has figured out that it's best to be soft-spoken and tread gently.

Nobody is better at figuring things out than God.

Bear in mind, later in the story, that when I say *God said*, I really mean that words were formed in my head as thoughts. I heard no audible voices. Honest. God communicates most of the time by implanting an idea, not by talking. In our society, in our culture, hearing voices is just too freaky for most people, even if it is God's voice.

Especially if it is God's voice.

Having said all that, here's something that might surprise you: I don't believe in God.

I don't believe in God, yet God talks to me. And furthermore, I talk to God. In fact, we carry on conversations all the time, God and I, like a couple of old gossips chatting over the back fence.

How is that possible?

You have to understand that I am a firm believer in Paradox Theory. In fact, I am the only believer in Paradox Theory. In fact, I invented Paradox Theory.

The Basic Rule of Paradox Theory is this: For every truth in the universe, its exact diametric opposite is also true. This theory is not very useful in understanding scientific method or most Western religions. However, Kabalistic Jews, Buddhists, Hindus, Taoists, Native Americans, Animists, and Earth Mothers all find it perfectly logical. Or at least those Jews, Buddhists, et al., to whom I've explained my theory said they found it logical. Some of them, anyhow.

If I had several hours, I could prove to you the truth of the Basic Rule of Paradox Theory. Of course there is a Prime Corollary to the Basic Rule, which states that the Basic Rule also applies to the Basic Rule. But we won't get into that.

Suffice it to say, I think it's possible to believe in God, deeply and fervently, with all your heart and soul, while at the same time not believe in God, with all the force and conviction of a die-hard skeptic. In fact, I submit to you that a lot of people regard God as I just described, although most will not admit their skepticism for fear of being struck dead if they are wrong. In the Western mind-set, you cannot believe two diametric opposites at the same time. Or at least you cannot admit that you do.

So even though I don't believe in God, I very much believe in God, pray to God every day, and talk to God. And God talks to me.

One last little point before I get on with the story: When I write about God, I try to be gender neutral if at all possible. When backed into a corner, with no way out, I have used the word *he*. I could just as easily have used the word *she*. My rationale is that according to the Bible, I was created in God's image. And I happen to be male. Therefore, the aspect of God that is most relevant to Art Bernstein is correspondingly male. Were I female, my God would be female.

Not that God's female aspects aren't relevant to me.

Anyhow, this is a story about an interesting little conversation I once had with God, and about a lesson God taught me in patience. It wasn't a thunder-and-lightning kind of lesson in which I ended up cowering on my knees in terror, begging forgiveness and fearing for my eternal soul. It was a sweet little lesson involving softness and gentle urging.

I like that kind of lesson the best. I suspect God does, also.

The story goes like this:

The deepest canyon in the United States is called Hells Canyon. It is 2,000 feet deeper than the Grand Canyon, which is only a mile deep. Unfortunately, visiting Hells Canyon is far more difficult than a trip to the Grand Canyon. Hells Canyon occupies a remote stretch of the Snake River along the Idaho–Oregon border.

When I say *remote*, I'm not kidding. The only spot on the canyon rim accessible by car, called Hat Point, lies exactly 600 miles from my house in

Grants Pass, Oregon. The last 24 miles to Hat Point, I'd heard, were over an unpaved roller coaster of an access road. Only an A. J. Foyt, with four-wheel drive, would dare attempt its ruts, grades, twists, turns, bumps, and grinds.

I was told precisely that by a student, a nature-loving grandma in her late fifties, at the community college where I taught for a while.

"It's a terrible, terrible road," she warned, wagging a finger an inch from my nose. "It's full of chuckholes and potholes and bottomless drop-offs. I never thought I'd make it. But it was worth it."

"I wonder why they call them 'chuckholes'" I said.

"Who knows?" said my student, slightly annoyed at my intellectual tangent. "Maybe because you get chucked out of our seat when you hit one. Maybe because the first ones were made by woodchucks."

I'd wanted to see Hells Canyon ever since I first heard of it, in college in Michigan in the late 1960s. But somehow, despite living in Oregon for twenty years, I'd never made it. I liked the idea of driving 600 miles without ever leaving the state. Grants Pass is nestled in a valley in the state's southwest corner while Hat Point occupies a mountaintop in the state's extreme northeast corner. It is nearly 700 miles from Brookings, Oregon, on the south coast, to Hat Point, but that trip involves nipping a corner of California.

My wife, Patricia, and I finally made it to Hat Point in October 1987. I was working as a private consulting forester at the time, and the state of Oregon had passed a law requiring all owners of commercially zoned forest property to submit Forest Management Plans to the state, written by private consulting foresters. It was a huge windfall for me. When the deadline passed, on September 30, it seemed like the perfect time to take a trip.

So, three weeks later, off we went.

PART 2

WILL YOU RELAX, BERNSTEIN, YOU'RE RUINING THE TRIP."
Pat probably said those words to me forty times as we drove the 400-some miles from Grants Pass to the eastern Oregon city of LaGrande. The first time she said them was just before we left the house. I had it in my head to leave at seven in the morning and arrive in LaGrande at around six, with short visits to the Painted Hills and John Day Fossil Beds. Pat, however, managed to putter around the house

until seven-twenty. I couldn't figure out what she was doing or why she took so long. I wanted to get to LaGrande at a reasonable hour, while we could still find a motel room.

For some reason, getting to LaGrande at a decent hour was very important to me. Inordinately important to me. I get that way on trips. The trait might have to do with my once having been diagnosed with a mild case of attention deficit disorder, one manifestation of which is that I get extremely impatient in certain circumstances, although I can be very patient in others. Or I might have the trait simply because it is my nature to worry too much. Or perhaps I have it because I'm a latent control freak whose obsessive tendencies come flooding out when stimulated by the stress of trips.

Logically, even if Pat and I didn't quite make it to LaGrande, and instead spent the night, say, in John Day, it would not be a tragedy. But when I travel, I get a schedule fixed in my head and I am never comfortable until I've arrived at my destination and know everything is all right. I realized that Pat's admonition to relax was absolutely correct and that my fixation with keeping on schedule prevented me from enjoying trips as fully as I might. Of far greater consequence was that my little quirk sometimes prevented Pat from enjoying trips as fully as she might. Not to mention any kids who happened to be with us.

There were no kids on this particular trip.

I have the same problem on airplane trips. If I have multiple connections, I can never relax or quit worrying until I am safely aboard the last connection and the airliner has taken off without crashing. Only then can I kick back and enjoy the ride. Until then I am impossible, a quivering mass of discharging nerve synapses and exhortations to "hurry up."

My attitude remains steadfast and unaffected even when unexpected diversions turn out to be the best part of the trip. Pat and I once took our youngest daughter, Anna, and oldest granddaughter, Jacqueline, who are two years apart in age, on a car trip to Michigan. On the way back we stopped at Fort Laramie National Historical Site, in Wyoming. I had in mind half an hour for the visit, forty-five minutes at the most.

On arrival, we discovered that the fort had a living history program, with actors in period costumes. As we entered, the National Park Service gave the kids questionnaires and instructed them, if they wanted, to interview several of the actors about life on the frontier a-hundred-and-some years ago. If the kids talked to a certain number of the actors, and correctly answered so many questions on the sheet of paper, they got a prize. It was the best time the kids had the entire trip, especially when they talked to the "Commanding Officer's Wife," a cute, very sweet and friendly young college student wearing a dress with a bustle.

We spent three hours at Fort Laramie. I was biting my nails the entire time, anxious to get back on the road. But we arrived home when we arrived home. The three lost hours made no appreciable difference.

But sheesh, I kept telling myself as I waited for Pat to get in the car the day we left for Hat Point. *If we did it Pat's way, we'd stop at every single produce stand and out-of-the-way curio shop between our house and LaGrande. It would take a month to reach our destination.* And we only had three days, so we needed to budget our time wisely.

I figured to spend half an hour at the Painted Hills and another half hour at the John Day Fossil Beds. It nearly drove me crazy when the side trip to the Painted Hills, in the central Oregon desert, swallowed up more than an hour of our precious day. The Painted Hills are a series of barren dirt slopes with exposed soil revealing bedding layers of all different colors, mostly yellow and purple. They're a unit of John Day Fossil Beds National Monument. I nearly became hysterical, soon after, when Pat spent fifteen minutes browsing through postcards in a convenience store in the nearby town of Mitchell. I tried, for the sake of peace in the family, to limit my remarks on the subject to gentle urging, but it was difficult.

We made up the lost time, or some of it, at the Fossil Beds, a gorgeous series of desert bluffs and side canyons along the John Day River containing many dinosaur excavations. We could have hiked up one of the side canyons alongside the highway, and we could have spent time in the little visitor center. Pat certainly wanted to. I wanted to also, but I had to hurry to compensate for the extra time spent at the Painted Hills. So all we did was pull into a roadside turnout for a couple of minutes. According to my calculations, we were now on track to arrive at LaGrande at seven instead of six. This was unacceptable.

I nearly panicked when a carefully selected shortcut through the Blue Mountains, from John Day to LaGrande, turned out to be much slower than I had estimated from the map. We lost nearly twenty more minutes. It was an interesting drive, though. Most of the road traveled through forested mountains that, unlike the western Oregon forests, contained a large percentage of western larch trees. There are no larch trees in western Oregon (well, very few, and none whatsoever in southwest Oregon). Larch is a conifer and a member of the Pine family, except its needles are deciduous. They turn bright orange and drop off in autumn, just like the leaves of maples and aspens. They were in full fall color when we visited.

Vast areas of the Blue Mountains, at that time, had been devastated by the gypsy moth, which had almost completely defoliated all the Douglas-fir trees for mile after mile. It was more than a little creepy.

We arrived at LaGrande at 5:30 P.M., half an hour earlier than my target arrival time. I don't know how that happened. The motel, a very nice, surprisingly inexpensive AAA establishment, had rented only two other rooms when we pulled up. They rented only four more rooms the entire night (a Thursday in October).

We spent the next two hours wandering around LaGrande looking for something to do. We had dinner at Denny's, checked out the campus of Eastern Oregon State College, and went for a walk in the pretty little tree-lined community. It was only eight o'clock when we retired to our room for the night, with virtually nothing else to occupy ourselves with but watching TV and sleeping until the sun rose and we could finally leave for Hat Point, eleven hours later.

Note that I said *virtually*.

The LaGrande TV stations, we quickly discovered, were all in Boise, Idaho, a hundred miles away. Boise is on Mountain Time. For some reason network TV shows are aired an hour earlier in the Central and Mountain Time Zones. *The Tonight Show*, for example, comes on at ten-thirty instead of eleven-thirty. Except that LaGrande was in the Pacific Time Zone. So the *Tonight Show* from Boise came on at nine-thirty. This did not help me sleep.

After eating breakfast, at eight in the morning, we departed from LaGrande for the Wallowa Valley and Hat Point. We'd made reservations at the same motel in LaGrande for the next night. I'd wanted to leave for Hat Point at six-thirty instead of eight but Pat would have none of it.

"Will you relax, Bernstein," she said, "you're ruining the trip."

LaGrande is located between the Wallowa Mountains and the Blue Mountains in a wide, grassy basin called the Grande Ronde Valley, which is French for "Big Round Valley." The Grande Ronde Valley is a magnificent agricultural valley, one of the most beautiful and productive valleys anywhere. I would not have been surprised to encounter the Jolly Green Giant, sitting in a wheat field, eating lunch.

Gradually as we drove, the Grande Ronde Valley gave way to the much smaller but equally beautiful Wallowa Valley. The road follows the Wallowa River, a tributary of the Grande Ronde River, to the small towns of Enterprise and Joseph. Somewhere along the route the mighty Wallowas come into view, rising up like the Front Range of the Rockies from the Kansas prairie. The rise is steep, abrupt, and dramatic. Up close you can see that the range is cut by deep glacial canyons, with old lateral moraines, appearing as huge elongated gravel piles, spilling out onto the flat valley floor. Most of the valley, in fact, is glacial outwash from the last Ice Age.

The Wallowas are considered the most rugged peaks in Oregon. They rise to almost 10,000 feet (Matterhorn Peak, 9,832), with several peaks over 9,500 feet (Eagle Cap, Sacajawea Peak). The Wallowas are the only chunk of the Rocky Mountains to enter Oregon.

Because the Wallowa Mountains, and the Wallowa Valley, are technically part of the Rockies, several native Rocky Mountain tree species have their only Oregon occurrence here. Paper birch is one such species. Another is Rocky Mountain juniper.

I didn't see any birch but I found lots of juniper. I'd read in a tree guide that the way to distinguish Rocky Mountain juniper from the western juniper that inhabits the rest of the state is that western juniper has "pitch encrustations" between its leaflets. After observing Rocky Mountain juniper during my trip to the Wallowas, I discovered a better way to tell them apart. Because of the pitch encrustations, western juniper, from a distance, is a sort of an olive color. Because of the lack of pitch encrustations, Rocky Mountain juniper is a deep green.

Also, I read somewhere that *wallowa*, and *walla-walla* are actually the same Native American word, meaning "beautiful valley." That's probably true, I guess, except it doesn't account for the extra *la* at the end of *walla-walla*.

Joseph turned out to be a charming little tourist-oriented community capitalizing on its location as gateway to the Wallowas, which they call the "Oregon Alps." Pat desperately wanted to check out a couple of gift shops in Joseph. I sidestepped the issue by promising that she could spend all the time she wanted after we got back from Hat Point, which I figured would happen at around two o'clock. Also, if we had time after Hat Point, I wanted to take the drive up the Lostine River Canyon. It was supposedly a beautiful route up a narrow, forested, steep-walled glacial valley that cut deeply into the Wallowas' main flank. The gravel access road, according to the map, ended with the only auto-accessible views of Matterhorn Peak and Eagle Cap, the core summits from which all the major Wallowa ridges radiated.

The Lostine River Road was only 17 miles long. How much extra time could it take? Also, I'd have given anything to go hiking in the Wallowas. But that would have to be saved for another trip. Again, there just wasn't enough time.

We did take in Wallowa Lake before heading out to Hat Point. The lake is the region's main tourist focus, a beautiful, very large natural body of water with the high Wallowas pressed against two sides and huge lateral and terminal glacial moraines damming up the other two. An aerial tramway supposedly offered a fantastic view of the mountains and lake from an 8,000-foot peak. But it was closed for the season.

We didn't have time anyhow.

PART 3

FROM WALLOWA LAKE WE DROVE 40 MILES UP A DESERT CANYON LINED with brown volcanic rimrock. A stream called Little Sheep Creek ran along the canyon bottom. The road took us to the tiny village of Imnaha. There we started up the dreaded 24 miles of gravel and dirt to Hat Point. The road wasn't nearly as bad as rumored. It had a few rough spots, especially near the beginning, but many of the back roads around Grants Pass were far worse.

For the first 17 miles, Hat Point Road peered down with ever more mind-boggling views into the canyon of the Imnaha River, of which Little Sheep Creek is a tributary. The Imnaha River is a spectacular gorge in its own right, with the Wallowas rising on the other side. Were it not overshadowed and overwhelmed by Hells Canyon, the Imnaha Canyon would rank among Oregon's most scenic drives. As it is, hardly anybody goes there because they all turn off onto the Hat Point Road, just as Pat and I did.

After mile 17, according to the map, Hat Point Road arrived at the top of a sort of mesa, leveled off, and began a broad, 180-degree sweep around to the Hells Canyon side. Supposedly, that's where the real scenery lay. Not that there was anything wrong with the Imnaha/Wallowa panorama. If for some reason I had been unable to make it all the way to Hat Point, my alternate plan was to drive a few miles up the Imnaha River Road.

I couldn't wait to get to the Hells Canyon side of the Hat Point Road, which might have been why Pat kept telling me to slow down. I thought 30 to 40 miles per hour was plenty cautious. But she wanted me to go no more than 5 miles an hour. I understood her concerns and tried my best to oblige, without much success. The road was very narrow and the drop-offs were very steep, with no guardrails and a long, long way to the bottom. But I was in a hurry. I'm not very good at going slow.

The one cloud on the horizon, as the road finally made its way around to the Hells Canyon side, was . . . the *clouds* on the horizon. Lots of them. It had snowed in the Wallowas the day before, and the weather remained blustery and overcast. Hat Point's elevation is 6,900 feet and we started growing extremely nervous when, at mile 14, it began snowing. It snowed on and off all the way to Hat Point, mostly in the form of flurries that didn't stick to the ground.

Eventually we pulled into the small, gravel Hat Point parking lot feeling exceedingly grateful to have made it despite the snow but concerned that thus far, we hadn't seen the slightest trace of Hells Canyon, the allegedly deepest canyon in the United States.

Hat Point turned out to be a lovely little flat with a fire lookout tower and a short trail leading through the woods to an observation deck. The setting was a grassy meadow with artistically placed clumps of subalpine fir and mountain hemlock. Both are high-elevation trees adapted to biting wind, bitter cold, and tons of snow.

I poked around taking pictures of the lookout while Pat walked down to the observation deck, a little wooden patio with a split-rail fence around it, glued to the canyon rim. When I finally got around to walking the 300-foot trail to the observation deck, she was on her way back to the car to get warm. It had stopped snowing by then but it was still windy and plenty cold. We passed each other at the halfway point.

"Don't waste your time," Pat warned. "The whole canyon is completely fogged in and you can't see a thing."

Pat was never a big-time nature enthusiast. Little time, yes. Big time, no.

My heart sank as I arrived at the observation deck and confirmed that she was correct. White mist swirled everywhere, hanging heavily in the frigid, damp air. My breath added to the swirling mist. A dank, musty smell filled the air, of which I was aware only briefly, when my nasal passages thawed out enough to be able to smell. The view of the canyon was limited to a few feet of gray lava rock on either side of the platform.

I felt like crying. After eighteen years and 600 miles, I could not permit my quest to go unfulfilled. I had to see Hells Canyon. I just had to.

Despite my stoic determination, I felt very discouraged. The thick, heavy fog appeared to have settled in for an extended duration and was not about to lift anytime soon. Short of suddenly acquiring X-ray vision, or waiting a week, I could think of no reasonable solution to the problem.

Then, for no apparent reason—"out of the blue," if you will— a sentence from the Old Testament of the Bible popped into my head. Now you must understand that I am not a religious person. I respect religion, and I believe in God, sort of, but I don't practice any particular faith. I didn't then and I don't now. And I am certainly not a Bible-quoting type, although I have read the Bible.

The quote that popped into my head was this: "Keep your mind on the Lord."

I looked it up when I arrived home and found it was from Isaiah 26:3.

It seemed like a reasonable suggestion. Obviously, no other force was going to part the fog and allow my long-awaited gander at Hells Canyon. Why not prayer?

"How about it?" I said out loud. "Will you help me out, God?"

My writing sometimes gets verbose but my prayers tend to be short and to the point, along the lines of "Thanks for the grub," or "Please take my daughter's fever away." As an impatient type, I find myself annoyed by prayers that begin, "We give thanks unto thee, oh Lord, Ruler of the Universe, for thy merciful blah blah blah." I figure that with all God has to do, he (or she) doesn't need to wade through ten pages of verbiage to find out what you want.

I pray frequently, by the way, on the theory that (1) it can't hurt and (2) there is a spiritual and psychological benefit to going through my day aware of, and grateful for, the little blessings and miracles that happen constantly, not the least of which is the miracle of my own existence. Such a view prevents me from getting too wrapped up in myself.

I get wrapped up in myself anyhow, of course.

My interest in prayer is strong enough for me to have attended church prayer meetings a couple times, even though I am unaffiliated with any faith or religious organization. I've visited all sorts of churches over the years, from Native American to Jewish to Buddhist to Baha'i to Islam to several Christian denominations.

Almost immediately after speaking my little nine-word prayer, a peacefulness descended on me. And a feeling of absolute confidence that the fog would lift shortly. Furthermore, I now knew what I had to do to make that happen.

The feeling of peace, of God's presence, might have had something to do with standing on a mountaintop at the edge of a vast abyss, with no other people around for miles (except Pat), at the end of a 24-mile dirt road. I can think of no better setting in which to engender a sense of God's presence. Not that God isn't present everywhere. I don't know if high, lonely places are closer to God or not. But you're less likely to get distracted in such settings, so they seem closer to God.

In any case, I paced back and forth on the platform, gathering my will and strength, then I reared up like Moses at the shore of the Red Sea.

"Okay, God," I commanded, "part the fog."

I gestured my mightiest Charlton Heston gesture. Then I peered once again into the empty whiteness. It looked like a polar bear building a snowman in a blizzard.

Dang!

Then God, or somebody, spaketh unto Art Bernstein once again:

"Wait upon the Lord," it said.

I later verified that God was quoting himself from Isaiah 40:31.

Immediately I felt ashamed. How impudent of me to think that God was at my beck and call rather than the other way around.

Okay, I thought, *if God wants me to wait, I'll jolly well wait.*

"Waiting" consisted of counting to a hundred, then commanding the fog to part once more. Needless to say, nothing happened.

"Come on," I pleaded, out loud, feeling a little stupid for talking to the air and glad that no people were around. "I don't have all day. Besides, Pat's waiting for me."

I counted to a hundred a second time, much more slowly, pacing all the while. When I was done, I peered as hard as I could into the formless void, to see if something, anything, was materializing through the haze.

I saw only a formless void.

You might be wondering why I believed God was at the other end of my dialogue. It might have been Satan talking to me, or the sprit of the trees and mountains, or one of my many alternate personalities. Or just me carrying on an internal conversation, as I frequently do. Or it could have been all of those things. Or none of them. Whether I was actually speaking with the Big Kahuna and Creator of the Universe, I cannot say. I submit, however, that anything that says godly things and urges you in a godly direction, be it a voice from on high, an internal conversation, or simply your own conscience, probably comes from God.

What do I mean by *godly things?* Had the internal voice instructed me to jump over the railing into the canyon, I'd have terminated the discussion posthaste. God isn't likely to ask you to do something that crazy or frightening. That doesn't mean God won't plant the thought to take a bold step, or that you will never experience anxiety over the things God would like from you. But while God may urge you, it is not like him (or her) to force the issue unless you really screw up your life. Above all, love will accompany everything God does.

And that's how I knew I was speaking to God. If there is a God.

"Wait," the voice in my head repeated. And I waited. Ten minutes. Fifteen minutes. Twenty minutes. I thought I'd go nuts. I couldn't stand the tedium. It was worse than fishing, which I avoid like Swiss chard because I lack the patience.

Am I missing something? I wondered. *Is there something else I need to do? Some formula?* I waited a couple more minutes, trying to reassure myself while hunching down in my jacket against the wind.

"Shout 'Praise God,' " a thought in my head suggested.

Forget it. I'd sooner not see Hells Canyon. I didn't mean to be ungrateful or insolent. But such a shout would have made me very uncomfortable. It would have felt foolish, not praiseful or uplifting. Fortunately, God understands my quirks. I make sure of that. And he sometimes overlooks them.

"Don't worry," the voice reassured. "You don't have to shout. Go get your wife instead. If I'm going to work a miracle, I need witnesses."

That evoked even more excuses than the shouting edict. *She's not that interested,* I rationalized. *And it's too cold for her to wait out here. And it's a long walk back to the car. And I might miss something if I leave. And . . .*

"Get your wife," the voice repeated.

I continued to stall, believing that my primary duty was to wait, as God had instructed. I leaned against the railing and stared into the emptiness. Fortunately God was growing tired of my stubbornness. He resolved the issue by getting my wife for me.

"Hi, Art."

Hearing Pat's voice behind me, I turned to greet her so that my back faced the canyon.

"Hi," I answered. "Sorry to take so long but I was hoping the fog would lift enough to let me see down to the bottom. No such luck, though."

"What are you talking about?" she said, staring at me as though I'd lost my mind, an all-too-familiar look. "The view is gorgeous."

I turned back toward the gorge. It was as though the fog had been slit with a knife. A mile or more below, we could see with perfect clarity the churning riffles of the Snake River. The hole in the fog, perhaps an eighth of a mile wide, enabled us to look down our side of the canyon to the river, then halfway up the far wall on the Idaho side. It was worth every second of my forty-minute wait.

"Wow," I whispered. That was the best I could muster. To say that I felt awed wouldn't have done it justice. I squeezed my wife's hand as we both stared at the display until the hole closed up five minutes later, never to reopen.

I know, I know. The story of how God let me see into that canyon seems trivial compared to other miracles like parting the Red Sea or the walls of Jericho falling down. That's where the real drama lies. Still, if God chose to work a "minor" miracle just to make me happy, give me material for a short story, or teach me a little lesson, it's definitely worth repeating.

Especially considering for whose domain the canyon is named.

Before we left Hells Canyon, I cupped my hands around my mouth and bellowed, "Praise God," as loudly as I could, into the abyss. My salute reverberated through the canyon and across to the Seven Devils Mountains beyond. The strength of my voice startled me.

If there were devils in the Seven Devils Mountains, they're gone now.

"Praise God," the hills shouted back, over and over. "Praise God."

PART 4

EXACTLY ONE DECADE LATER I VISITED HAT POINT FOR THE SECOND TIME, WITH MY friend Steve Polinger. This time the weather was clear, sunny, and hot. Hat Point Road remained mostly gravel but had been improved considerably since 1987. There were dozens of cars on the road, with two or three stopped at every turnout and vista point.

The biggest difference was that most of the beautiful subalpine fir and mountain hemlock trees had burned down, leaving only spooky, depressing skeleton forests. The trees would grow back eventually but until they did, the high-country charm was slightly diminished.

At Hat Point I discovered that the parking lot had been blacktopped and expanded to accommodate a hundred vehicles instead of ten. And a blacktopped nature trail had been built along the rim. They, too, diminished the experience.

More than slightly.

Hells Canyon was still worth visiting, though. And that second time I could see the entire range of the Seven Devils Mountains on the far side, from which the canyon's 7,300-foot depth is measured.

What I did not see was the little observation deck. I walked the paved trail twice looking for pilings, or some remnant or indication that it once existed. But I found nothing.

That also diminished the experience. A lot.

PART 5

IN 1999 I HIKED THE GRIZZLY PEAK TRAIL UP A MOUNTAIN NEAR ASHLAND, OREGON, which leads to a sandstone bluff high above the valley in which Ashland is located. I'd heard that the view straight down from 5,400 feet was mighty impressive. But it was overcast that day, and when I arrived at the vista point on the summit, the entire valley was filled with fog, not unlike Hat Point on my first go-round. Being only 40 miles from home instead of 600, I wasn't nearly as worried as I'd been at Hat Point. It was a very pretty place even without the view, and I was more than willing to come back another day.

I sat on a sandstone rock outcrop that looked down into the fog, and ate my lunch.

After about twenty-five minutes a narrow slit suddenly appeared in the fog that enabled me to see down to Ashland and up the other side of the valley. Three minutes later, the slit closed back up. I hadn't prayed about it and I certainly hadn't carried on any extensive conversations with God Almighty about it.

When you think about it, fog banks are actually clouds. And clouds have clearly defined edges that constantly change. So sudden dramatic breaks are probably not that uncommon.

They sure are nice, though.

I could be wrong, but I like to think that both "fog liftings," the one at Hat Point and the one on Grizzly Peak, were gifts from God, little miracles whose sole purpose was to surprise and delight me.

I believe God enjoys surprising and delighting me. It happens often enough.

THE HIKE: *Hells Canyon National Recreation Area, Oregon.*

LENGTH *(one way): 100 yards (the trail is not there anymore).*

DIRECTIONS: *First, get to Joseph, Oregon, on the Wallow River plain at the foot of the Wallowa Mountains. To reach Joseph, take OR 82 east from I-84 at LaGrande. After 70 miles, in Joseph, follow the paved Little Sheep Creek Highway left, toward Imnaha, 40 miles away. Hat Point Road #4240 begins in Imnaha. It's 22 miles to the Memaloose Guard Station and landing strip. Turn right at Memaloose onto Spur 315 and proceed 2 more miles to Hat Point.*

ABOUT THE AUTHOR

ART BERNSTEIN IS THE AUTHOR OF THIRTEEN nature and hiking guides, including Falcon's *Hiking Oregon's Southern Cascades and Siskiyous.* An avid hiker and naturalist, he holds a master's degree in natural resource management from the University of Michigan. He lives in Grants Pass, Oregon.